International acclaim for Camille Paglia's

BREAK, BLOW, BURN

"A solid and impressive achievement that stands with the very best American writing on poetry." —*Los Angeles Times*

"It will have students storming the walls of tomorrow's English departments, mad for poetry again." —*St. Petersburg Times*

"Paglia has put down her Molotov cocktails and picked up the lyre. . . . [She] approaches poetry with a . . . reverence for craft." —*Newsday*

"Intensive, well-informed, and largely persuasive. . . . When it comes to understanding what and how a poem means, she is right." —*The Boston Globe*

"A treasury of knowledge. . . . The latest shot in her campaign to save culture from theory . . . shows her at her true worth. . . . She is humble enough to be enthralled by [poetry]; enthralled enough to be inspired; and inspired enough to write the sinuous and finely shaded prose that proves how a single poem can get the whole of her attention. . . . She has the powers of discrimination to show what talent is—powers that add up to a talent in themselves. . . . Her readings of Shakespeare are close, fully informed by the scholarship and—a harder trick—fundamentally sane. . . . Her sensitivity to George Herbert is the best early sign of her range of sympathy. . . . Infectious." —*The New York Times Book Review*

"This excellent handbook will defuse the fear with which novices instinctively approach poetry. . . . Paglia has a brisk, intense and powerful understanding of poetry. . . . She reminds us that poetry—art—is mankind's rebuttal against the transitory. And in a culture that is more flotsam than sea, this brief, enthusiastic book is a needed reminder." —*The Globe and Mail* (Toronto)

"Plainspoken and direct—exactly the kind of writing that will appeal to the general reader who's afraid of modern literary criticism. . . . Paglia offers the sort of lucid textual criticism you'd expect from a good college professor. . . . Paglia also pays meticulous attention to language, which can produce delightful insights as well as writing that's a pleasure in itself." —*Austin American-Statesman*

"A blast to read. . . . Amusing, original, and irreverent."
—*Interview Magazine*

"The liveliest form of practical criticism—the sort that stirs you to pull dusty anthologies from the shelf and immerse yourself in the music, rhythm and emotional theater of lyrics. . . . Her manner is that of the most stimulating lecturer. . . . She will provoke you into honing your own interpretations. That alone makes *Break, Blow, Burn* a creative read." —*The New Leader*

"Insightful and punchy, erudite yet approachable. . . . Paglia enjoys a privilege that eludes most academics—a rapt mainstream audience." —Canadian Broadcasting Corporation

"She succeeds brilliantly. . . . Paglia writes clearly, avoids jargon and over-interpretation, provides just enough historical context, and repeatedly scores a bull's-eye. . . . [She] is amazing at teasing meaning from the barest bones of verse. . . . No matter how much you know about poetry, *Break, Blow, Burn* may be read with profit and delight." —*Mobile Register*

"Beautifully lucid. . . . An indisputably terrific primer for all students of literature in English." —*Kirkus Reviews*

"*Break, Blow, Burn* marks the triumph of Camille Paglia the critic. . . . Again and again [she] soars." —*The Star-Ledger* (Newark, NJ)

"Paglia is clearly in love with poetry. . . . The poems included . . . are well chosen." —*Time Out New York*

CAMILLE PAGLIA

BREAK, BLOW, BURN

Camille Paglia is University Professor of Humanities and Media Studies at the University of the Arts in Philadelphia. She is the author of *Sexual Personae: Art and Decadence from Nefertiti to Emily Dickinson*; *Sex, Art, and American Culture*; and *Vamps & Tramps*. She has also written *The Birds*, a study of Alfred Hitchcock. She lives in Philadelphia.

Please visit Camille Paglia on the Web:
www.breakblowburn.com.

ALSO BY CAMILLE PAGLIA

The Birds

Vamps & Tramps: New Essays

Sex, Art, and American Culture: Essays

Sexual Personae:
Art and Decadence from Nefertiti to Emily Dickinson

BREAK, BLOW, BURN

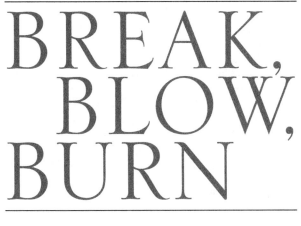

BREAK, BLOW, BURN

CAMILLE PAGLIA

VINTAGE BOOKS
A Division of Random House, Inc.
New York

CONTENTS

INTRODUCTION

This book is intended for a general audience. The unexpected success of my first book, *Sexual Personae,* which juxtaposed painting and sculpture with poetry, proved that there were serious readers outside academe who were craving an introduction to literary and cultural history and its enduring artistic principles.* In *Break, Blow, Burn,* I have tried to write concise commentaries on poetry that illuminate the text but also give pleasure in themselves as pieces of writing.

The readings of poetry here are based on my more than three decades of experience as a classroom teacher. I believe that close reading, or what used to be called "explication of text," not only is the best technique for revealing beauty and meaning in literature but is a superb instrument for the analysis of all art and culture. Through it, one learns how to focus the mind, sharpen perception, and refine emotion. I have used close reading with students of widely different preparations, from freshmen to writing majors to adults in night classes, and I have extrapolated this microscopic, sequential method to other genres in my slide lectures on art as well as my writing on film.

The foundation of my literary education in college and graduate school in the 1960s was a technique known as the New Criticism, which studied the internal or formal qualities of poetry. I was impatient with what I regarded as its genteel sentimentality, its prim

---

*Camille Paglia, *Sexual Personae: Art and Decadence from Nefertiti to Emily Dickinson* (Yale University Press, 1990; Vintage Books, 1991). See the annotated bibliography for prior publications that expand on points made in this introduction.

evasion of the sex and aggression in artistic creativity. Urgent supplementation was needed by psychology as well as history, toward which I had been oriented since adolescence, when I began exploring books about Greco-Roman and Near Eastern archaeology. The New Critics' admirable reaction against a prior era of bibliographic pedantry had eventually resulted in an annihilation of context, an orphaning of the text. New Criticism was also hostile or oblivious to popular culture, the master mythology of my postwar generation. For that I had to look to bohemian artists like Andy Warhol or dissident academics like Marshall McLuhan and Leslie Fiedler.

But the New Criticism, attuned to paradox and ambiguity, was a sophisticated system of interpretation that has never been surpassed as a pedagogical tool for helping novice as well as veteran readers to understand poetry. Its destruction by the influx of European poststructuralism into American universities in the 1970s was a cultural disaster from which higher education has yet to recover. With its clotted jargon, circular reasoning, and smug, debunking cynicism, poststructuralism works only on narrative—on the longer genres of story and novel. It is helpless with lyric poems, where the individual word has enormous power and mystery and where the senses are played upon by rhythm, mood, and dreamlike metaphors.

Poetry was at a height of prestige in the 1960s. American college students were listening to rock music but also writing poetry. There were packed readings by poets on campuses and at political demonstrations. In 1966, for example, I attended an antiwar "poetry read-in" staged by visiting poets Galway Kinnell, James Wright, and Robert Bly at Harpur College (my alma mater at the State University of New York at Binghamton). Harpur was then a hotbed of antiacademic poetry. Among other poets who read during my years there were Denise Levertov, W. D. Snodgrass, George Starbuck, A. R. Ammons, Babette Deutsch, Donald Justice, Robert Creeley, John Logan, Richard Hugo, Muriel Rukeyser, Richard Wilbur, Isabella Gardner, Francis Ponge, Jon Silkin, Robert Hazel, Adrienne Rich, and John Berryman. During graduate school at Yale University, I attended readings by W. H. Auden, Robert Lowell, Elizabeth Bishop, and many others. In 1969, Allen Ginsberg and Gregory Corso appeared at the Yale Law School in an event significantly not sponsored by the English Department, where there was open disdain for Beat poetry (one of my primary influences).

At that magic moment, professors specializing in poetry criticism had stratospheric reputations at the major universities. But over the following decades, poetry and poetry study were steadily marginalized by pretentious "theory"—which claims to analyze language but atrociously abuses language. Poststructuralism and crusading identity politics led to the gradual sinking in reputation of the premiere literature departments, so that by the turn of the millennium, they were no longer seen even by the undergraduates themselves to be where the excitement was on campus. One result of this triumph of ideology over art is that, on the basis of their publications, few literature professors know how to "read" anymore—and thus can scarcely be trusted to teach that skill to their students. Cultural studies, for example, despite its auspicious name, has been undone by its programmatic Marxism and is a morass of misreadings or overreadings. During the past quarter century, humanistic principles and honest practical criticism could more reliably be found among low-paid adjuncts faithfully teaching service courses at community colleges than in the vain, showy professoriat of the elite schools.

Though I had read and written poetry in high school (I adored Gerard Manley Hopkins and Edna St. Vincent Millay and loathed Robert Frost), my real education in it came at Harpur. I took courses in Metaphysical poetry and John Milton from an expert in seventeenth-century literature, Arthur L. Clements, whose close readings and innovative integration of Western and Asian religions made a deep impact on me. I had what can only be described as a conversion experience in the classes of Milton Kessler, a poet who had been a student of Theodore Roethke at the University of Washington. I took or audited four of his courses: "Introduction to Poetry," "Visionary Poets," "Poetry as Play," and "The Confessional Poets." Kessler's theory of poetry was based on sensory response and body rhythms. Partly because he had been trained in voice and opera, he endorsed emotional directness and amplitude in art. His classroom explications were dramatic, celebratory, and ingeniously associative, bringing *everything* to bear on the text. That intense way of reading poetry was definitely not the norm in graduate school. The first paper I submitted at Yale ("Exoticism in Wallace Stevens") came back with the dismissive note that it was a "qualitative appreciation, which we find so often in reviews of contemporary poetry."

The next stage in my comprehension of poetry came from Harold Bloom, whom I did not know (I had never taken his seminars) until I was drafting the prospectus for my doctoral thesis, then titled "The Androgynous Dream" but later called *Sexual Personae*. Hearing of my psychoanalytic topic via the grad student grapevine, Bloom summoned me to his office and offered to be my adviser. (He announced, "My dear, I am the *only* one who can direct that dissertation!" And of course he was right.) Bloom's massive, interdisciplinary erudition and electrifying insights into the spiritual dimension of literature were exactly what I needed for the development of my work. He was then the scholar who had revolutionized Romantic studies with his extraordinary books on Blake and Shelley. (It was several years before he published *The Anxiety of Influence*, the book that made him an international celebrity.) Though he was tartly skeptical of my zeal for mass media, I found Bloom's thinking otherwise completely in sync with the neo-Romanticism of the sixties' cultural insurgency. Both Bloom and Kessler, with their profound empathy and fiery, prophetic temperaments, seemed to me more visionary rabbis than professors.

My attraction to poetry has always been driven by my love of English, which my family acquired relatively recently. (My mother and all four of my grandparents were born in Italy.) While my parents spoke English at home, my early childhood in the small factory town of Endicott in upstate New York was spent among speakers of sometimes mutually unintelligible Italian dialects. Unlike melodious Tuscan or literary Italian, rural Italian from the central and southern provinces is brusque, assertive, and consonant-laden, with guttural accents and dropped final vowels. What fascinated me about English was what I later recognized as its hybrid etymology: blunt Anglo-Saxon concreteness, sleek Norman French urbanity, and polysyllabic Greco-Roman abstraction. The clash of these elements, as competitive as Italian dialects, is invigorating, richly entertaining, and often funny, as it is to Shakespeare, who gets tremendous effects out of their interplay. The dazzling multiplicity of sounds and word choices in English makes it brilliantly suited to be a language of poetry. It's why the pragmatic Anglo-American tradition (unlike effete French rationalism) doesn't need poststructuralism: in English, usage depends upon context; the words jostle and provoke one another and mischievously shift their meanings over time.

English has evolved over the past century because of mass media and advertising, but the shadowy literary establishment in the United States, in and outside academe, has failed to adjust. From the start, like Andy Warhol (another product of an immigrant family in an isolated Northeastern industrial town), I recognized commercial popular culture as the authentic native voice of America. Burned into my memory, for example, is a late-1950s TV commercial for M&M's chocolate candies. A sultry cartoon peanut, sunbathing on a chaise longue, said in a twanging Southern drawl: "I'm an M&M peanut / Toasted to a golden brown / Dipped in creamy milk chocolate / And covered in a thin candy shell!" Illustrating each line, she prettily dove into a swimming pool of melted chocolate and popped out on the other side to strike a pose and be instantly toweled in her monogrammed candy wrap. I felt then, and still do, that the M&M peanut's jingle was a vivacious poem and that the creative team who produced that ad were folk artists, anonymous as the artisans of medieval cathedrals.

My attentiveness to the American vernacular—through commercials, screwball comedies, hit songs, and AM talk radio (which I listen to around the clock)—has made me restive with the current state of poetry. I find too much work by the most acclaimed poets labored, affected, and verbose, intended not to communicate with the general audience but to impress their fellow poets. Poetic language has become stale and derivative, even when it makes all-too-familiar avant-garde or ethnic gestures. Hence I don't agree with the assessments (pro or con) of contemporary poetry by most of the leading poetry critics and reviewers. Those who turn their backs on media (or overdose on postmodernism) have no gauge for monitoring the metamorphosis of English. Any poetry removed from popular diction will inevitably become as esoteric as eighteenth-century satire (perfected by Alexander Pope), whose dense allusiveness and preciosity drove the early Romantic poets into the countryside to find living speech again. Poetry's declining status has made its embattled practitioners insular and self-protective: personal friendships have spawned cliques and coteries in book and magazine publishing, prize committees, and grants organizations. I have no such friendships and am a propagandist for no poet or group of poets.

In gathering material for this book, I was shocked at how weak *individual* poems have become over the past forty years. Our most honored poets are gifted and prolific, but we have come to respect them for their intelligence, commitment, and the *body* of their work. They ceased focusing long ago on production of the powerful, distinctive, self-contained poem. They have lost ambition and no longer believe they can or should speak for their era. Elevating process over form, they treat their poems like meandering diary entries and craft them for effect in live readings rather than on the page. Arresting themes or images are proposed, then dropped or left to dribble away. Or, in a sign of lack of confidence in the reader or material, suggestive points are prosaically rephrased and hammered into obviousness. Rote formulas are rampant—a lugubrious victimology of accident, disease, and depression or a simplistic, ranting politics (people good, government bad) that looks naive next to the incisive writing about politics on today's op-ed pages. To be included in this book, a poem had to be strong enough, as an artifact, to stand up to all the great poems that precede it. Hence there may be some surprising choices and omissions here. One of my aims is to challenge contemporary poets to reassess their assumptions and modus operandi.

In the 1990s, poetry as performance art revived among young people in slams recalling the hipster clubs of the Beat era. As always, the return of oral tradition had folk roots—in this case the incantatory rhyming of African-American urban hip-hop. But it's poetry on the page—a *visual* construct—that lasts. The eye too is involved. The shapeliness and symmetry of the four-line ballad stanza (descending from medieval England and Scotland and carried by seventeenth-century émigrés to the American South and Appalachia) once structured the best lyrics of rhythm and blues, gospel, country and western music, and rock 'n' roll. But with the immense commercial success of rock music, those folk roots have receded, and popular songwriting has gotten weaker and weaker. In a course I created on song lyrics at the University of the Arts, I encourage aspiring songwriters to look at their lyrics on the page and to evaluate them for visual balance. Hence this book ends with a great lyric, Joni Mitchell's "Woodstock," which became an anthem for my conflicted generation.

The first half of this book contains canonical poems from the Renaissance through Romanticism that have proved most successful for me in the classroom. In one case, I have excerpted a grisly passage from Shakespeare's *Hamlet* (the ghost's speech) and treated it as a poem. Emily Dickinson is a specialty: I wrote my college senior thesis on her, devoted a long chapter to her in *Sexual Personae* ("Amherst's Madame de Sade"), and teach an upper-level Dickinson course under the inter-arts rubric "Major Artists." Other poems here—such as those by William Carlos Williams, Theodore Roethke, Robert Lowell, and Sylvia Plath—stunned and bewitched me when I first read them in Milton Kessler's classes. The case of Plath illustrates the signal differences between Bloom's critical code and mine: he has colorfully rejected her work, while I have elsewhere called "Daddy" a central poem of the twentieth century.

For the other modern poems reprinted here, I conducted a long search through library collections and bookstores to locate texts that I could enthusiastically recommend to the general reader. My desire was for poems that would reward close scrutiny and withstand repeated rereadings—as many as five or six in a row. Because translation is so problematic, I decided to use only poems written in English. (Among poets originally considered for inclusion were Sappho, Catullus, Petrarch, Schiller, Baudelaire, and Lorca.) While I strongly support multiculturalism and global perspectives in education, the writers I selected demonstrate the ancestry and enduring vitality of Anglo-American literature. Because of my commitment to Old Historicism, the poems are organized chronologically rather than thematically. Similarly, my discussion of each poem proceeds line by line from start to finish, as one would read it or as I would analyze it in class.

My title comes from a poem in this book, John Donne's Holy Sonnet XIV: "That I may rise, and stand, o'erthrow me, and bend / Your force to break, blow, burn and make me new." Donne is appealing to God to overwhelm him and compel his redemption from sin. My secular but semimystical view of art is that it taps primal energies, breaks down barriers, and imperiously remakes our settled way of seeing. Animated by the breath force (the original meaning of "spirit" and "inspiration"), poetry brings exhilarating spiritual renewal. A good poem is iridescent and incandescent, catching the light at unexpected angles and illuminating human universals—whose very existence is denied by today's parochial theorists. Among those looming universals are time and mortality, to which we all are subject. Like philosophy, poetry is a contemplative form, but unlike philosophy, poetry subliminally manipulates the body and triggers its nerve impulses, the muscle tremors of sensation and speech.

The sacred remains latent in poetry, which was born in ancient ritual and cult. For Donne, God is an eternal, transcendent judge and king. For Wordsworth, the divine suffuses nature and manifests itself in numinous moments of intensified consciousness. For Roethke, the divine is a ghostly Muse who emanates from his own psyche—a pattern seen differently in *Hamlet,* with its purgatorial stalking father. Poetry's persistent theme of the sublime—the awesome vastness of the universe—is a religious perspective, even in atheists like Shelley. Despite the cosmic vision of the radical, psychedelic 1960s, the sublime is precisely what poststructuralism, with its blindness to nature, cannot see. Metaphor is based on analogy: art is a revelation of the interconnectedness of the universe. The concentrated attention demanded by poetry is close to meditation. Reading a poem requires alert receptivity, perceptual openness, and intuition. Commentary on poetry is a kind of divination, resembling the practice of oracles, sibyls, augurs, and interpreters of dreams.

Poets have glimpses of other realities, higher or lower, which can't be fully grasped cognitively. The poem is a methodical working out of fugitive impressions. It finds or rather projects symbols into the inner and outer worlds. Poets speak even when they know their words will be swept away by the wind. In college Greek class, I was amazed by the fragments of Archaic poetry—sometimes just a surviving phrase or line—that vividly conveyed the sharp personalities of their authors, figures like Archilochus, Alcman, and Ibycus, about whom little is known. The continuity of Western culture is demonstrated by lyric poetry, which from its birth in ancient Greece has played so significant a role in the emergence of individualism, spawning in turn our concept of civil rights.

Another of my unfashionable precepts is that, like Bloom and Kessler, I revere the artist and the poet, who are so ruthlessly "exposed" by the sneering poststructuralists with their political agenda. There is no "death of the author" (that Parisian cliché) in my worldview. Authors strive and create against every impediment, including their doubters and detractors. Despite breaks, losses, and revivals, artistic tradition has a transhistorical flow that I have elsewhere compared to a mighty river. Poems give birth to other poems. Yet poetry is not just about itself: it does point to something *out there,* however dimly we can know it. The modernist doctrine of the work's self-reflexiveness once empowered art but has ended by strangling it in gimmickry.

Artists are makers, not just mouthers of slippery discourse. Language, the poets' medium, should not be privileged over the protean materials of other artists, who work in pigments, stone, metals, and fibers. Poets are fabricators and engineers, pursuing a craft analogous to cabinetry or bridge building. I maintain that the text emphatically exists as an object; it is not just a mist of ephemeral subjectivities. Every reading is partial, but that does not absolve us from the quest for meaning, which defines us as a species. Thus, from my archaeological perspective, Sappho's poems, while open to arguable and even contradictory interpretation, are also tangible manuscripts that have been imperfectly recovered from strips of recycled papyri in a trash heap in Egypt's Fayum. The idea of contingency properly applies to the gaping lacunae in Sappho's poems that scholars have so delicately and provisionally filled.

In writing about a poem, I try to *listen* to it and find a language and tone that mesh with its own idiom. We live in a time increasingly indifferent to literary style, from the slack prose of once august newspapers to pedestrian translations of the Bible. The Web (which I champion and to which I have extensively contributed) has increased verbal fluency but not quality, at least in its rushed, patchy genres of e-mail and blog. Good writing comes from good reading. Humanists must set an example: all literary criticism should be accessible to the general reader. Criticism at its best is re-creative, not spirit-killing. Technical analysis of a poem is like breaking down a car engine, which has to be reassembled to run again. Theorists childishly smash up their subjects and leave the *disjecta membra* like litter.

For me poetry is speech-based and is not just an arbitrary pattern of signs that can be slid around like a jigsaw puzzle. I sound out poems silently, as others pray. Poetry, which began as song, is music-drama: I value emotional expressiveness, musical phrasings, and choreographic assertion, the speaker's theatrical self-positioning toward other persons or implacable external forces. My commentaries are sympathetic redramatizations that try to capture defining gestures and psychological strategies. But prose readings are a costly shift in format, as when turning a novel or biography into a screenplay. It's a translation in which much is inevitably lost. I am not that concerned with prosody except to compare strict meter (drilled by my Greek and Latin teachers) to the standard songs that jazz musicians transform: I prefer irregularity, syncopation, bending the note.

My advice to the reader approaching a poem is to make the mind still and blank. Let the poem speak. This charged quiet mimics the blank space ringing the printed poem, the nothing out of which something takes shape. Many critics counsel memorizing poetry, but that has never been my habit. To commit a poem to memory is to make the act of reading superfluous. But I believe in immersion in and saturation by the poem, so that the next time we meet it, we have the thrill of recognition. We feel (to quote singer Stevie Nicks) the hauntingly familiar. It's akin to addiction or to the euphoria of being in love.

In the title of his classic 1947 manual of New Criticism, Cleanth Brooks compared a poem to Donne's "well wrought urn," housing funeral ashes from which the phoenix will rise again. A poem for me is more like an aquarium: it is both impenetrable and transparent, its wall like the glass curtain of a modern skyscraper. We are transfixed by motion within the frame—not unlike a movie or television screen. What flashes obscurely through poetry is the ceaseless, darting energy of words. The best route into poetry is through the dictionary (Emily Dickinson's bible). Words accumulate meaning over time. Studying the dictionary teaches you the art of condensation as well as the nuances and genealogy of language that poets twist and turn.

At this time of foreboding about the future of Western culture, it is crucial to identify and preserve our finest artifacts. Canons are always in flux, but canon formation is a critic's obligation. What lasts, and why? Custodianship, not deconstruction, should be the mission and goal of the humanities. As a student of ancient empires, I am uncertain about whether the West's chaotic personalism can prevail against the totalizing creeds that menace it. Hence it is critical that we reinforce the spiritual values of Western art, however we define them. In the Greco-Roman line, beauty and aesthetic pleasure are spiritual too. Poetry does not simply reconfirm gender or group identity; it develops the imagination and feeds the soul.

And art generates art: where will our future artists come from? In an era ruled by materialism and unstable geopolitics, art must be restored to the center of public education. If the humanities expect support and investment from society, there must be a reform of academe, which can come only from idealistic graduate students and junior faculty. But they cannot do it alone. Poets must remember their calling and take stage again.

BREAK, BLOW, BURN

ONE

WILLIAM SHAKESPEARE

Sonnet 73

That time of year thou mayst in me behold
When yellow leaves, or none, or few, do hang
Upon those boughs which shake against the cold,
Bare ruined choirs, where late the sweet birds sang.
In me thou see'st the twilight of such day   5
As after sunset fadeth in the west;
Which by and by black night doth take away;
Death's second self that seals up all in rest.
In me thou see'st the glowing of such fire,
That on the ashes of his youth doth lie,   10
As the deathbed whereon it must expire,
Consumed with that which it was nourished by.
This thou perceiv'st, which makes thy love more strong,
To love that well which thou must leave ere long.

The sonnet was a medieval form perfected by the Italian poet Petrarch, who was inspired by the courtly love tradition of southern France. From him, the fad of sonnet writing spread throughout Renaissance Europe. Sir Thomas Wyatt and the Earl of Surrey introduced the sonnet to England, though the style they favored was highly artificial and ridden with "conceits," showy metaphors that became clichés. Sir Philip Sidney and Edmund Spenser restored Petrarch's fluid lyricism to the sonnet. But it was Shakespeare who rescued an exhausted romantic genre and made it a supple instrument of searching self-analysis. By treating the sonnet as a freestanding poem rather than a unit in a sonnet sequence, Shakespeare revolutionized poetry in the same way that Donatello, liberating the statue from its medieval architectural niche, revolutionized sculpture.

No writer before Shakespeare had packed more into a sonnet or any other short poem. Sonnet 73 has a tremendous range of reference and a fineness of observed detail. Shakespeare's mobile eye prefigures the camera. Love, the sonnet's original raison d'être, recedes for a melancholy survey of the human condition. The poem is interested less in individual suffering than in the relationship of microcosm to macrocosm—mankind's interconnection with nature.

Structurally, Sonnet 73 follows Surrey's format. In the Italian sonnet adapted by Wyatt, fourteen lines were divided into two quatrains (a quatrain is a set of four lines) and a sestet (six lines). The Elizabethan sonnet, afterward called the Shakespearean, used three quatrains and a couplet—two lines with the bite of an epigram. Shakespeare treats the three quatrains in Sonnet 73 like scenes from a play: each has its guiding metaphor, a variation on the main theme. These metaphors split off, in turn, into subordinate metaphors, to end each quatrain with a witty flourish. The insertion of "in me" to start each quatrain gives the poem immediacy and urgency and encourages us, whether justified or not, in identifying the speaker with the poet (1, 5, 9). The regular repetition of that phrase makes us hear and feel the poem's triple structure. "In me" operates like a stage cue, prompting the entrance of each metaphor from the wings.

In the first quatrain, man's life is compared to a "year" in a northern climate of dramatically changing seasons. The aging poet pinpoints his location on life's spectrum as the transition from maturity to old age, when autumn shifts to winter. The opening metaphor of "time" yields to a bleak image of man's body as a tree: the bare "boughs" shaken by the "cold" wind are like the weak limbs of an elderly man, trembling with fear at approaching death (1–3). The branches tossed and outlined against the sky resemble the imploring arms of victims trying to escape fate. It's as if man is crucified on his own frail body. Scattered "yellow leaves" clinging to the branches evoke other afflictions and losses of age, such as fading, thinning hair (an issue for Shakespeare, if our one portrait of him is accurate). The sporadic drift of leaves to earth (like sands through an hourglass) is re-created in the hesitant, tapping rhythm: "yellow leaves, or none, or few." Core energy is tapering off.

As the quatrain ends, the ravaged, skeletal tree melts into a broken building (4). The "bare ruined choirs" belong to a medieval abbey, like those destroyed a half century earlier by Henry VIII when the Church of England seceded from Rome. The picturesque scene evokes a vanished civilization, now reclaimed by nature. So too, Shakespeare implies, do all human efforts end. The "sweet birds" who "late" (lately) sang from the trees but have now fled south recall the boy choirs who once filled the chapel with music. ("Choir" is also the area of a church where services are held.) The waning of song suggests that poetry came more easily to the young Shakespeare than it does now. The "bare ruined choirs" may also obliquely refer to the theaters where his career once flourished (and which were vulnerable to fire as well as closure by city authorities).

The second quatrain compares man's life to a "day" (5). This metaphor is as ancient as Oedipus. (The Sphinx asked Oedipus, "What walks on four legs in the morning, two at noon, and three at night?" He replied, "Man.") Again Shakespeare visualizes precise degrees in a process of gradual change. Our "twilight" years are stages in sunset. The poem unveils a brilliant western tableau: the sun, symbolizing our physical vitality, has dropped below the horizon, but the sky is still ruddy with the afterglow (6). That too, like all earthly colors, will shortly ("by and by") dissolve into the "black" of night (7). The second quatrain concludes as the first one did, with an ornate apposition elaborating a prior line. Night is personified as "Death's second self"—his twin or alter ego—obliterating the sun and "seal-[ing] up all in rest" (8). The implication is unsettling: sleep is a daily rehearsal for our final repose. At night, the world is a graveyard of sleepers, shrouded and entombed in their soft beds. The mental movement sketched by this quatrain is extraordinary: our eye flies out to the earth's inflamed edge, then falls back and goes black, leaving us with only the helpless, tactile sensation of sleep. Six sibilants in line 8 produce a sound of "sh-h-h," hushing but also paralyzing.

The third quatrain compares man's life to a "fire," an everyday utility endowed by Shakespeare with a dynamic biography (9–10). He projects himself into the fire's "glowing" phase, when the blaze is long gone and even the small, darting tongues have sputtered out. All that remains is hot coals, embers lying on a thick layer of "ashes," debris of the fire's flaming "youth." Shakespeare's metaphor makes our body temperature an index of ambition, physical stamina, and sexual passion. When it cools, we too will slowly "expire," that is, breathe our last (11). The acrid ashes are a "deathbed"—the second bed of the poem—because they are the funeral pyre of worldly desires. The fire metaphor ingeniously returns us to the start of the poem: these logs burned down to ash were cut from the "boughs" of the man-tree in the first quatrain (3). For Shakespeare, the human body is on fire from our day of birth. The thought is extended by a paradox: as living beings, we are simultaneously "nourished" and "consumed" (12). Creation and destruction are wed: the hotter the fire, the swifter it dies.

The final couplet is a direct address to the reader as well as the poet's stern self-reminder: "This thou perceiv'st, which makes thy love more strong, / To love that well which thou must leave ere long." Whatever we seek or crave—a person, a profession, a high ideal—is evanescent. Nothing survives the ash pit of the grave. Though surrender and farewell are cruelly built into human life, there is value in the doing. Our sense of life's transience intensifies its pleasures.

The sonnet's three submerged quatrains are like fleeting, elegiac self-portraits: the poet as a year, a day, and a fire. Shakespeare, like Darwin, sees humanity beset by impersonal forces. There is no reference here to God or an afterlife. Consciousness itself is elemental, an effect of light and heat that dissipates when our bodies are reabsorbed by nature.

TWO

WILLIAM SHAKESPEARE

Sonnet 29

When, in disgrace with Fortune and men's eyes,
I all alone beweep my outcast state,
And trouble deaf heaven with my bootless cries,
And look upon myself, and curse my fate,
Wishing me like to one more rich in hope,   5
Featured like him, like him with friends possessed,
Desiring this man's art and that man's scope,
With what I most enjoy contented least;
Yet in these thoughts myself almost despising,
Haply I think on thee, and then my state,   10
Like to the lark at break of day arising
From sullen earth, sings hymns at heaven's gate;
For thy sweet love remembered such wealth brings
That then I scorn to change my state with kings.

Poetic design in Shakespeare's Sonnet 29 is a tour de force that makes Sonnet 73's symmetrical, self-contained units look almost stodgy. Ignore the modern punctuation: Sonnet 29 is essentially a single sentence, cascading down the lines with the virtuosity of the natural speaking voice that Shakespeare mastered in his career as an actor and playwright. He treats sonnet structure with audacious, jazzlike improvisation, as if it weren't even there. Syntax too is plastic in his hands. Most of the poem is just a prelude, a piling up of subordinate and participial clauses. The main body of the sentence (subject and verb: "I think") doesn't arrive until the tenth line, where it acts as a pivotal point of transformation.

The sonnet re-creates an episode of severe depression that appears all too familiar to Shakespeare. (He was probably in his forties.) The litanylike cadence catches us up in an obsessive mental rhythm, so that we see things as he does. Direction is ingeniously indicated by theatrical "blocking": we are made to look one way and then another in a psychologically distorted world. At the same time, we feel burdened by heavy emotion, sinking to the nadir of the poem in the word "despising" (9). The overall effect is prophetically avant-garde: it's as if the poet, like an actor in tortured soliloquy, stands spotlit on a bare black stage.

Two-thirds of the poem consists of a list of half-imaginary grievances. It begins with an allegorical tableau, as crisply limned as in a late-medieval panel painting. Shakespeare (if we may identify him with the speaker) claims he is "outcast," ostracized, "in disgrace with Fortune and men's eyes" (1–2). To be in disfavor with "men's eyes" means to have lost social status: the disparaging male eyes glare or, more woundingly, glance and turn indifferently away. But important female eyes don't see him at all: he has been abandoned by Fortune (some editions wrongly drop the capitalization), the ancient goddess Fortuna, who turned a rudder or wheel and who would later become Lady Luck, patroness of gamblers. Nothing breaks Shakespeare's way. Fortune is blind to him, and the Christian God is "deaf" or perhaps nonexistent. The poet's "cries," or prayers, like those of *Hamlet*'s guilty but unrepentant king, are "bootless"—futile, useless—as they rise toward heaven and fade like echoes (3).

Self-absorbed and cursing his fate, the poet is momentarily braced by angry energy (4). But seething dissatisfactions erupt, a catalog of lacks and wants. He seems to gesture this way and that toward a parade of envied others who do not see him, since he has become an invisible man. The man "more rich in hope" has reason for cheer since he is on the fast track toward a splendid future (5). The second is well "featured," that is, handsome, a boon that in any age draws attention and brings preferment (6). (We could infer that the poet thought his own looks unimpressive or mediocre.) The third has "friends" in high places, family connections or contacts critical for advancement in the premodern court world. There are hints of petty rivalries among the cultural elite: Shakespeare, incredible to us, envies another's "art," that is, literary skill, probably because it is of a more regular, polished, and fashionable kind (7). And he feels intimidated by yet another's "scope," or intellectual power, presumably owed to a university education. (The middle-class Shakespeare had a solid Stratford primary schooling, where he acquired, according to a contemporary satire, "little Latin and less Greek.")

Art makes a disturbing reentry. That he is least "contented" with what he most enjoys suggests Shakespeare's writing career is in crisis (8). Uninspired, he is merely going through the motions. But his identity is so centered in art making that any threat to it worsens his sense of extremity. "Myself almost despising": he tastes the surfeited self-loathing that leads Hamlet to the brink of suicide (9).

At the corrosive word "despising," when the poem seems about to self-destruct, rescue "haply" (luckily) comes as a happy thought—the memory of a precious face (10). Is it a man or a woman? The poet blurs it. But since the sonnet's human dramatis personae have all been male, we might well conjecture that the beloved is the "fair youth" whom Sonnet 144 calls an "angel," a role he plays here over the distance of time. His effect on the poem and on Shakespeare's "state" of mind is immediate: the mood darts upward like "the lark at break of day arising" (11). It's a new dawn.

The plot line of the poem resembles a modern business graph that veers dizzyingly downward to bottom out in bankruptcy (9). At his lowest, the poet is sluggishly mired in "sullen earth," the gloom upon the hills just before sunrise, when the sky has already brightened (12). The lark bursts into song for the sheer joy of being alive. Its "hymns" follow the same arcing path as the poet's earlier "bootless" prayers, but a bird doesn't care if "heaven's gate" is locked. It makes music because it can. So does poetry flow from him, Shakespeare implies, when love is the goad. The beating of the lark's wings surely mimes the beating of his own heart, which quickens at the mere idea of the beloved.

The poem concludes in unqualified direct address: "For thy sweet love remembered such wealth brings / That then I scorn to change my state with kings" (13–14). Perhaps the sonnet was sent as a gift to its inspirer, but the beloved has already half materialized as a luminous presence. The friend's "sweet love" may or may not have been physical, but it is enduringly restorative. Lady Luck's stinginess has been neutralized by a bonanza of spiritual "wealth." Love allows the revitalized poet to "scorn" ambition and materialism: high rank and power now seem paltry. Emotional exaltation brings salvation. Shakespeare's art is reborn, crystallizing in the poem before us.

THREE

WILLIAM SHAKESPEARE

The Ghost's Speech
HAMLET I.V.34–40, 59–88

Now, Hamlet, hear.
'Tis given out that, sleeping in my orchard,
A serpent stung me. So the whole ear of Denmark
Is by a forgèd process of my death
Rankly abused. But know, thou noble youth,   5
The serpent that did sting thy father's life
Now wears his crown. . . .
      Sleeping within my orchard,
My custom always of the afternoon,
Upon my secure hour thy uncle stole   10
With juice of cursed hebona in a vial,
And in the porches of my ears did pour
The leperous distillment, whose effect
Holds such an enmity with blood of man
That swift as quicksilver it courses through   15
The natural gates and alleys of the body,
And with a sudden vigor it doth posset
And curd, like eager droppings into milk,
The thin and wholesome blood. So did it mine,
And a most instant tetter barked about   20
Most lazarlike with vile and loathsome crust
All my smooth body.
Thus was I, sleeping, by a brother's hand
Of life, of crown, of queen at once dispatched,
Cut off even in the blossoms of my sin,   25
Unhouseled, disappointed, unaneled,

No reck'ning made, but sent to my account
With all my imperfections on my head.
O, horrible! O, horrible! Most horrible!
If thou hast nature in thee, bear it not.   30
Let not the royal bed of Denmark be
A couch for luxury and damnèd incest.
But howsomever thou pursues this act,
Taint not thy mind, nor let thy soul contrive
Against thy mother aught. Leave her to heaven   35
And to those thorns that in her bosom lodge
To prick and sting her.

Shakespeare the poet often burns through Shakespeare the dramatist, not simply in the great soliloquies that have become actors' set pieces but in passages throughout his plays that can stand alone as poems. A remarkable example is the ghost's speech in *Hamlet,* an excerpt from the midnight encounter of father and son on Elsinore's windy battlement. The description by Hamlet the elder of his grisly murder by a treacherous brother, who stole his throne and wife, is a magnificent flight of strange, lurid poetry. The packed images twist and turn with a Mannerist sophistication, fascinating yet repulsive.

"Now, Hamlet, hear": with unnerving intensity and overbearing paternal authority, the ghost (whom Shakespeare himself reputedly played onstage) presses his heavy revelation on his agitated son (1). Hearing is the medium of first shock, but as the saga unfolds, the visual and the tactile take over. Words seem sticky, insinuating, invasive as we are drawn closer and closer to the grotesque scene. The speech builds from a fabrication, the official story issued by the palace bureaucracy: "'Tis given out that, sleeping in my orchard, / A serpent stung me" (2–3). The cover-up misleads a nation, stunned by grief into a single thought: "So the whole ear of Denmark / Is by a forgèd process of my death / Rankly abused" (3–5). The people are the body politic: unsettled, manipulated, paranoid, they are reduced to a giant, collective "ear" poisoned by lies—miming the king's secret murder. Government, which should serve truth, has become a fount of lies. The tale has been craftily "forgèd" because Claudius, the new king, is himself a forgery or fake, never destined by God for the throne. An ear "rankly abused" suggests force and trauma, a brutalizing of soft tissue. "Rank" also has a stench of squalor and decay, the pollution caused in *Hamlet* (as in Sophocles' *Oedipus Rex*) by corruption at the top.

The ghost's narrative of the murder begins with the hypnotic lilt of a lullaby: "Sleeping within my orchard, / My custom always of the afternoon"(8–9). "Custom," or routine, is predicated on trust, the illusion of safety craved by all human beings. Taken unawares in his "secure hour" by a disloyal ally, Hamlet senior recalls another king,

Duncan of Scotland, slain in his bed by his host, Macbeth ("Sleep no more! Macbeth does murder sleep," *Macbeth* II.ii.33–34). For the head of state to be at ease on leisurely afternoons means the nation is at peace. In medieval and Renaissance iconography, a king napping in his orchard would symbolize the harmony of nature and society: cultivated land is nature ordered by human reason and design. The well-managed garden, a major metaphor in *Hamlet*, is a paradigm of the wisely governed state. When the true gardener is gone, the world becomes (as young Hamlet complains) "an unweeded garden / That grows to seed," possessed by "things rank and gross in nature" (I.ii. 135–36). Mold, fungi, spiders, and rodents run wild, and fertility is aborted. ("A rat?" cries Hamlet, mistaking Polonius for Claudius and jamming his rapier through a bulging curtain; III.iv.23.)

The Danish royal garden was once Eden before the Fall, with Hamlet senior as Adam in the state of innocence. Thus the spurious report of the king's death by snakebite is figuratively true: the ghost says, "The serpent that did sting thy father's life / Now wears his crown" (6–7). Claudius the crowned reptile (like a quaint emblem in alchemy) is the primordial serpent with its inexplicable malice toward God's creation. Shakespeare's serpent succeeds in capturing Eve: "O Hamlet, what a falling-off was there," laments the ghost, wounded by his wife Gertrude's quick coupling with Claudius (I.v.47). The young prince inherits a world of disillusion after the Fall where, thanks to the serpent's machinations, human life is under sentence of death. The ghost's bitter sexual jealousy is magnified by voyeurism, his exiled watching and his later aggressive solicitude for Gertrude. Spying (a constant motif in this play) is also implicit in the stealth ("stole") with which Claudius ambushes his sleeping brother, who is rendered passive and robbed of potency (10). The hushed sense of trespass gives the murder a homoerotic tinge, as if its violation of a hidden pocket of the body rehearses male-on-male rape. Incest is a shadowy undercurrent in the play: Hamlet is obsessively focused on his mother's bedroom activities, while Laertes, bullying his sister Ophelia about her love life, wars with Hamlet for her affections.

In Renaissance England, poisoning, like stabbing in the back, was a dishonorable way to kill, associated with cowards, fickle women, and devious Italians. Hence the regicide Claudius is prima facie unmanly. Murder by ear is so esoteric that it makes the body (our own as well as the king's) seem hideously vulnerable. Quietly tipping his vial in the orchard, Claudius resembles a gardener tenderly watering a prize plant. An ancient architectural metaphor is also at work: the true king (as in Egypt) is conflated with the palace, a citadel that proves woefully easy to infiltrate and subvert. His ear is the palace vestibule ("porches"), and his veins are "the natural gates and alleys of the body" through which the poison, "swift as quicksilver," slithers like a snake or a draft of bad air, the medium of plague (12, 15–16). The poison's stunning speed and amorphousness are dramatized in Shakespeare's weaving of its multiple effects through eleven dizzyingly headlong lines. The poison's "enmity with blood of man" is suggestively satanic ("Satan" means "the Adversary"), blocking and canceling God's work (14). "With a sudden vigor it doth posset / And curd, like eager droppings into milk, / The thin and wholesome blood": the toxin mysteriously changes the blood chemically, clotting and curdling it as when acid ("eager") is dripped into milk (17–19). The pure stream is churned to sludge—our mother's milk of natural emotion gone sour (compare "th' milk of human kindness," *Macbeth* I.v.16). Drumming rhythms capture the choking of the king's system with mushrooming tumors and blobby growths like cottage cheese.

The poison is a "leperous distillment," causing or feigning the gangrene in leprosy (13). The surface of the king's skin massively erupts, while his warrior's sinews and muscles melt away. The realm's supreme power is now a pitiable outcast ("most lazarlike," like the biblical beggar Lazarus, a leper covered with sores; 21). His flesh is a raw wound, with the heroic human contours lost in a nauseating mass of undifferentiated tissue. A scab ("a most instant tetter") shoots around his body: his skin crawls, along with ours—replicating the sensation of the serpent-murderer creeping up on his prey (20–22). Suppurating and drying in a magic flash, the king's "smooth body," with its aristocratic refinement, is encased in a "vile and loathsome crust." It is bizarrely "barked about"—covered with bark like a tree (a good example of Shakespeare's typical conversion of nouns to verbs). Animal to vegetable: the king has tumbled down the great chain of being to the subhuman, where he becomes a worthless thing, a rotting log in a grove. The passage exploits a sensuous concreteness of language to activate our atavistic horror at death and decay. We recoil at the staccato fusillade of consonants that make us hear the crackling of the victim's mammoth scab (20–21).

Robbed of his life, the king has also nearly lost his soul. He was denied last rites ("unhouseled, disappointed, unaneled") whereby he could make confession and receive absolution (26). He was, he protests, "cut off even in the blossoms of my sin" (25). This image sees man after the Fall as a plant bearing (in Baudelaire's phrase) flowers of evil. It's as if sin is intrinsic to organic life. Indeed, "cursed hebona," the plant (possibly henbane) crushed by Claudius for its poison juice, represents a minute segment of nature damned by heaven and charged with the death force (11). There is a striking contrast between the king's physical vulnerability and the severe mathematic imposed by divine judgment: "No reck'ning made, but sent to my account / With all my imperfections on my head" (27–28). The weight of those "imperfections" is ominously transferred to Hamlet ("thou noble youth") through this very speech (5). If the son has "nature" in him—that is, filial love—he must rise to duty (30). Sensitive, indecisive Hamlet will be expected to "bear it not"—to avenge his father's loss of absolution by dragging the murderer to his own bloody reckoning.

The ghost's journey into the painful past comes full circle with his reference to "the royal bed of Denmark"—or more precisely to its female occupant, whom the bed wraps like a pod (31). Claudius is curiously erased from the picture. He is implicitly present as a contaminant, polluting and perverting the bed into "a couch for luxury and damnèd incest"—sloth and unbridled lust divorced from dynastic procreation (32). (Whether a woman's remarriage to her husband's brother constitutes incest is debatable, though Hamlet, like John the Baptist denouncing Herodias, clearly believes it is.) The royal bed as valuable artifact and symbol of succession is found in literature as early as Homer's *Odyssey*. *Hamlet*'s royal bed—declined by the king for his open-air siestas—is repeatedly identified with the queen, possession of whom is at issue throughout the play. The ghost's program of vengeance requires a liberation and purgation of the bed where Hamlet himself may well have been conceived and born.

In forbidding his son to take punitive action against Gertrude

("Taint not thy mind, nor let thy soul contrive / Against thy mother aught"), the ghost can be seen as motivated by compassion or by cruelty (34–35). "Leave her to heaven"—the highest court—"and to those thorns that in her bosom lodge / To prick and sting her": the brambles of the unweeded garden have invaded the palace (35–37). Does the king spare his queen out of sadism? Does he relish seeing her suffer? His metaphor winds her heart (like the Sacred Heart of Jesus) with a thorny vine: it's the parasitic embrace of the serpent usurper, Claudius. The queen is a fleshy fruit clutched, snared, stung, and blighted. Sexual intercourse is imagined as intimate torture, an excruciating love-death with the penis ("prick") as a darting tongue or poisoned fang. The hovering ghost suffers from his own witness and incapacity. Gertrude's conscience, he insists, will be her own best torturer: her erotic pleasures will always be commingled with spiritual pain.

The ghost's sinister speech is decadent insofar as it shows civilization collapsing into the realm of gross matter. Divine creation is reversed as supersubtle evil dissolves forms and beings. Shakespeare moves swiftly from suffocation and extinction in the garden to bondage and torment in the bedroom. The king's triple cry—"O, horrible! O, horrible! Most horrible!"—is an aria close to a howl, requiring consummate skill from an actor (29). Our ear, like the king's, is invaded by poison via the revolting images, which can barely be intelligibly processed. The abandonment of a mutilated corpse like trash is an affront to human dignity (compare "garbage" as the food of "lust," I.v.55–57). The king's encrusted body is ugly as offal: is this why he wears armor for his nightly walk? The charismatic warrior whom his intellectual son fulsomely compares to Hyperion, the sun god, is physically ravaged and shamed (I.ii.140). His armor warns of Norway's looming threat but also signifies a state of war among his nearest and dearest—those lifetime conflicts of Freudian family romance that Shakespeare so presciently grasped. The garden now breeds pestilence: the king's corpse, restless because of an unavenged murder, exudes the sulfurous bad smells that fill the play.

In eerie mood and macabre detail, the ghost's speech has a style that would later be called Gothic. The flamboyant ghoulishness of such passages in Shakespeare's plays was disdained as vulgar by Neo-classicists, particularly in France. But the Gothic was triumphantly reclaimed by Romanticism, which would in turn engender modern horror films. The ghost's serpentine speech, like the monumental Hellenistic sculpture *Laocoön* (which shows a Trojan priest and his sons strangled by sea snakes), reflects the anxieties of a turbulent "late" phase of culture. The mature Shakespeare of the jittery Jacobean period may have lost faith in politics and public ethics. Idealism fails in *Hamlet*, as man regresses to the reptilian.

FOUR

JOHN DONNE

The Flea

Marke but this flea, and marke in this,
How little that which thou deny'st me is;
It suck'd me first, and now sucks thee,
And in this flea, our two bloods mingled bee;
Thou know'st that this cannot be said   5
A sinne, nor shame, nor losse of maidenhead,
  Yet this enjoyes before it wooe,
  And pamper'd swells with one blood made of two,
  And this, alas, is more than wee would doe.

Oh stay, three lives in one flea spare,   10
Where wee almost, yea more than maryed are.
This flea is you and I, and this
Our mariage bed, and mariage temple is;
Though parents grudge, and you, w'are met,
And cloysterd in these living walls of Jet.   15
  Though use make you apt to kill mee,
  Let not to this, selfe murder added bee,
  And sacrilege, three sinnes in killing three.

Cruell and sudden, hast thou since
Purpled thy naile, in blood of innocence?   20
Wherein could this flea guilty bee,
Except in that drop which it suckt from thee?

Yet thou triumph'st, and saist that thou
Find'st not thy selfe, nor mee the weaker now;
'Tis true, then learne how false, feares bee;   25
Just so much honor, when thou yeeld'st to mee,
Will wast, as this flea's death tooke life from thee.

J ohn Donne, whose career overlapped Shakespeare's, was the lead-
ing figure of the loosely affiliated Metaphysical school of Brit-
ish poetry. The literary idiosyncrasies of the Metaphysicals, always
controversial, would be denounced by eighteenth-century critics like
Samuel Johnson. Few Romantics were admirers of this witty, cerebral
style; an exception was Emily Dickinson. Interest in Metaphysical
poetry revived in the twentieth century, when it was championed for
its intellectuality by modernists like T. S. Eliot.

"The Flea" is one of the oddest love poems ever written. It's
a good illustration of the Metaphysicals' effrontery, incongruities,
and ostentatious use of conceits (elaborate metaphors). Like so many
poems of the period, it's a cunning strategy of seduction. Here, how-
ever, the poet satirizes his own sexual desperation. The date of com-
position is unknown, but it presumably precedes Donne's secret
marriage to Anne More in 1601. (Their union was opposed by her
high-ranking parents, who objected to Donne's Catholicism.) The
poem purports to show Anne resisting his advances until they can be
legally married. As his wife, she would inspire Donne's great poem "A
Valediction Forbidding Mourning," but she was not the woman ad-
dressed in his early, bawdy "To His Mistress Going to Bed."

The three long stanzas of "The Flea" are like scenes from a play.
The abrupt opening (a feature of Metaphysical poetry) has a dra-
matic immediacy partly inspired by London theater, then booming.
Donne also shows a feel for the printed page here that was rare when
poets circulated their work in manuscript. He uses the blank space
between stanzas as eloquently as words themselves. The poem begins
in the vernacular, as if the reader has dropped into the middle of a
conversation. Donne may have learned this from Shakespeare, who
often starts scenes and even plays in an offhand manner. However,
the overall structure of "The Flea" is formal. Its appeal to the beloved
is based not on romantic emotion but on logic, almost as if it were a
court brief. (Donne studied law before entering government service.)

"Marke but this flea": observe this. Our attention, as well as the lady's, is seized, as we are drawn into an intimate, sheltered space. Fleas were a mundane annoyance, infesting bedding and upholstery even in wealthy homes. The Mannerist grotesquerie of the flea metaphor flouts the faded Petrarchan tradition of love poetry. Donne exploits the mock-epic contrast between the insect's size and the burden of meaning it's asked to carry. Allusions and homilies—the lavish attention normally paid to devotional symbols like the crucifix—are heaped on it as if it were a patient pack mule. The hapless flea will actually end up as a holy martyr to love. Its transformation begins with its theft of human blood—first the poet's and then the lady's, which are "mingled" like potion in a beaker (3–4).

As it magically "swells with one blood made of two," the flea becomes their weird child (8). The couple have somehow vaulted to procreation without sexual intercourse, for which a virgin always pays a blood price. The poet tries to minimize the latter: "How little" is the "losse of maidenhead"—the hymen as inconvenient barrier (2, 6). Since it's neither "sinne, nor shame" to lose a drop of blood to a flea, why fixate on a useless shred of tissue? The flea, in its bustling animal drive, "enjoyes," or takes its pleasure, "before it wooe" (7). Fleas, in other words, are rapists. "This, alas, is more than wee would doe": the first stanza ends with Donne's rueful assurance that, even in high heat, he will woo and never rape. As a gentleman, he knows his pleasure depends on a woman's consent.

In the pause (a heartbeat) between stanzas, there's activity we don't see. "Oh stay," cries the poet: spare that flea (10)! The lady has clearly moved to kill it; hence the rest of the stanza consists of Donne's oratorical plea for clemency. It's an amusing reversal of conventional melodrama, where a weeping woman (like Pocahontas, who visited England in 1616) intercedes to beg mercy from a grim executioner. To distract her from her lethal project, the poet blows up a blizzard of whimsical metaphors. The flea becomes the Holy Trinity ("three lives in one"; compare the poem's three stanzas). The flea is their "mariage bed" and "mariage temple," a chapel made of "living walls of Jet"— the insect's black shell (13, 15). In the flea's mixed blood, they "more than maryed are," having in effect already become lovers (11). Gratitude is owed the flea, which has protectively "cloystered" or closeted them (like monks and nuns living without sex) against a hostile world where "parents grudge"—that is, ungenerously forbid true lovers' happiness (14–15).

But she too "grudge[s]" in torturing her suitor by making him wait and wait (14). He needles her with hackneyed Petrarchanisms: "Though use make you apt to kill mee" (16). Habit and overfamiliarity, he claims, make her treat him with excruciating indifference, so that she has become a passé type—the frosty Petrarchan mistress, killing her lover with scorn. Surely she's more sensible and au courant than that! Don't add suicide ("selfe murder") to homicide, he pleads (17). It would be "sacrilege" too, since the flea's death would mean desecration and razing of their "mariage temple"—as if a flea's extermination were a historic atrocity comparable to the Romans' destruction of Herod's temple (18).

The lady's response to the poet's torrent of images is short and sweet: during the pregnant pause between the second and third stanzas, the flea meets a swift end at her hands. She is serenely impervious to the poet's dazzling flights of rhetoric. He is stung but hardly stopped. "Cruell and sudden" he calls her in feigned despair, casting her again as yesteryear's imperious Petrarchan lady (19). She has "purpled" her fingernail (still a fail-safe way to kill fleas) in "blood of innocence" and thus turned tyrant, like Herod slaughtering the Innocents or Pontius Pilate washing his hands of the blood of a just man (20).

The beloved's silence has its own power. Fond but weary of her chatterbox suitor, she may just be trying to take a nap! Determined to rouse a reaction, the poet peppers her with questions. She has acted arbitrarily, he charges, like a ruthless hanging judge: what was the flea "guilty" of except "that drop" it sucked from her (21–22)? This seems to make her laugh ("thou triumph'st") and blithely reply that she finds neither herself nor him any "the weaker" from loss of blood (23–24). The poet pounces on this as if it were the first false move by an opponent in a wrestling match. " 'Tis true," he exults, taking the weight of her lunge and turning it against her: her own statement is proof of "how false" her "feares" of sex are (25). The loss of "honor" in chastity's end is infinitesimal—no graver in the cosmic scheme than the death of a flea (26–27).

Whether Donne's ingenious indictment of the perennial double standard was then or ever effective, we don't know. The poem's juxtaposition of desire and disgust would be a risky maneuver in any courtship. But "The Flea" makes us feel the evolution in personal relationships at the English Renaissance, when marriage acquired the romantic idealism that adultery had had in medieval literature. Though Donne's fiancée says little, the poem's precosity is a tribute to her intelligence. He will jump through hoops to win her admiration. The poem's self-conscious artificiality captures the fragility of the complex rituals with which society has always tried to contain and control sexual energy.

In its arch absurdity, "The Flea" resembles Surrealist art. It has the grandiloquence and sexual explicitness of Salvador Dalí's dream paintings, where crawling ants signify itching lust. Dalí's fascinated subordination to his challenging wife, Gala, resembles the romantic pattern in "The Flea." Donne portrays himself, like Dalí, as a showy phallic swordsman baffled and bemused by a forceful, alluring woman, who brushes him away like a pesky fly.

FIVE

JOHN DONNE

Holy Sonnet I

Thou hast made me, And shall thy worke decay?
Repaire me now, for now mine end doth haste,
I runne to death, and death meets me as fast,
And all my pleasures are like yesterday;
I dare not move my dimme eyes any way,   5
Despaire behind, and death before doth cast
Such terror, and my feeble flesh doth waste
By sinne in it, which it t'wards hell doth weigh;
Onely thou art above, and when towards thee
By thy leave I can looke, I rise againe;   10
But our old subtle foe so tempteth me,
That not one houre my selfe I can sustaine;
Thy Grace may wing me to prevent his art,
And thou like Adamant draw mine iron heart.

John Donne's body of writing falls into two parts, secular and sacred. After he converted and took holy orders in the Church of England, Donne turned away from love poetry and focused his artistic energy on sermons and devotional verse. His sonnets show Shakespeare's influence, most blatantly in Holy Sonnet I, whose fluid rhythms and falling pattern recall Shakespeare's Sonnet 29. The imperious Petrarchan lady of sonnet tradition has metamorphosed into God, whom the love-starved poet begs and berates. From the arguable evidence of his plays and poems, Shakespeare was probably an agnostic, but Donne clearly believed in a personal God, with whom he conducted a long, wrangling, sometimes rancorous relationship.

Holy Sonnet I is a drama of mankind's spiritual struggles that transcends the Christian frame of reference. It begins with trademark Metaphysical abruptness: "Thou hast made me, And shall thy worke decay?" The poet demands God's attention and even rebukes him for negligence. Scripture says we are made in God's image—so why has he let us slide into sin and imperfection? "Repaire me now," Donne insists—using the imperative mood, which would have been startlingly inappropriate for a subordinate addressing a superior (2). There is no flattering honorific, no gesture of deference. He treats God like a superintendent responsible for maintenance and upkeep.

Donne's excuse for rudeness is a claim of emergency: death fast approaches, as it does for every man. "I runne to death," he says in fatigue, as if the body were an hourglass through which our disintegrating flesh trickles like grains of sand (3). The image of running to death introduces the poem's complex directional theme. On the road of life—an ancient metaphor in world literature—we press forward through daily distraction and agitation. But is the poet running *from* something? "All my pleasures are like yesterday": the lusts and ecstasies of young adulthood, now so distant and unreal, will return to haunt him when he meets his maker (4).

"I dare not move my dimme eyes any way": where can one look for salvation (5)? The poet's sight is "dimme" from human weakness and limitation as well as the eternal twilight of earthly illusion. "Despaire behind, and death before doth cast / Such terror": life unfolds amid macabre shadows (6–7). Thanks to past errors and indiscretions, "despair" threatens from the road already traveled, but "terror" waits ahead in death and judgment. Push-pull: buffeted by contrary impulses, the poet feels yet another sensation, as his "feeble flesh," withered by age and illness and burdened by sin, begins to sink toward hell. Paradoxically, sin "doth waste" or emaciate him even while making him denser. He is trapped in matter and crushed by internal and external forces.

"Weigh," with its sagging, extended vowel, is the poem's nadir, where we feel hell's black, oppressive gravitational pull (8). Rescue takes time but is launched by the transitional phrase "Onely thou art above," which makes us glance upward (9). "Onely [only]" is grammatically dual: as a conjunction meaning "however," it starts the escape from hell; as an adjective modifying "thou," it's a stirring profession of faith. Donne is saying, in effect, "There is only one God." From that simple declaration, energy surges into him and the poem. When glimmering hope lets him "looke" expectantly toward heaven again—something possible only by God's "leave" or permission—his dire descent is checked (10). "I rise againe," he exults, following the model of Jesus, who fell and staggered to his feet again on the way to Calvary and who harrowed hell before his resurrection, the happy ending promised to all faithful Christians.

In life, however, there can be no final victory. Satan remains "our old subtle foe," invisible as well as cunning (11). The wraithlike conspirator, the spoiler of God's plan, always tests or "tempteth" man with flashy baubles. Human strength is not enough: Donne cannot "sustaine" himself even for "one houre" without God's providential hand, which dips into every detail of earthly life (12). Special intervention by "Grace" is urgently needed—the merciful Third Person of the Trinity, usually depicted as a shaft of light or a white dove. Rapid, darting rhythms capture the dove's flight as it swoops in to "wing" the poet's soul to safety (13). The honorific coarsely missing from the second line now appears as a pun: "Thy Grace" as a term of respect conveys Donne's recognition of God's royal majesty and also heralds their reconciliation.

The sonnet's allegorical climax is cinematic, like the windswept episodes of Dante's *Inferno*. The faltering soul is snatched in midair by the dove with beating wings. Divine action must "prevent" Satan's "art" or devious craft: the dual meanings of "prevent"—to stop and to precede—are punned on (13). It's a chase scene, with the soul eluding the clutches of a demon predator. Meanwhile, the First Person of the Trinity, the stern Father, enters the poem as "Adamant"—a diamond-hard lodestone—whose irresistible magnetism pulls Donne's dull, stubborn "iron heart" toward redemption (14).

Pictorially, the poem is a cruciform emblem. The earthly horizontal—Donne's path from yesterday's fleshpots to tomorrow's tomb—is crossed by the embattled vertical extending from heaven to hell. As in Shakespeare's Sonnet 29, there is a slow, steady sinking into gloom, interrupted two-thirds of the way through by a winged savior, who bears the heart skyward. In Shakespeare, a human beloved, potent even in memory, is identified with the cheerful lark of sunrise. In Donne, the benefactor is the Holy Ghost, airlifting the soul from certain damnation.

Sonnet's end is the finality of salvation, when time stops and eternity begins. "Adamant," positioned at the midpoint of the last line like the keystone of an arch, makes us feel God the Father's overwhelming masculine power, as Donne characteristically perceives and honors it. With its brusque consonants, "Adamant" is massively resolute in sound. Its capital peaks like a holy mountain embedded in the text. It marks the spot where the quester, a tainted heir of old Adam, sees the face of God, who is the Alpha and Omega, the first and last. The poet's impure heart, having shed its envelope of "feeble flesh," is drawn toward God's adamantine touch, which turns iron into spiritual gold.

SIX

JOHN DONNE

Holy Sonnet XIV

Batter my heart, three-person'd God; for you
As yet but knock, breathe, shine, and seek to mend;
That I may rise, and stand, o'erthrow me, and bend
Your force to break, blow, burn and make me new.
I, like an usurp'd towne, to another due,   5
Labour to admit you, but Oh, to no end,
Reason, your viceroy in me, me should defend,
But is captiv'd, and proves weak or untrue.
Yet dearly I love you, and would be loved faine,
But am betroth'd unto your enemie: 10
Divorce me, untie, or break that knot againe,
Take me to you, imprison me, for I
Except you enthrall me, never shall be free,
Nor ever chaste, except you ravish me.

In Renaissance and Baroque art, sex and religion are often startlingly intertwined. The source of this motif was the Old Testament's Song of Songs, admired by mystics like Saint Teresa of Avila, the great Spanish Carmelite reformer shown in ecstasy in a famous Bernini sculpture. The Song of Songs consists of canticles of sensuous Hebrew love poetry, interpreted by Christian theologians as an allegory of the bridegroom Jesus knocking at the door of the female soul.

The Petrarchan sonnet was rarely as sexually explicit as Donne makes it in Holy Sonnet XIV, where he portrays himself—or rather his heart—as a kidnapped virgin crying out for a virile liberator. The poem begins with the same brash imperative mood of Holy Sonnet I: "Batter my heart, three-person'd God." Strong action is needed to rescue the poet from sin. Of the three persons of the Trinity, God has thus far ineffectually acted only through the milder two: "for you / As yet but knock, breathe, shine, and seek to mend" (1–2). Jesus has too politely rapped on his bride's door, which must be broken down by the overwhelming power of God the Father—a warlike battering ram rather than the tender Lamb of God.

In the second line, Donne's door metaphor seamlessly blends into a new image, drawn from common objects of the workaday world, with which the poet as maker aligns himself. (Such breaches of literary decorum in Metaphysical poetry are historically analogous to Caravaggio's controversial painting—rejected by the patron—of Saint Matthew as a humble peasant with calloused feet.) Jesus, the foster child of a Nazareth carpenter, has become a craftsman—a silversmith or kettle maker to whom a broken pot (the poet's heart) is brought for repair. Still hoping to "mend" or patch it, the smith tests the vessel's strength by knocking and tapping all around it to hear where the metal has worn thin. The breath with which he mists it before polishing (the final stage in writing too) is the Third Person of the Trinity, the Holy Spirit or "breath of life" with which God infused the dust to create Adam (Genesis 2.7). The old pot's buffed-up "shine" is the Son as "the true Light" (John 1.9).

For deliverance from life's thronging temptations, however, Donne needs radical, even violent aid: "bend / Your force to break, blow, burn and make me new" (3–4). The soul-vessel must be hacked to pieces and melted down over high heat to purge its impurities. The aggressive alliteration—a barrage of explosive *b* sounds—makes us feel the trauma of destruction before rebirth. There are sexual innuendos in "make me new" and also in "That I may rise, and stand, o'erthrow me," a paradox conflating erection with resurrection (3). Spiritual victory strangely requires defeat by God, since man is too weak to achieve redemption on his own. A higher self must be forged from the wreckage of his old identity.

The main metaphor of the sonnet's first quatrain is the heart as leaky pot; that of the second quatrain is the heart as a citadel under siege: "I, like an usurp'd town, to another due" (5). A king, the rightful ruler, is away and has left a "viceroy" (literally, vice king; compare vice president) as the town's steward and defender (7). But the viceroy, identified with "reason," is "captiv'd" (captured) and has buckled under pressure (8). Coward or traitor (he "proves weak or untrue"), he has surrendered the town to the "enemie" (10). It's an allegorical saga: returning to heaven after creating mankind, God the king left reason (the divine spark distinguishing us from animals) as his viceroy. In other words, logic should be enough to persuade us to avoid sin. But human intellect is "weak" and easily duped by Satan, who cleverly infiltrates the heart and hardens it to God's grace. Dante makes a similar point in the *Divine Comedy:* Vergil, the epic poet who symbolizes reason and language, can lead Dante only so far; at the gates of Paradise, the beautiful Beatrice, symbolizing faith, takes over as tour guide in the ascent to truth.

Holy Sonnet XIV fuses politics and romance. Donne's soul is a maiden "to another due"—that is, promised to God. But she has been coerced and "betroth'd" to the invader, as if she were Persephone carried off by the prince of hell (5, 10). Like a loyalist resistance fighter, she struggles vainly to open the city gates to the true king: "I . . . / Labour to admit you, but Oh, to no end" (5–6). All she can do is swear her love for God and assure him she would gladly ("faine") be loved by him in turn (9). The heroine's emotions accelerate in a torrent of imperatives and paradoxes: she longs to be divorced and cut off from the vile usurper so that she can be safely sequestered or even jailed ("imprison") by her Lord (11–12).

By projecting himself into female anguish, victimization and bondage ("break that knot"), the poet is playing with transsexual and homoerotic effects (11). Most of his contemporaries, however, would probably have understood the poem as simply a provocative fantasia on the popular Renaissance theme of sacred and profane love. True freedom, Donne asserts, comes only through servitude to God (in philosophical terms, the good; 12–13). He appeals to God to "enthrall" him, a verb meaning to enamor or entrance but also to subjugate (a "thrall" was a medieval slave or serf; 13). The city of the heart, prefiguring the New Jerusalem, must be destroyed in order to save it. The brutal paradox of Donne's last line still stuns: "Nor ever chaste, except you ravish me." We will never be pure until we are abducted and raped by God.

SEVEN

GEORGE HERBERT

Church-monuments

While that my soul repairs to her devotion,
Here I intombe my flesh, that it betimes
May take acquaintance of this heap of dust;
To which the blast of death's incessant motion,
Fed with the exhalation of our crimes,   5
Drives all at last. Therefore I gladly trust

My bodie to this school, that it may learn
To spell his elements, and finde his birth
Written in dustie heraldrie and lines;
Which dissolution sure doth best discern,   10
Comparing dust with dust, and earth with earth.
These laugh at Jet and Marble put for signes,

To sever the good fellowship of dust,
And spoil the meeting. What shall point out them,
When they shall bow, and kneel, and fall down flat   15
To kisse those heaps, which now they have in trust?
Deare flesh, while I do pray, learn here thy stemme
And true descent; that when thou shalt grow fat,

And wanton in thy cravings, thou mayst know,
That flesh is but the glasse, which holds the dust   20
That measures all our time; which also shall
Be crumbled into dust. Mark here below
How tame these ashes are, how free from lust,
That thou mayst fit thy self against thy fall.

In 1630, George Herbert became rector of Bemerton in a country parish near Salisbury. When he died three years later at the age of forty, he left a large body of unpublished poetry, all of it devotional. Some of Herbert's poems are witty and tricky in the Metaphysical manner, while others are quietly contemplative, with a sweet simplicity reminiscent of the fragments of Sappho.

"Church-monuments" is a profound allegory in charmingly amusing form. The poet—or rather his rational mind—assumes the dramatic role of a gentleman arriving at church with two companions. The first is his spouse, his feminine soul, who "repairs" (departs) to her prayers in the chancel (1). The other is his body ("my flesh"), imagined as a child left by his parents at Sunday school (2). The entire text of the poem consists of the father's firm warning to the child to tend to his lessons.

School is being rather uncomfortably held in the crypt—one of those picturesque old chapels where nobles were buried in elevated sarcophagi or in wells under the stone floor. The title's church monuments would include the vault and memorial stones, as well as any life-size images of the dead laid out in fancy dress or suits of armor. The "dustie heraldrie"—medieval shields colorfully painted with family crests—suggests these people were important in their time (9). (Herbert belonged to a noble Welsh family.)

The poet temporarily "intombe[s]" his body in the crypt with "this heap of dust"—the corpses, who are eccentric teachers as well as sluggish fellow pupils (2–3). All of us, swept along like withered autumn leaves by a relentless "blast," will eventually end up at this grisly school (4). That stormy force is "death's incessant motion," pushing us day by day from birth toward extinction. There is no shelter, even in church, from its implacable pressure. The wind is intensified by the putrid "exhalation of our crimes"—gas from rot, including the living human body corrupted by sin (5).

The poet "gladly trust[s]" his body to this school, which offers elementary education in the facts of life (6–7). First assignments are anatomy and genealogy, where the student will "learn / To spell his elements" and find his birth "written" in the dust of earthly matter (7–9). The "lines" parsed like a classroom alphabet are the chapel's death dates and epitaphs—germane to body but not soul. The master lesson is "dissolution" or decay, illustrating death's creeping omnipresence (10). "Comparing dust with dust, and earth with earth," the body gazes at its own bleak future in the crypt's moldering masses (11). The reference text for today's sermon is Ecclesiastes: "All are of the dust, and all turn to dust," alluding in turn to God's creation of man from "the dust of the ground" (Ecclesiastes 3.20; Genesis 2.7).

Despite its ghoulish theme, "Church-monuments" has the disarming sprightliness of a fairy tale. Planted in their dank stronghold, the corpses "laugh" at pompous "signes"—the gravestones fabricated of costly materials like "Marble" and "Jet" (a jewel-like black anthracite; 12). All that paraphernalia simply gets in the way to "spoil" the party. The dead revel in their own splinter congregation, where coffins and tombs impede "the good fellowship of dust" (13). No matter how strenuously self-deluded potentates try to preserve class barriers, the cadavers' prayer "meeting" should be a jovial mixer, like a country pub. There's nothing to fear, anyhow, after the body has lost thought and sensation. The church monuments themselves will inevitably crack and disintegrate: what will memorialize *them,* "when they shall bow, and kneel, and fall down flat / To kisse those heaps, which now they have in trust" (14–16)? The monuments' slow fall over centuries seems to unfold before our eyes by time-lapse photography. These grand ornaments, commissioned by the high and mighty, will eventually humble themselves at the feet of a greater lord—death. Stripped of beauty, they will be forced to embrace as kin the gruesome human remains they hold "in trust"—like corroded coins in an ancient, buried hoard.

Affectionately charging his body ("Deare flesh") to be a good pupil, the poet rejoins his soul, already in prayer, and fuses with her (17). By implication, his spirit rises while his body waits below, learning its "stemme / And true descent," the family tree rooted in slippery mutability (17–18). From this uncanny encounter with its ancestors, the body will take away a mental souvenir for the perilous times when it grows "fat / And wanton in [its] cravings"—when slothful complacency and animal appetite defeat the soul's higher promptings (18–19). The memento mori takes the form of an hourglass with the curvilinear silhouette of the human body: "flesh is but the glasse, which holds the dust / That measures all our time; which also shall / Be crumbled into dust" (20–22). As the sands flow through his hourglass, Herbert makes us hear and feel faint, regular pulses (like a water clock) on the words "flesh," "glasse," "dust," and "time." Then, with the end of time, the hourglass wobbles and tumbles off the end of one line onto the next, where it smashes to powder ("crumbled into dust").

The summation is sterner: "Mark" (observe), the poet admonishes his body, how "tame" and docile and how "free from lust" are these sad heaps of mortal "ashes" (22–23). All of life's noise, flurry, and pretension vanish when our hour is up. The rigorous curriculum of the crypt puts the body through its paces to "fit" or prepare it for its fate—the "fall" that none can escape ever since man's Fall brought death into the world (24). The poem is in fact structured like a fall— a formal cascade like a Baroque fountain: Herbert ignores the stanza breaks and lets his sentences spill over the gap. The effect is refreshing, like soft rain dribbling off a roof. The poem's playful, soothing rhythms distance its unsettling imagery of death and decay. Teasing yet compassionate, Herbert makes his schoolroom crypt a crowded capsule of earthly life, where grief and loss coexist with pleasure and joy.

EIGHT

GEORGE HERBERT

The Quip

The merrie world did on a day
With his train-bands and mates agree
To meet together, where I lay,
And all in sport to geere at me.

First, Beautie crept into a rose,   5
Which when I pluckt not, Sir, said she,
Tell me, I pray, Whose hands are those?
But thou shalt answer, Lord, for me.

Then Money came, and chinking still,
What tune is this, poore man? said he: 10
I heard in Musick you had skill.
But thou shalt answer, Lord, for me.

Then came brave Glorie puffing by
In silks that whistled, who but he?
He scarce allow'd me half an eie.   15
But thou shalt answer, Lord, for me.

Then came quick Wit and Conversation,
And he would needs a comfort be,
And, to be short, make an Oration.
But thou shalt answer, Lord, for me.   20

Yet when the houre of thy designe
To answer these fine things shall come;
Speak not at large; say, I am thine:
And then they have their answer home.

This poem has the bouncy vitality of an illustrated children's book. Its brand of moral allegory had gone out of literary fashion after Shakespeare's generation brought naturalism to theater. "The Quip" is a comic version of dramatic episodes in Edmund Spenser's allegorical epic, *The Faerie Queene* (1590–96), with its medieval setting and archaic language. In its appealing accessibility, however, Herbert's poem prefigures one of the most popular books in history, John Bunyan's *Pilgrim's Progress* (1678).

In "The Quip," the poet is beset by temptation by four personified vices, who try to distract him from his commitment to God. He is secluded yet undefended, like Jesus harried in the wilderness. The "merrie world," depicted as male, conspires to ambush him: this is the contemporary smart set, consumed by power and ambition (1). Its "train-bands and mates" (militias and henchmen as well as pals), roaming around like a gang of armed bandits, gather to "geere" at him "in sport," like the Roman soldiers who mock Jesus (2–4).

In the first stanza, the crowd streams toward the pensive poet as if he were the main attraction at a bearbaiting. In the second stanza, his personal space is invaded by a half-occult presence ("Beautie"). In the next three stanzas, a parade passes by, with each marcher pausing to upbraid him, as if he were a prisoner shamed in the town stocks. The poem is episodically structured in symmetrical scenes, each with its master character. The sequential design resembles that of late-medieval panel paintings by Duccio or Giotto.

Beautie, stealthy, seductive, and explicitly female, creeps into a nearby rose, as if she were a crafty fusion of Eve and serpent in nature's garden (5). When the poet declines to "pluck" her—succumb to her charms and yield to lust—she taunts him, "Whose hands are those?" (6–7). He's acting, she insinuates, like a serf or bondman rather than like a real man or free Briton. He doesn't take her bait; swallowing his humiliation, he refuses all reply. His remedy is to turn his mental focus away from the sensuous outer world toward his inner vision of God, to whom his hands—and by extension his life's work—are dedicated.

"*But thou shalt answer, Lord, for me*": this haunting refrain is itali-cized because the line is silent and hovers in another dimension (8). It's a prayer blazing a trail to heaven. It illuminates the connection be-tween a believer under duress and the personal Savior of Protes-tantism. Whenever it appears (four times in all), the refrain vaults the poet out of reach of his aggressive tempters, whose rebuke is deferred until the Second Coming of Jesus, when the good will be justified.

Greed, the vice of the third stanza, is a walking money bag, "chink-ing" or clinking with the clatter of coins (9). When he gets no homage from the poet, Money dismisses him and his poetry with condescend-ing pity: You, "poore man" (literally true of a man of the cloth in an obscure parish), are playing a "tune" no one wants or understands (10). Why aren't you writing the kind of song that sells? Herbert is tone-deaf to the world's favorite "Musick," the tinkle of lucre (11). His eccentric, old-fashioned literary style (he was also an accomplished musician) has evidently gotten him tagged for lack of "skill"—the usual fate of those who go their own way.

The fourth stanza's snobbish autocrat is so drunk with self-love that even acknowledging the poet would be beneath him. "Glorie" is vanity, an immoderate desire for fame and reputation (13). His nose is so high in the air that he can spare only "half an eie" for the unfor-tunates beneath him on the social ladder (15). There's a lot of noise in this stanza but significantly no speech. Glorie is huffing and "puff-ing" as he hurries by, as if he is fat and swollen (puffed up) with pride. His "silks that whistled" are his fancy silk pantaloons rubbing together—a silly, empty sound (14). Glorie is "brave" not because he's courageous but because he's all surface and show.

The fourth temptation would be the most agonizing for a poet in love with words: "quick Wit and Conversation"—imagined as a sin-gle, hybrid being—stands for intellect or cleverness for its own sake (17). This character is one of those great talkers whose brilliance has evaporated into thin air because they lacked the will or patience to get it down on paper. As with Glorie, self-love is again the fault, just as appetite and acquisitiveness were perils for Beautie and Money. Bewitched by his own voice, Wit inflates every "short" point into a long-winded exegesis; whatever "comfort" (guidance) he offers is lost in the pedantry of a pompous "Oration" (18–19). That Herbert had been public orator at Cambridge University suggests he was well aware of the trap of preciosity, when language loses meaning because it has become narcissistically self-referential (a problem for medieval scholasticism as well as modern poststructuralism).

The worldly ideals promenading before him are all "fine things," concludes the poet, but they are evanescent. When God returns on doomsday ("the houre of thy designe"), society and history will end (21–22). The poet's present renunciations will bring a future reward, the ultimate "answer" to vice's scornful challenges (24). He asks God to speak neither lengthily nor publicly ("at large") but directly to his soul in the intimate language of love: "I am thine" (23). These simple, unadorned words will strike "home" like an arrow to the heart (24). By his Christlike turning of the other cheek, the lonely poet has built up treasure in heaven, his true "home." Thus the title's "quip" or joke will be on his antagonists, when heaven's gate slams in their faces.

NINE

GEORGE HERBERT

Love

Love bade me welcome: yet my soul drew back,
     Guiltie of dust and sinne.
But quick-ey'd Love, observing me grow slack
     From my first entrance in,
Drew nearer to me, sweetly questioning,   5
     If I lack'd any thing.

A guest, I answer'd, worthy to be here:
     Love said, You shall be he.
I the unkinde, ungratefull? Ah my deare,
     I cannot look on thee.   10
Love took my hand, and smiling did reply,
     Who made the eyes but I?

Truth Lord, but I have marr'd them: let my shame
     Go where it doth deserve.
And know you not, sayes Love, who bore the blame?   15
     My deare, then I will serve.
You must sit downe, sayes Love, and taste my meat:
     So I did sit and eat.

L ike Donne's Holy Sonnets I and XIV, "Love" (one of three poems of this name by Herbert) treats religion with the erotic language of Petrarchan courtship. However, Donne's two sonnets are brash, punchy, and confrontational, while Herbert's poem is quiet, modest, and refined. Its languid, hypnotic atmosphere is curiously seductive.

In form, the poem is a dramatic dialogue, like a debate in Plato. Unexpectedly, it is also as annotated for physical gesture as a screenplay. The triple stanzas presumably correspond to the Trinity, whose Second Person is Jesus, the character Herbert calls "Love." The latter (spelled "luv") remains a common British term of endearment, equivalent to "dear" or "darling." Herbert's Godhead of choice is the mild, merciful Son, not Donne's implacable, robust Father with his seething energy.

The setting is a banquet, a love feast or agape, as practiced by early Christians. The Greek word *agape* means "charity" or "brotherly love," which would usually be distinguished from eros, sexual love. But Herbert deftly intermingles the two types of love in the manner of the Song of Songs: his lines become a melting series of gentle caresses. There is no piercing climax like that reported by the swooning Saint Teresa of Avila when her heart was struck by an angel's dart. On the contrary, Herbert creates a diffuse sensation of restrained, prolonged ecstasy.

In the poem's master metaphor, a host is graciously reassuring an awkward guest who feels embarrassed and out of place. Two biblical stories have been combined. First is Jesus' parable of the kingdom of heaven as a wedding feast for which passersby are gathered off the highway when invited guests fail to appear (Matthew 22.1–14). Next is the Last Supper, where Jesus identifies his body and blood with bread and wine, thus instituting the sacrament of Holy Communion (Luke 22.19–20). At that Passover meal, Simon Peter protests his unworthiness when Jesus tries to wash his feet (John 13.6–9).

"Love bade me welcome": the cordial host is beckoning at the door, but the shy, travel-worn guest, "guiltie of dust and sinne," recoils (1–2). The dust comes from the long road that humanity has traveled since Adam and Eve were driven from the Garden of Eden. It is also our weak flesh itself, tainted by original sin. Consciousness of past faults makes the guest shrink back—as though anything could be hidden from God's gaze. Is the "soul" of the first line female, like Herbert's soul-spouse in "Church-monuments"? Perhaps, but the human speaker in "Love" is definitely male ("You shall be he," 8), as is the divine host ("Lord," 13). Thus the language of tumescence and penetration ("grow slack," "entrance in") is suggestively homoerotic (3–4). An amiable doorkeeper rather than the traditional bridegroom who impatiently knocks, Jesus has been cast in the receptive role of the sequestered bride.

As the arriving guest hesitates and goes "slack" from lack of confidence, the perfect host springs tenderly to his aid. Love is called "quick-ey'd" because he is preternaturally perceptive and also because his eyes "quicken"—that is, give energy and life (3). We too feel Love drawing "nearer" and hear his "sweet," solicitous voice. We are smoothly enveloped in the poem's eerie aura of charged intimacy. It does not require Christian belief to appreciate Herbert's clairvoyance and shivery, tactile effects, as at a séance.

Host and guest spar in polite point and counterpoint. The poem poses four questions—three by Love and one by the visitor. The sinful guest claims he is not "worthy" of God's presence. By failing to respond to God's gifts, he has been "unkinde, ungratefull," since we are God's "kin," made in his divine image (7, 9). (Compare Hamlet's dig at his unsavory uncle: "A little more than kin, and less than kind," *Hamlet* I.ii.65.) The guest addresses Love familiarly ("Ah my deare") but is overcome with shame: he casts his eyes down ("I cannot look on thee"), unable to meet his host's all-seeing gaze (9–10).

Love's response is Zen-like: to illustrate how self-entrammeled is humanity by fallible words, he uses touch and punning to circumvent everyday logic. Taking the guest's hand, Love asks, "Who made the eyes but I?" (11–12). This brilliant sally asserts that man cannot look away from God, since everything we look at—and indeed our mental faculties as well as our organs of sight—were made by God. These "eyes" include the "I" of personal identity. Love is implying—and accentuating it by electric physical contact—that our boundaries of personality are an illusion and that we can find blessed relief in surrendering to the limitlessness of God.

But the guest is stubbornly recalcitrant, preserving his self-thwarting anxiety in the face of Love's easy manner and indulgent smile. "Truth Lord": he concedes the justice of Love's pun but insists that his own sins have "marr'd" or misused his eyes, the windows of apprehension (13). Clinging to his debased view of his worst self, the guest nearly masochistically requests expulsion: "let my shame / Go where it doth deserve" (13–14). But Love parries this by citing the huge price he paid to redeem fallen man—the torture of the crucifixion, where he as scapegoat "bore the blame," literally the weight of the cross as well as that of his own torn body (15).

Love is imploring humanity: Set down your burden of doubt; in perfect faith there is neither fear nor struggle. The guest makes one last protest, vowing to "serve" at table—another feint, paradoxically, by false pride. Now Love loses patience and, dropping the Socratic questions, issues a direct command: "You must sit downe . . . and taste my meat." "Meat" means any meal but also mortal flesh, the Eucharist transubstantiated into Christ's sacrificed body. Love says in effect, "Eat me"—a carnal come-on with a spiritual zinger, since the Communion wafer utterly transforms its taker from inside out.

In the last line, talk ends, replaced by simple action: "So I did sit and eat." Man in proper relation to God does not kneel, cower, or grovel, nor does he suffer the agony of separation. Indeed, the poem's dialogue, devoid of modern quotation marks, is seamlessly intertwined. (Inserting those marks may aid comprehension: the guest speaks in lines 7, 9–10, 13–14, 16; the host speaks in lines 6, 8, 12, 15, 17.) Again as in Zen, truth is in the process, and the conclusion is implicit in the premises.

"Love" is strictly organized: each stanza contains a rhyming quatrain ("back"/"slack"; "sinne"/"in"), completed by a couplet ("questioning"/"thing"). But the regular alternation of long and short lines produces a rocking feeling, a dreamy ebb and flow. The firm frame has built-in uncertainties. We follow the path of the all-too-human quester as he advances toward God, then retreats in confusion. But the poem ends in blissful union, a sacred marriage where consumption, sexual consummation, and salvation coincide.

TEN

ANDREW MARVELL

To His Coy Mistress

Had we but World enough, and Time,
This coyness, Lady, were no crime.
We would sit down, and think which way
To walk, and pass our long Love's Day.
Thou by the Indian Ganges' side   5
Shouldst Rubies find; I by the Tide
Of Humber would complain. I would
Love you ten years before the Flood,
And you should, if you please, refuse
Till the Conversion of the Jews.   10
My vegetable Love should grow
Vaster than Empires, and more slow;
An hundred years should go to praise
Thine Eyes, and on thy Forehead gaze;
Two hundred to adore each Breast: 15
But thirty thousand to the rest.
An Age at least to every part,
And the last Age should show your Heart.
For, Lady, you deserve this State;
Nor would I love at lower rate.   20
    But at my back I always hear
Time's wingèd Chariot hurrying near;
And yonder all before us lie
Deserts of vast eternity.
Thy Beauty shall no more be found.   25
Nor, in thy marble Vault, shall sound
My echoing Song; then Worms shall try

That long-preserved Virginity,
And your quaint Honor turn to dust,
And into ashes all my Lust: 30
The Grave's a fine and private place,
But none, I think, do there embrace.
    Now therefore, while the youthful hue
Sits on thy skin like morning dew,
And while thy willing Soul transpires   35
At every pore with instant Fires,
Now let us sport us while we may,
And now, like amorous birds of prey,
Rather at once our Time devour
Than languish in his slow-chapped power.   40
Let us roll all our Strength and all
Our sweetness up into one Ball,
And tear our Pleasures with rough strife
Thorough the Iron gates of Life:
Thus, though we cannot make our Sun   45
Stand still, yet we will make him run.

This is the most famous as well as the most intricate carpe diem poem. The term means "Seize the day"—that is, "Live now," a brazen pagan message descending from Greco-Roman literature. Marvell's oratorical plea for a young woman's sexual surrender builds like a legal argument from evidence to summation. The three long stanzas (really verse paragraphs of rhyming couplets) mimic the structure of a simple syllogism in formal logic. To paraphrase the three parts: (1) If we had all the time in the world . . . (2) But we don't . . . (3) So let's make love.

The poem's driving theme is the transience of time: all things must pass. This sober insight, fostering detachment from earthly illusion, is shared by classical philosophers (such as Heraclitus and the Roman Stoics), Christian theologians, and Buddhist monks. But Marvell, quite the opposite, wants to reclaim and intensify the sensual present: "Now . . . now . . . now," he insists (33, 37, 38). By creating an alarming sense of urgency, he lures the lady (called "mistress" not for her sexual status but for her social position or power over her admirers) to side with him against the hostile forces of the universe.

The lady's coyness—her reserve, distance, or affectation of disdain—is not merely a frustration for the poet but a "crime": we must make the most of life's gifts (2). The poem's first section is a vivid, cinematic fantasy of how immortals might loiter and wander. "Had we but World enough, and Time"—if humanity had all of space and all of time—flirtation could drag on forever (1). The phrases ("our long Love's Day") stretch and spread, simulating an indolent holiday (4). The lady's off to India, fabled for its luxury: strolling the banks of the Ganges, she idly collects "Rubies" as if they were pebbles or seashells (5–6). Meanwhile, back in England, the poet sits "complaining"—writing unhappy love poems—beside another river, the Humber, an estuary in his native Lincolnshire in northern England (6–7). Perhaps it is to the Humber's medieval port of Hull that the lady will return from her Asian voyage: normally, it is men who blithely roam and women who pine and wait. The couple would defy time too: patiently enduring her whims and rejections, the poet would blanket history with his love, from the primeval era of Noah's flood to the Second Coming, when Jews will allegedly turn Christian (7–10). The casual anti-Semitism, so dismaying to modern readers, shouldn't obscure the audacity of Marvell's premise: he is sacrilegiously conflating Christianity with his pagan cult of love, where either he or Eros displaces Christ.

Free from external constraint, Marvell claims, his desire would steadily grow and ripen like "vegetable Love" until it covered terrain "vaster than Empires" (11–12). He is playing with Aristotle's notion of the "vegetable soul," the procreative principle. Here it swells like a giant, lumbering, phalliform squash, settling across continents. It fertilizes the world, which becomes a paradise garden where politics seem trivial. (Garden imagery is persistent in Marvell's work.) Powered by "vegetable Love," his poetry massively proliferates: one hundred years are needed for due homage to the lady's eyes and forehead, two hundred years for each of her breasts, and a hyperbolic thirty thousand years for "the rest"—that is, her shadowy, undiscovered nether realm (13–16). Marvell's clinical itemization of body parts parodies the Petrarchan blazon, a rhetorical catalog of an adored lady's impossibly perfect charms—which were always rose red and snowy alabaster, even if, as Shakespeare jokes, her cheeks were really pallid and her breasts "dun" (Sonnet 130). Her "Heart," or emotional depth, should have its own "Age" of praise—but it is not, of course, the main object of the poet's dogged siege (18). She does "deserve this State" (ceremony), and were all things equal, he still would not woo her "at lower rate"—a less dignified pace (19–20).

But something is pushing them forward: they can hear and feel but not see it. Personified Time is speeding toward them in his "wingèd Chariot," like the car of the sun god (22). "Time flies" *(Tempus fugit)* was an ancient maxim. Marvell's Time is the master charioteer of life's race and is simultaneously a cold wind whipped up by the chariot's mechanically beating wings, from which no creature can escape. The poet turns terrorist to force the lady to see what lies before them: "deserts of vast eternity," fusing space and time like so much else in the poem (24). "Desert" in the seventeenth century would conjure up an uninhabited wilderness and not necessarily the sand dunes of Arabia or North Africa. Marvell means to cast a chill: the lady is being manipulated to snuggle closer to her ardent suitor. They are like Adam and Eve driven by the avenging angel out of Eden toward the unknown.

Having distracted and disoriented the lady with his bleak vision of a cosmos emptied of humanity as well as God, Marvell now unfurls a harsh list of the ravages of Time. Her alluring "Beauty" will vanish, he prophesies (25). The Petrarchan beloved's iconic alabaster skin becomes this lady's "marble Vault"—the frigid, pristine vagina as sealed tomb (26). The poet's "echoing Song"—as if bouncing off stone walls—will not be heard, since he too will be dead and unable to mourn her (26–27). The only victors will be the "Worms," gang rapists who will "try" (test) her "long-preserved Virginity"—a cleverly sustained phrase conveying the unpalatable mustiness of age (27–28). Marvell's mischievous strategy is a taunt: if you hang on to that thing too long, he warns, no one will want it! Pleasure is trumped by decay: her "quaint Honor" (chastity) and his phallic "Lust" will crumble into "dust" and "ashes" (29–30). Her attachment to honor is "quaint" because it is intriguing yet unfashionable and antiquated. "Quaint" also puns on "queynte," a medieval word (it appears in Chaucer) for female genitalia. Her charms, he implies, will soon wither: why let life go to waste? For all its sheltered privacy, the "Grave" is an unsuitable love nest, since its isolated, crippled tenants can never "embrace" (31–32).

In his conclusion ("Now therefore"), Marvell tries to spark and fan the lady's desire (33). His delectable portrait of her nubile readiness brings exhilarating relief from the imagery of rot and suffocation. The poem itself is reborn, as we glimpse her skin moist as "morning dew" and flushed pink with "youthful hue" (33–34). The gap closes between spirit and sense: her "willing Soul transpires" (breathes) through "every pore" of her body, which shimmers with "instant Fires," eager and unstoppable (35–36). It's as if perspiration sublimates to purifying steam. So let's play ("let us sport us"), the poet urges, while we still can (37). They too gain wings: they become not Venus's tame, white doves but "amorous birds of prey," fierce raptors feeding on each other in a fine frenzy (38). They will turn the tables on Time, devouring him instead of being devoured (39). Time's personification has shifted to a dragon with mammoth jaws: humans agonizingly "languish in his slow-chapped power"—meaning we are passive morsels in his mighty, grinding chops (40).

Vigorous action is needed against voracious Time. By joining "Strength" and "sweetness," energy and delight, lovemaking is creative and redemptive (41–42). In the "rough strife" of the bedchamber, male and female battle but finally fuse, their intertwined bodies forming "one Ball," like Aristophanes' hybrid couples in Plato's *Symposium* (42–43). They will "tear" their "Pleasures" out of Eden without begging permission of a jealous deity. The "Iron gates of Life" must close on everyone, but passion's heat and light can remake our world (44). The sun, as measurer of time, will never "stand still" (45–46), though Jupiter stopped the dawn for his adulterous night with Alcmene. But lovers can nevertheless make the sun god "run"—that is, make time fly—as they celebrate their feverish rites of sexual joy.

ELEVEN

WILLIAM BLAKE

The Chimney Sweeper

When my mother died I was very young,
And my father sold me while yet my tongue
Could scarcely cry weep wcep weep weep.
So your chimneys I sweep & in soot I sleep.

Theres little Tom Dacre, who cried when his head   5
That curl'd like a lambs back, was shav'd, so I said,
Hush Tom never mind it, for when your head's bare,
You know that the soot cannot spoil your white hair.

And so he was quiet, & that very night,
As Tom was a-sleeping he had such a sight,   10
That thousands of sweepers, Dick, Joe, Ned, & Jack,
Were all of them lock'd up in coffins of black

And by came an Angel who had a bright key,
And he open'd the coffins & set them all free.
Then down a green plain, leaping, laughing they run   15
And wash in a river and shine in the Sun.

Then naked & white, all their bags left behind,
They rise upon clouds, and sport in the wind.
And the Angel told Tom, if he'd be a good boy,
He'd have God for his father & never want joy.   20

And so Tom awoke and we rose in the dark
And got with our bags & our brushes to work.
Tho' the morning was cold, Tom was happy & warm,
So if all do their duty, they need not fear harm.

Romantic writers glorified childhood as a state of innocence. Blake's "The Chimney Sweeper," written in the same year as the French Revolution, combines the Romantic cult of the child with the new radical politics, which can both be traced to social thinker Jean-Jacques Rousseau. It is the boy sweep, rather than Blake, who speaks: he acts as the poet's dramatic persona or mask. There is no anger in his tale. On the contrary, the sweep's gentle acceptance of his miserable life makes his exploitation seem all the more atrocious. Blake shifts responsibility for protest onto us.

The poem begins as autobiography, a favorite Romantic genre. Having lost his mother, his natural protector, the small child was "sold" into slavery by his father (1–2). That is, he was apprenticed to a chimney-sweeping firm whose young teams would probably have worked simply for food, lodging, and clothing—basics that the boy's widowed working-class father might well have been unable to provide for his family. Children, soberly garbed in practical black, were used for chimney sweeping because they could wriggle into narrow, cramped spaces. The health risks of this filthy job were many—deformation of a boy's growing skeleton as well as long-term toxic effects from coal dust, now known to be carcinogenic. Chronic throat and lung problems as well as skin irritation must have been common. (Among the specimens floating in formaldehyde at Philadelphia's Mütter Museum, a nineteenth-century medical collection, is a chimney sweep's foot deformed by a bulbous tumor on the instep.)

Blake's sweep was so young when indentured into service that, he admits, he still lisped (2–3). The hawking of products and services by itinerant street vendors was once a lively, raucous feature of urban life. "Sweep, sweep, sweep!" cried the wandering crews seeking a day's employment. But this tiny boy couldn't even form the word: "Weep weep weep weep!" is how it came out—inadvertently sending a damning message to the oblivious world. It's really the thundering indictment of Blake as poet-prophet: Weep, you callous society that enslaves and murders its young; weep for yourself and your defenseless victims.

"So your chimneys I sweep & in soot I sleep": this singsong, matter-of-fact line implicates the reader in the poem's crimes—a confrontational device ordinarily associated with ironically self-conscious writers like Baudelaire (4). The boy may be peacefully resigned to the horror of his everyday reality, but we, locked in our own routines and distanced by genteel book reading, are forced to face our collective indifference. The boy represents the invisible army of manual laborers, charwomen, and janitors who do our dirty work. Scrubbing the infernal warren of brick and stone tunnels, he absorbs soot (symbolizing social sin) into his own skin and clothes, while we stay neat and clean.

The anonymous sweep—made faceless by his role—chatters cheerfully away about his friend "little Tom Dacre," whom he has taken under his wing (5). In this moral vacuum, where parents and caretakers are absent or negligent, the children must nurture each other. When the newcomer's curly hair was shaved off (to keep it from catching fire from live coals), he cried at his disfigurement, experienced as loss of self. Head shaving is a familiar initiatory practice in military and religious settings to reduce individuality and enforce group norms. To soothe little Tom, the solicitous sweep resorts to consolation of pitiful illogic: "When your head's bare, / You know that the soot cannot spoil your white hair" (7–8). That's like saying, "Good thing you lost your leg—now you'll never stub your toe!" Tom's white (that is, blond) "lambs back" hair represents the innocence of the Christlike sacrificial lamb: children, according to Blake, have become scapegoats for society's amorality and greed (6). Their white hair seems unnatural, as if the boys have been vaulted forward to old age without enjoying the freedoms and satisfactions of virile adulthood. For modern readers, the bald children's caged sameness is disturbingly reminiscent of that of emaciated survivors of Nazi concentration camps, where liberation was met with blank stoicism.

Amazingly, the sweep's desperate reassurance works: Tom goes "quiet," and for the next three stanzas, the whole center of the text, we enter his dreams (9–20). The poem seems to crack open in an ecstatic allegory of rebirth: the children of industrial London escape by the "thousands" from a living death, the locked "coffins of black" that are their soot-stained bodies as well as the chimneys where they spend their days (11–12). Alas, Tom's vision of paradise is nothing more than a simple, playful childhood—the birthright that was robbed from them. The poem overflows with the boys' repressed energy and vitality, as "leaping, laughing they run" across the "green plain" of nature, then plunge into the purifying "river." Bathed "white," they "shine" with their own inner light, bright as the "Sun" (15–18).

But something goes terribly wrong. The "Angel" with the "bright key" who was their liberator inexplicably turns oppressor (13, 19). As the sweeps "rise upon clouds" toward heaven and "sport in the wind" like prankish cherubs casting off their burdens (the "bags" of brushes and collected soot), an officiously moralistic voice cuts into the dream and terminates it: "And the Angel told Tom, if he'd be a good boy, / He'd have God for his father & never want joy" (17–20). That Tom wakes right up suggests that the voice actually belongs to the boss or overseer, briskly rousing his charges before dawn. The angel's homily, heavy with conventional piety, stops the children's fun and free motion dead: If you'll be good boys—that is, do what we say—you'll win God's approval and find your reward in heaven. (In British English, to "never want joy" means never to *lack* it.) But God is another false father in this poem.

The trusting, optimistic children grab their bags and brushes and get right to work in the "cold" and "dark" (21–23). They want to do right, and their spirit is unquenched. But they've been brainwashed into pliability by manipulative maxims such as the one recited by our first sweep in the ominous last line: "So if all do their duty, they need not fear harm" (24). This bromide is an outrageous lie. If the children were to rebel, to run away to the green paradise lying just outside the city, they would be safe. Their naive goodwill leads straight to their ruin—a short, limited life of sickliness and toil. The final stanza's off rhymes ("dark"/"work," "warm"/"harm") subtly unbalance us and make us sense the fractures in the sweep's world. The poem shows him betrayed by an ascending row of duplicitous male authority figures—his father, the profiteering boss, the turncoat angel, and God himself, who tacitly endorses or tolerates an unjust social system. As Tom's dream suggests, the only deliverance for the sweep and his friends will be death.

TWELVE

WILLIAM BLAKE

London

I wander thro' each charter'd street,
Near where the charter'd Thames does flow.
And mark in every face I meet
Marks of weakness, marks of woe.

In every cry of every Man,   5
In every Infants cry of fear,
In every voice: in every ban,
The mind-forg'd manacles I hear

How the Chimney-sweepers cry
Every blackning Church appalls   10
And the hapless Soldiers sigh
Runs in blood down Palace walls

But most thro' midnight streets I hear
How the youthful Harlots curse
Blasts the new-born Infants tear   15
And blights with plagues the Marriage hearse

The poet in his role as Hebrew prophet steps front and center. In "London," Blake broadens the exposé of commercial society implicit in "The Chimney Sweeper" to include the older institutions of church and state. The poem achieves epic sweep in only four stanzas, as the corrupt city comes to represent the moral condition of all of European civilization.

Wandering through London's hell, Blake follows the model of Dante as poet-quester cataloging the horrors of the Inferno. A visitor to the storied British capital in 1793 would have seen a grand, expanding city in economic boom. But the poet, with telepathic hearing and merciless X-ray eyes, homes in on the suffering, dislocation, and hidden spiritual costs of rapid social transformation. The Industrial Revolution, which began in England in the 1770s and would spread globally over the next two centuries, profoundly altered community, personal identity, and basic values in ways we are still sorting out.

"London" is darkly paranoid, as claustrophobic and hallucinatory as an Expressionist nightmare. Everyone and everything in it are in bondage to obscure, malevolent forces. The streets and even the river Thames are "charter'd"—mapped, licensed, controlled, and choked with commerce (1–2). (Boats, buses, and airplanes in the United States are still "chartered"—reserved and rented—in this sense.) In Blake's vast system, the mathematical grid, produced by the draftsman's compass, is identified with reason, law, and an oppressor Father-God who curtails human imagination and natural energy. When "London" was written, the threat of revolutionary agitation from France, then plunging into the Reign of Terror, had moved the British government to suspend liberties considered "charter'd" by the medieval Magna Carta (Latin for "Great Charter").

As the people flow through London's streets, a moral darkness seems to hang over the land. The poem may begin in the workday but ends in the pitch of night, so that the poet's walking tour seems haunted and driven. "I . . . mark in every face I meet / Marks of weakness, marks of woe": he notes (to "mark" means to remark or

observe) the signs and scars of illness, exhaustion, anxiety, and de-
spair, the afflictions of the damned in a city rushing to its doom (3–4).
Working-class faces had indeed changed: Blake's generation was the
first to see the pasty pallor of factory workers cut off, as their farmer
forebears had never been, from the sun's burnishing, life-giving rays.

In the second stanza, sight yields to sound as the poet-prophet
is besieged by "cry" after "cry" of the tortured (5–6). On the literal
level, Blake is simply hearing ordinary street noise—the banter of
pedestrians; the calls of hucksters, fishwives, and teamsters; and the
squalling of babies, whose wails he interprets as "fear" of life itself.
It's as if infants have been torn from the womb and tossed among
wolves. The sounds gradually become stranger: "In every voice: in
every ban, / The mind-forg'd manacles I hear" (7–8). Blake means
that human beings labor in chains of their own making. Surreally,
bustling passersby seem to plod past like prisoners, the shackles rat-
tling on their wrists and ankles and making a harsh machine music.
These bonds come from a metaphor in Rousseau's *Social Contract,*
which opens with the famous salvo "Man is born free, but every-
where he is in chains." If the poem's manacles are forged in the
mind—that is, if they are imaginary—then they can be broken by
simple alteration of consciousness. Blake hears them "in every ban"—
in every political or religious regulation, prohibition, and proclama-
tion, including marriage banns. "Mind-forg'd manacles" are, finally,
all the conventions or invisible premises of thought, including our
daily dimensions of time and space.

"I hear" is a swing phrase at the poem's midpoint: it follows the
prior stanza's cries and clanks while setting up the final stanzas' in-
genious sequence of fragile sound effects (8). Sight and sound con-
verge: things heard now turn by magic synesthesia into things seen.
"The Chimney-sweepers cry," that jaunty street call masking a help-
less child's misery, trails up and "appalls" the "blackning Church"—
or rather it *should* appall the church into horrified action but
shamefully does not (9–10). The soot staining the church facade is
what the sweeps give their lives to scrape away. Acid pollution pour-
ing from factory chimneys would soon start to erode the imposing
stone monuments of Europe. By failing to respond to the sweeps' suf-

fering and, in Blake's view, to the hijacking of society by rapacious commercial interests, the church is also blackening on the inside. If it is "appalled" (literally, gone pale with shock), it's because a Christian citadel that should defend the poor has turned into a "whited sepulcher"—Jesus' scathing term for the pharisaical religious establishment: they are ornate marble sarcophagi that "appear beautiful outward, but are within full of dead men's bones, and of all uncleanness" (Matthew 23.27). Hence, for Blake, the English church is "appalled" only because it is a coffin draped in a pall, its telltale coat of funereal soot.

The next auditory image similarly turns visual: the "sigh" of a "hapless" (unlucky) soldier strikes the deaf walls of another coldly impersonal building, the "Palace," residence and ministry of hereditary authority (11–12). Where is the soldier, and why is he sighing? The dramatic effect of that slight sound suggests this must be his last breath on a distant battlefield. He has paid the ultimate price for a cause he incompletely understands and that is certainly not, at this point in British history, in defense of his homeland. He is cannon fodder, like the boy sweep a proletarian pawn of selfish higher powers. But the soldier will have his revenge: his wispy sigh seems to float on the wind to foggy London, where it turns to rain that runs down the walls in sheets of blood. The palace's red-streaked walls (paralleling the church's blackened walls) betray the callousness and irresponsibility of Europe's frivolous kings, who have blood on their hands from centuries of war games pursued for their own prestige. In "London," the sighs of the powerless, feeble in isolation, gather to form an irresistible storm. The grisly drizzle is also an omen, like the disembodied hand at Belshazzar's feast whose writing on the wall foretold the fall of Babylon (Daniel 5.5). Blood running down palace walls, as happened very recently in France, may one day be that of the British ruling class. Hence Blake's poem, like Moses' warning to Pharaoh about the approaching plagues, contains a prophecy (never fulfilled) of the overthrow of the British monarchy.

The poem's series of exploited persons, begun by sweep and soldier, is completed by the "youthful Harlot," the smudged heroine of the last stanza (14). As a streetwalker, she occupies the most dangerous and debased realm in prostitution. "Youthful" for that time might well mean she is in her early teens. Through no choice of her own, she may already be a mother. She fends for herself in the mean streets by the only trade she knows. Her "curse" is her come-on, the soft, flirtatious invitation in which the poet intuits her hidden hatred. Her curse is also the "plagues" of venereal disease, the whore's revenge covertly transmitted over the sexual network to her clients' respectable virgin brides (16). In Blake's radical philosophy, prostitution is created by religious prudery and social hypocrisy: middle- and upper-class men, their desires frustrated by pious, unresponsive wives, hunt down working-class women by night whom they would treat as invisible or subhuman by light of day. The poem presents sexuality, like the Thames, as a natural but potentially torrential force. Its distortion or blockage has catastrophic consequences. By poisoning posterity, syphilis, which would spread throughout nineteenth-century cities, threatens to bring history to a halt (15). The "new-born Infants tear" is "blasted" like a sapling by the winter wind: a baby's tear ducts can be contaminated in his or her passage through an infected mother's birth canal (a medical risk avoided today by cesarean section). That such infants cry without shedding tears implies a stunting of emotion and a brutalized future.

The poem's final, chilling image takes us forward to a festive scene, as a happy couple set off from church for their life together. But their carriage is really a "Marriage hearse" bound for the graveyard, since its secret cargo is the groom's syphilitic seed (16). The forgotten, unassuming harlot is proxy for tyrannous Mother Nature herself, whose judgment will fall on a society where exploitation—economic, political, religious, and sexual—has become the law of the land.

THIRTEEN

WILLIAM WORDSWORTH

The World Is Too Much with Us

The world is too much with us; late and soon,
Getting and spending, we lay waste our powers:
Little we see in Nature that is ours;
We have given our hearts away, a sordid boon!
This Sea that bares her bosom to the moon;   5
The winds that will be howling at all hours,
And are up-gathered now like sleeping flowers;
For this, for everything, we are out of tune;
It moves us not.—Great God! I'd rather be
A Pagan suckled in a creed outworn;   10
So might I, standing on this pleasant lea,
Have glimpses that would make me less forlorn;
Have sight of Proteus rising from the sea;
Or hear old Triton blow his wreathèd horn.

Not until midway through this sonnet, which opens with general reflections about life, do we realize that the poet is gazing out to sea from a bluff or meadow ("this pleasant lea"; 5, 11). Wordsworth's very specific, open-air point of view prefigures that of the Impressionist painters who set up their easels on hills or country roads. The poem relies on quick notations and atmospheric impressions, but its impulse is emotional rather than documentary. Somber and pensive, Wordsworth strikes his characteristic pose of isolation and detachment.

"The world is too much with us": the tone is flat, severe, dismissive. This "world" is the secular realm of wealth and power, about which Roman generals in triumph, like the popes after them, were admonished with the warning *"Sic transit gloria mundi"* (Thus passes the glory of the world). Bunyan's Vanity Fair in *Pilgrim's Progress* is a symbol of that pomp and glory, with their heady distractions. Wordsworth's "world" is civilization as Rousseau taught the Romantics to see it—oppressive, avaricious, and implicitly male-dominated. It is "too much with us" because it has seeped into our brains and become us.

"Late and soon"—yesterday, today, and tomorrow—"we lay waste our powers," exhausting and debasing our best instincts in meaningless activity (1–2). We're caught in a vicious cycle of "getting and spending": Wordsworth boldly fuses economics with sex—the go-go commercialism of industrial England with predatory libertinage, a showy male sport. Materialism feeds on itself, while "getting" (procreating, as in "begetting") without emotional investment or commitment is an affront to Mother Nature. Heedless "spending" (an old colloquialism for ejaculation) reduces sex to selfish mechanical release—what Shakespeare calls "lust in action," where pleasure is followed by shame and disgust (Sonnet 129).

"Little we see in Nature that is ours": though we sprang from nature, we act like self-created units who owe it nothing (3). From Blake on, the Romantics put the blame for modern alienation on Cartesian rationalism and Newtonian physics, which sees the universe as a machine. "We have given our hearts away, a sordid boon": like Faust, who sought dominance through knowledge, Western culture has sold its soul to the devil—to false idols whose reward ("boon") is filthy lucre (4). For Wordsworth, affluence brings desensitization, a deadening of the heart.

Burdened with negatives, the poem sinks into melancholy but regenerates itself in a series of ecstatic perceptions: we see nature come alive. "This Sea that bares her bosom to the moon": the sea's undulating swells become the ample breasts of female nature, offering both maternal and erotic invitation to the sky. The poet's beguiling vision of interconnectedness makes his sense of desolation momentarily ebb. Tranquillity and gentleness rule: the fierce sea "winds" normally buffeting the shore are happily laid up like sated infants worn out by their "howling" (6). "Up-gathered now like sleeping flowers," the winds are like an armful of blossoms embraced by Mother Nature, or perhaps they are magically sealed in slumber in the cradle-like chalices of wildflowers (7).

But as in "Tintern Abbey," Wordsworth finds it difficult to sustain his faith in nature: "For this, for everything, we are out of tune; / It moves us not" (8–9). We have become too self-conscious, too sophisticated to be touched or inspired by nature alone. We no longer hear the soothing lullaby of natural energy. The phrase "out of tune" contains a buried image, a favorite metaphor of the Romantic poets: the human mind or body as an Aeolian lyre (wind harp) played upon and vibrated by nature. Wordsworth is implying that our lives in industrial society are so unbalanced that the music wrung from us is harsh, jangling, and dissonant.

"Great God!": this cry, breaking into a line, snaps it in half (9). It changes the poem's mood for the third time: the poet has rapidly passed from spleen to sensuality to aching longing. "I'd rather be / A Pagan suckled in a creed outworn": the wish openly flouts the Judeo-Christian Father-God (9–10). Wordsworth claims he would gladly exchange contemporary conveniences and privileges to be reborn in raw, pre-Christian Britain. In a parallel passage in *The Prelude*, he pictures a primitive Briton, clad in "wolf-skin vest" and "barbaric majesty," roving the sacred ground on Salisbury Plain near Stonehenge (XIII.312–26). Paganism is "a creed outworn" because it has been superseded, but for Wordsworth it "suckled" or fed its followers because it was predicated on the harmony of man and nature, identified by the Romantics with the fertile female principle. Wordsworth means to shock: he is saying, in effect, "I wish Jesus had never been born."

Paganism, as the poet perhaps too optimistically sees it, was holistic: under its more generous dispensation, we would have redemptive "glimpses" of cosmic unity wherever we looked and would thus be at least partly relieved of loneliness and anxiety ("less forlorn," 12). Nature would no longer be the fallen realm of gross matter disdained by Christianity, nor would it be science's cold clockwork universe. The elements would teem with friendly spirits, mentors to mankind. Wordsworth imagines the female sea churned by masculine apparitions: Proteus, the mercurial shape-shifter, symbolizes nature's constant metamorphoses, while the hybrid Triton, "old" but still virile, represents in his half-fish form the archaic continuum of man with nature (13–14). Proteus and Triton were not suave sky gods residing on Mount Olympus but elemental forces robust with the sexuality erased from the Christian Trinity. Triton's "wreathèd horn" is either a conch shell, traditionally blown by gamboling mermen, or a more phallic bull's or ram's horn (like the shofar), summoning the faithful to worship. It is twined with ivy, serpentine vines from the paradise garden, where there is eternal holiday. The poem's pagan festival will be loud, exuberant, and orgiastic, in contrast to the solemn austerity of Christian services, which dwell on Jesus' crucifixion or the misty afterlife. Pagan restoration, as the mythmaking Wordsworth dreams it, heals our estrangement. His rowdy demigods—whom he longs to see but cannot—celebrate the here and now in perfect concord with primal nature.

FOURTEEN

WILLIAM WORDSWORTH

Composed upon Westminster Bridge
SEPTEMBER 3, 1802

Earth has not anything to show more fair:
Dull would he be of soul who could pass by
A sight so touching in its majesty:
This City now doth, like a garment, wear
The beauty of the morning; silent, bare,　　　　　5
Ships, towers, domes, theatres, and temples lie
Open unto the fields, and to the sky;
All bright and glittering in the smokeless air.
Never did sun more beautifully steep
In his first splendour, valley, rock, or hill;　　　10
Ne'er saw I, never felt, a calm so deep!
The river glideth at his own sweet will:
Dear God! the very houses seem asleep;
And all that mighty heart is lying still!

In his preface to the second edition of *Lyrical Ballads,* a revolutionary collection he cowrote with Samuel Taylor Coleridge, Wordsworth called poetry "the spontaneous overflow of powerful feelings." The new Romantic values were immediacy and emotional truth, replacing the cooler, more formal standards of Neoclassicism, such as symmetry, perfection, and control.

With its journalistic dateline, "Composed upon Westminster Bridge" is the most vivid of Wordsworth's you-are-there poems, which absorb us into his consciousness and make us see what he does. Here the drama resides in the poet's surprise at his own response to the city spread out before him. Like Rousseau, Wordsworth is normally repelled by the noise and furor of urban life: nature alone restores his equilibrium and sense of self. Hence this sonnet is really written to himself; it's a process of sorting through the tumult of his thoughts.

The poet is stopped in his tracks as he crosses Westminster Bridge, which links London's raffish South Bank to the prestigious enclave of Westminster Abbey and the Houses of Parliament. The whole of the old city stretches northward and eastward from Westminster along the riverbank. Though Wordsworth is mesmerized, his approval, as we shall see, is conditional. Physical beauty is his startled first impression: "Earth has not anything to show more fair" (1). "Fair" means clean, pure, or lovely (compare *My Fair Lady*). Wordsworth never dreamed that a cityscape could rival the lakes, groves, moors, and crags of his beloved Cumberland in northern England. There is a touch of self-rebuke for his past indifference: only the "dull" of soul—the mundane or small-minded—could ignore this tremendous prospect, "a sight so touching in its majesty" (2–3). The attribute "touching" doesn't quite fit "majesty": the city has poignancy or vulnerability yet also grandeur, the spirit of the sublime—a touchstone of the cult of "sensibility" preceding Romanticism. The poet is intrigued by the disparity in his mixed feelings of tenderness and awe.

Only gradually do we realize, through accumulating details of the "silent" vista, how early the hour is (5). "The beauty of the morning," portrayed as a "garment" worn by the sleeping city, is probably a fine mist: its bewitching transparency (like that of a silken peignoir) suggests Wordsworth is imagining the city as feminine (4–5). The "City" is capitalized partly because of its nymphlike personification, but that term also remains current for central London. In the foreground along the Thames, the masts and rigging of docked ships would have been as dense as a forest, while in the middle distance loomed the dome of Saint Paul's Cathedral as well as the rooftops, spires, and turrets of other landmarks, such as the Courts of Justice, the medieval Temple Church, and the royal theaters of Covent Garden and Drury Lane. Hence the catalog—"ships, towers, domes, theatres, and temples"—succinctly captures the actual skyline from Westminster Bridge (6). The poet is confronting, without his usual suspicion and hostility, the political, legal, and commercial matrix of British society.

At this charged moment, nature and culture seem magically reconciled. Though the expanding city was then encroaching on the countryside, the poet sees integration rather than invasion: the city's monuments, invitingly "bare," "lie / Open unto the fields, and to the sky," suggesting guilelessness and even erotic surrender (5–7). But significantly, there are no hard-driving humans to spoil the scene. In personifying the city, the poem has oddly depopulated it. The problem, Wordsworth might say, is not what man has made but how it is used. London gleams like fairyland: the roofs ("bright and glittering") are silvered with overnight dew, while the atmosphere suffused by the rising sun (personified as male: "his first splendour") drenches the city in liquid gold ("steep"; 8–10). The man-made is restored to the pristine state of any "valley, rock, or hill." The key phrase is "smokeless air": the city's sanctification is possible only in the interlude before the hellish factories start up to do their dirty work. Night has purified but cannot stop the hectic social cycle. For Wordsworth, industrial smog is a spiritual as well as physical pollution, shortening our perspective and obscuring nature's elemental realities.

"Ne'er saw I, never felt, a calm so deep!": Wordsworth elsewhere calls such moments of illumination "spots of time" (11). Observation and emotion, merging, become sensuously tactile. From the stone bridge, with the stately Thames streaming beneath, Wordsworth contemplates the city without actually being *in* it. He simultaneously registers nature's adaptable, mobile energy along with society's stubborn fixity, so that existence seems fleetingly unified. The river, yet another personified male, "glideth at his own sweet will," combining languid mildness with inscrutable power (12). Making its wide, meandering turns through London, it seems to take pleasure in its brief nocturnal freedom from traffic. As the city's bloodstream, the river is the model for the easy, steady, flowing pressure of ideas in the poem itself.

The outburst ("Dear God!") in the penultimate line shows the poem moving toward prayer, though Christianity is conspicuously absent from Wordsworth's pagan panorama of animistic presences and imperial architecture, which reduces churches to the secular dimension (13, 6). If "the very houses seem asleep," they too must be alive, as packed with their charges as seed-bearing pods. It's as if the city is under a spell or in suspended animation. Everything seems possible as the new day dawns. Will the sleepers engineer their own deliverance and rebirth?

The poem's final effect, accentuated by a surprising exclamation point, is a strange image of the city as a "mighty heart" that is "lying still"—as living hearts can never do (14). During the workday, the heart hammers to excess but finds relief in the luxury of night. It's the poet's heart that is constricted: in heightened awareness he attains bliss and peace, but love for humanity is indiscernible. On the contrary, Wordsworth embraces the city only when its citizens are inert. When they wake, they will reclaim their social roles and descend into the harsh arena of warring egos. Having had his epiphany, Wordsworth moves on, preserving his solitude and estrangement by shutting down his expanded perception.

FIFTEEN

PERCY BYSSHE SHELLEY

Ozymandias

I met a traveller from an antique land
Who said: Two vast and trunkless legs of stone
Stand in the desert . . . Near them, on the sand,
Half sunk, a shattered visage lies, whose frown,
And wrinkled lip, and sneer of cold command,   5
Tell that its sculptor well those passions read
Which yet survive, stamped on these lifeless things,
The hand that mocked them, and the heart that fed:
And on the pedestal these words appear:
'My name is Ozymandias, king of kings: 10
Look on my works, ye Mighty, and despair!'
Nothing beside remains. Round the decay
Of that colossal wreck, boundless and bare
The lone and level sands stretch far away.

Compressed in size yet vast in scale, "Ozymandias" remains Shelley's most accessible poem, employing effects that are prophetically cinematic. Its punishing landscape descends directly from Marvell's "deserts of vast eternity," the wilderness beyond Eden in "To His Coy Mistress." This time, however, we are in Egypt, which had been opened to European exploration by Napoleon's 1798 invasion. Like Wordsworth's "The World Is Too Much with Us" and "Composed upon Westminster Bridge," "Ozymandias" is a traditional sonnet but also a spontaneous Romantic effusion, reportedly written straight out in less than an hour on the flyleaf of a borrowed book.

Only one line is ostensibly in the poet's voice: Shelley introduces the poem, then steps back and disappears. A second character, the shadowy "traveller," begins to speak in the second line, and though his voice continues to the end, he too recedes as the monumental artifacts take over. There is a third voice inset in the poem—that of a royal ghost as sonorous and demanding as Hamlet's stalking father.

Does the traveler really exist? Or is he a dream vision? In either case, he acts as a proxy for Shelley, the wanderer who was to die in exile. The traveler "from an antique land" may be a space traveler or, eerily, a time traveler, a messenger from antiquity (1). The poem's relay of voices distances the visual material and makes us feel the passage of time. As a framing device, however, the succession of speakers is incomplete, since we never return to the opening person or place. The lack of closure may be due partly to the poem's cataclysmic revelation: what the traveler sees is nature's total victory over culture.

"Two vast and trunkless legs of stone / Stand in the desert": a colossus has been lopped off at the groin, like a tree snapped in half by a storm wind (2–3). The torso, its core of strength, has vanished: the metaphor implicit in "trunkless," identifying human bodies with trees, is the same that Shakespeare used for the autumnal boughs of Sonnet 73. The stranded stone legs, stolidly pillarlike, attest to the weight of institutions now demolished. The only recognizable remnant is the statue's head with its "shattered visage" (face), symboliz-ing the brittle mask as well as the ideological obsessions of its model (4). Ozymandias is the Greek name given by the Roman-era historian Diodorus Siculus to the great Rameses II (who may be the Bible's obstinate pharaoh defied by Moses) in an account of the Ramesseum at Thebes. Shelley's colossus has a hard expression never in fact seen in the serene pharaonic portraits of any dynasty; it more resembles that of mammoth Olmec heads, then lost in the Central American jungle. We recognize the king's "frown, / And wrinkled lip, and sneer of cold command" as the face of fascism (Mussolini or the totalitarian Stalin), intimidating internal and external enemies and terrorizing ordinary citizens (4–5). Shelley may have one dictator in mind: the poem was written two years after Napoleon's defeat by British forces at Waterloo.

A secret message has been transmitted from artist to artist to pos-terity. The anonymous "sculptor," a manual laborer at the bottom of the social pyramid, has "well those passions read," capturing Pharaoh's megalomania and the sadistically tinged lust for power in all tyrants (6). The ancient artist's intuition and insight, "stamped" on the statue's scattered parts, have survived, while his sovereign's dazzling achievements have not (7). A commoner has triumphed over a living god. The artist's hand "mocked" Pharaoh in two senses: it imitated or mimicked, and it ridiculed or satirized (8). The artist's "heart," his ultimate inspiration, "fed" on his own skeptical thoughts, shared with no one but us, his future audience and true confidants. That such coded communication over time is possible in art is illus-trated by Raphael's revealing 1518 portrait of his patron, a sallow, jowly Pope Leo X (Martin Luther's excommunicator), flanked by two startlingly shifty cardinals, his nephews.

The Egyptian "pedestal," a humble block, has lasted longer than the royal statue itself (9). After so many centuries, the inscription, meant to instill fear and envy, has changed meaning. Ozymandias boasts that he is "king of kings," with divine dominion over other leaders of the bellicose Near East from Babylon and Assyria to Troy: "Look on my works, ye Mighty, and despair!" (10–11). No one, Ozy-mandias asserts, will ever match or surpass the massive temples, treasure cities, and glorious deeds of imperial Egypt. The motto, as if contaminated by the "decay / Of that colossal wreck," carries a terrible irony (12–13). Ozymandias's message, painfully deepened by experience, is now addressed to the "Mighty"—the kings and statesmen—of Shelley's own unstable era: Despair, says the mutilated statue, at the futility of power; these fragments are your future! The awesome record of a celebrated king, who ruled for sixty-seven years over a civilization that lasted three millennia, has been ground to dust. Only the handiwork of an invisible craftsman has kept Pharaoh's memory alive. Art is long, politics short. But even art is finally subject to nature, whose ruthless operations are like an ever-shifting sea (the stone head is "half sunk" in sand; 4).

Modern readers may find the clarity of conception and execution of "Ozymandias" especially compelling because Shelley's technique resembles that of the motion picture camera. The poem begins in medium range with a chance encounter between two men, probably in Europe. Then the scene dissolves to a North African desert where the truncated legs of a statue, brutal and totemic, loom up at center screen. Now our gaze is drawn down to small details in close-up, such as the "wrinkled lip" of the fallen head and the pedestal's ambiguous inscription. At the phrase "Look on my works," we nearly feel the spectral king gesturing, as the camera obediently pulls back and up to make a 360-degree pan of the "boundless and bare" landscape (11–14).

The last line, with its "lone and level sands" stretching to the horizon, seems simple but isn't. The scene is "lone" (lonely) because devoid of people as well as emotional consolation. It's as if, with no witnesses left, the poem itself is about to self-destruct. The sands are "level" because they are flat and unadorned by trees but also because they are literally leveling: time is the great equalizer, reducing pharaoh to serf. All idols are toppled in the poem, including God, whom the atheist Shelley disdained as simply another tyrant drunk with absolute power.

For the eighteenth and early nineteenth centuries, with their fashionable "grand tour," Rome's picturesque ruins were a melancholy parable of the evanescence of fame, wealth, and power. But contemporary Rome, for all its rubble, was still a living town, with cottages, churches, markets, and cows grazing in the half-buried Forum. With its pitilessly grinding sands of time, "Ozymandias" is far more extreme: it wipes out history and humanity in a godless apocalypse that prefigures modern nihilism.

SIXTEEN

SAMUEL TAYLOR COLERIDGE

Kubla Khan

OR, A VISION IN A DREAM. A FRAGMENT.

In Xanadu did Kubla Khan
A stately pleasure-dome decree:
Where Alph, the sacred river, ran
Through caverns measureless to man
 Down to a sunless sea. 5
So twice five miles of fertile ground
With walls and towers were girdled round:
And there were gardens bright with sinuous rills,
Where blossomed many an incense-bearing tree;
And here were forests ancient as the hills, 10
Enfolding sunny spots of greenery.

But oh! that deep romantic chasm which slanted
Down the green hill athwart a cedarn cover!
A savage place! as holy and enchanted
As e'er beneath a waning moon was haunted 15
By woman wailing for her demon-lover!
And from this chasm, with ceaseless turmoil seething,
As if this earth in fast thick pants were breathing,
A mighty fountain momently was forced:
Amid whose swift half-intermitted burst 20
Huge fragments vaulted like rebounding hail,
Or chaffy grain beneath the thresher's flail:
And 'mid these dancing rocks at once and ever
It flung up momently the sacred river.
Five miles meandering with a mazy motion 25

Through wood and dale the sacred river ran,
Then reached the caverns measureless to man,
And sank in tumult to a lifeless ocean:
And 'mid this tumult Kubla heard from far
Ancestral voices prophesying war!   30
  The shadow of the dome of pleasure
  Floated midway on the waves;
  Where was heard the mingled measure
  From the fountain and the caves.
It was a miracle of rare device,   35
A sunny pleasure-dome with caves of ice!

  A damsel with a dulcimer
  In a vision once I saw:
  It was an Abyssinian maid,
  And on her dulcimer she played,   40
  Singing of Mount Abora.
  Could I revive within me
  Her symphony and song,
  To such a deep delight 'twould win me,
That with music loud and long,   45
I would build that dome in air,
That sunny dome! those caves of ice!
And all who heard should see them there,
And all should cry, Beware! Beware!
His flashing eyes, his floating hair!   50
Weave a circle round him thrice,
And close your eyes with holy dread,
For he on honey-dew hath fed,
And drunk the milk of Paradise.

The theme of "Kubla Khan" is the power and danger of creative imagination. The poem prophetically describes the artist's plight in a hostile or indifferent society during the era of the avant-garde, which would begin in nineteenth-century Paris. Coleridge was dissatisfied with "Kubla Khan" and held on to it for nearly twenty years; it was finally published at the insistence of Lord Byron.

Sensitive about the poem's eccentric structure, Coleridge attached a preface whose peculiar claims were accepted as fact by early readers and critics. In it he says that, while recuperating from "a slight indisposition" in the countryside, he was lulled asleep by an "anodyne" (laudanum, an opiate to which he was addicted) just as he was reading a passage in a seventeenth-century travelogue describing the lavish palace of the Chinese emperor Kubla Khan. Awaking from three hours of "profound sleep," he began to write out the "two to three hundred lines" that had somehow coalesced during his dream. But a knock on the door suddenly called him away. Returning little more than an hour later, he found "to his no small surprise and mortification" that the rest of the poem had faded from memory.

The fifty-four-line text of "Kubla Khan" is therefore to be understood, according to the subtitle, as "a fragment." Was Coleridge's defensive strategy aimed at shadowy carpers or at his own festering doubts? The poem certainly does not feel incomplete to us, whose looser standards of form descend from the radical innovations of Romanticism and nineteenth-century realism. We no longer expect perfection, symmetry, or sharp closure in works of art. Indeed, modernist plays and dance pieces can end so ambiguously that raised houselights must signal the end of a performance. "Kubla Khan" anticipates the fractures and fragmentation in Western culture that would be registered in collage, the jigsaw medium invented by Picasso on the eve of World War I and applied by T. S. Eliot to the shards of literature sifted from rubble in *The Waste Land* (1922).

"A Vision in a Dream": this beautiful phrase, acknowledging the poem's hallucinatory genesis, also describes Romantic art-making.

The poet is a seer, inexplicably gifted with the power of divination. While the master vision of "Kubla Khan" is of then-exotic Asia, the poem also contains two subordinate visions: the first is a dream of a woman singing in Abyssinia (Ethiopia); the second is a cryptic self-portrait of the poet himself in creative ecstasy. Rejecting the cool discipline of Neoclassicism, the Romantics surrendered themselves to intense emotion and extreme experiences. They made themselves the subject of their art—a heady approach with its own limitations. The "dream" of Coleridge's subtitle takes in all of the Romantics' unorthodox new interests, such as fairy tales and ghost stories, gleaned from folk culture. Agrarian peoples at the mercy of nature traditionally view dreams as omens or messages from the spirit world. Freud credited the Romantic poets with discovery of the psychological meaning of dreams, which had been dismissed by Enlightenment thinkers as meaningless excitation of the nerves.

"In Xanadu did Kubla Khan / A stately pleasure-dome decree": the opening lines, even in their inverted syntax, closely follow Coleridge's seventeenth-century source. But the effect is thrillingly trumpet-like, instantly summoning up the luxurious milieu of an imperial court. The khan (a sovereign or chieftain) is a haughty despot, like Shelley's Ozymandias. The Chinese elite live like parasitic French aristocrats, normally loathed by the leftist Romantics. Kubla Khan (grandson of the ruthless Genghis Khan) both attracts and repels: hence the aptness of these famous lines to Orson Welles's classic 1941 film, *Citizen Kane,* where they are elegiacally intoned over a newsreel about a dead press lord (based on William Randolph Hearst) and his private wonderland.

Coleridge's poem is subtly allegorical: Kubla Khan represents the artist; fabulous Xanadu is the world of art; and the "stately pleasure-dome" is the intricate artwork, exemplified by the poem itself. The dome is literally created by "decree" or edict, since a poem is magically made of language. The dome is dedicated to "pleasure" because Romantic art frankly appeals to the senses. Virtue, the didactic goal of Neoclassicism, has been displaced by beauty.

Kubla's dome ultimately symbolizes all human constructions or fabrications, including the tissue of ideas. It is poised at a geologically unstable spot—where a "sacred river" flows into "caverns measure-less to man" and drops "down to a sunless sea" (3–5). Thus the earth's surface functions as a second dome, a brittle crust over suffocating darkness into which the pleasure palace could collapse at any time. The river is sacred because it is a force of pagan nature, the primary energy source of Romantic art. Its Greek name, Alph, sounds odd in a Chinese setting: it implies that nature, not Jehovah, is the poem's alpha and omega, its creator and destroyer. The name echoes that of a real river in Arcadia, the Alpheus, which flowed past the great tem-ple of Zeus at Olympia and, in legend, ran in a pure stream through the salt sea to rise again as a fountain in Sicily. Hence the Alpheus sig-nifies continuity through apparent breakage or separation. The cav-erns into which Coleridge's river falls are "measureless" because they represent metaphysical mysteries of life that cannot be quantified, much less solved, by science or mathematics.

The royal precinct is a "fertile" pocket paradise, ten miles around (6). It's a harmonious marriage of nature and culture, with towered walls enclosing "gardens bright with sinuous rills"—twisting brooks like nature's snaky signature (7–8). Visual contrasts abound: allur-ingly private glades ("sunny spots of greenery") are scattered like golden coins amid the gloomy ancient forests, while the gardens are dotted with blossoming trees heavily perfuming the air with incense, as at a sacred service (9–11). Lulled by these glimpses of mesmerizing beauty, we are jarred awake by a break in the text that mirrors what it describes: "oh! that deep romantic chasm" (12–13). The earth is split, slashed diagonally across a hill of grand cedar trees. This "sav-age place" shows nature at its harshest and least hospitable (14).

The chasm is "romantic" in the older sense of remote, fantastic, or picturesque. But the word's alternate erotic associations surface in the operatic scene depicted by Coleridge's stunningly pornographic simile: a possessed, lust-maddened woman, on the prowl beneath an eerie "waning moon," is "wailing for her demon-lover" (14–16). The primeval chasm, "holy and enchanted," is a site of black magic, a perilous point of contact between the human and nonhuman realms. Biology and geology are interconnected (an insight we usually attrib-ute to a later stage in science): the sex impulse, driving from infernal depths, is powered by the same elemental forces that shape the earth. For Coleridge, desire is primitive and uncontrollable: hence the raping touch of incubi brings such perverse pleasure that their victims howl like wolves for their return.

The chasm itself, with "ceaseless turmoil seething," is like a witch's cauldron (17). If Coleridge is thinking of the cleft or gorge as vulval, then his "mighty fountain" forced up by the earth with "fast thick pants" is blatantly ejaculatory (18–19). Nature is a perpetual-motion machine, autoerotic and self-fecundating (like a hermaphrodite deity in Egyptian myth). In the geyser's erratic pulses ("swift half-intermitted burst"), clouds of boulders are tossed up as if they were light as "rebounding hail, / Or chaffy grain" (20–22). The metaphorical "thresher" with his punishing "flail" is ultimately remorseless nature itself, which spares no living creature. There is abstract beauty amid frightful power: the "dancing rocks" follow nature's random pattern, too complex for human eyes (23).

This sublime scene contains the core of the poem's aesthetic theory: Romantic inspiration is sporadic, volcanic, and explosive. Art making draws on primitive, amoral, erotic energies, whose unpredictable, occult workings surprise even the artist. Coleridge's turbulent subterranean realm prefigures Freud's irrational id, where dreams and art are born. The "huge fragments" of rock sprayed skyward refer back to the poem's subtitle; "Kubla Khan," the stunted fragment, was born this way, violently expelled from imagination's underworld (21). "Flung up" on land, the raging river spreads out to flow for five tranquil miles through the pastoral "wood and dale" (24–26). Its "meandering with a mazy motion" represents the smooth surface yet intricate design of art, a labyrinth that invites and baffles. The barbaric convulsions of the work's creation are undetectable and forgotten, as the reader or viewer goes along for a pleasure ride and sees the world in a new way. Reaching the caverns again, the river sinks "in tumult to a lifeless ocean," its fall seeming to trigger its regeneration at earth's womblike center (27–28). With its constantly recirculating energies, Xanadu is a microcosm of nature, an ingeniously self-contained ecosystem.

Kubla Khan now reappears for the first time since the opening lines. Through the thundering cataract, the emperor hears or hallucinates "ancestral voices prophesying war" (29–30). Is this a premonition of Xanadu's destruction? Will its undoing be civil strife or outside attack? Perhaps the ghostly ancestors have been reassimilated by nature as guardian spirits—like Sophocles' banished Oedipus at Colonus. Or are Kubla's ancestors his real enemies? The rule-breaking, iconoclastic Romantic poet is at eternal war with his artistic forefathers.

The winding river has brought us full circle back to the pleasure-dome, whose shadow floats "midway" on the shimmering waves (31–32). The precarious edifice seems buoyed up by the roar of the waters, a "mingled measure / From the fountain and the caves," like sonorous orchestral music (33–34). "A miracle of rare device," the dome is a triumph of engineering but seems as fragile as a bubble or eggshell (35). "A sunny pleasure-dome with caves of ice": heat and cold, light and darkness (36). Coleridge wrote elsewhere that art synthesizes opposites; his favorite proverb was "Extremes meet." In "Kubla Khan," that includes moral extremes: the icy caves recall the pit of Dante's hell, where betrayers of brotherhood, such as Satan, are pinned for eternity in a frozen lake. An artist must confront and explore all passions and hatreds. The dome whose outline ripples in the water is finally the all-encompassing skull of the artist himself, a Narcissus who drowns in his creations.

At the poem's second break, we leave Xanadu behind. Or rather, Kubla's idyll recedes in space and time, while Xanadu as an internalized state will return at the climax. We travel first from Asia to Africa for the poet's remembered vision of an "Abyssinian maid" singing and playing a dulcimer (a stringed instrument struck with hammers; 37–41). She is the poem's second female vocalist: the first was the demon-infatuated vagrant with her banshee wail. But the mind of the Abyssinian maid is fixed on higher things—on Mount Abora, Coleridge's half-invented name for a remote locale that he may have identified with Eden and that he substitutes here for Mount Parnassus, home of the Greek Muses, whose European tradition has presumably been exhausted. The mysterious woman artist is Coleridge's African Muse. He longs to be inseminated with her exquisite "symphony and song" (42–44). Could he "revive" it, he would be reborn into artistic productivity, bringing a "deep delight" whose orgasmic intensity is suggested by the surging, chanting rhythm that now takes over the rest of the poem.

The finale transports us to imaginary space that may represent Europe remade by global vision. The poet himself bursts into view, the emperor Kubla Khan reincarnated as a half-mad artist in creative rapture. He is swept up in afflatus—a divine spirit-wind that brings knowledge and eloquence. The "music loud and long" that the poet prays for is the very poem before us (45–46). Whenever we read "Kubla Khan" aloud (as to a class of students), Coleridge lives again to "build that dome in air." The poem is literally made of air—the breath we use for speech. For a privileged moment, "that sunny dome! those caves of ice!" attain concrete form: "And all who heard should see them there" (47–48). Talented artists have the uncanny power to materialize their thoughts and fantasies, temporarily invading our minds and becalming our bodies. But great artists radically transform us, permanently repopulating our consciousness with their own obsessions.

What is the audience's response to such astonishing virtuosity? In "Kubla Khan," alas, neither gratitude nor respect. Even if the artist's achievements are eventually accepted, he is not. He remains a pariah, strange and uncouth. "Beware! Beware!": society must expel him, since he is contaminated by genius (49). Coleridge's artist is a crank or derelict, friendless and loveless. Yet at the height of inspiration, he seems to be dancing, like the rocks thrown up by the sacred river. His long, unkempt hair floats in the wind, caressed by nature. His eyes are "flashing" with inner visions, though he is blind to the here and now (50).

Coleridge grimly warns the world against himself and his kind. Close ranks, and cast a spell: "Weave a circle round him thrice," like a village May dance to contain and imprison him (51). "And close your eyes with holy dread": don't even look at him, since Judeo-Christianity cannot tolerate the artist's lurid pagan testament (52). The Romantic artist is both hero and criminal. Cut off from the vanished aristocratic patronage system, he will now starve for his art.

Like the ascetic prophet John the Baptist, who survived in the desert on locusts and honey, the modern artist abuses his body to feed his soul. Drugged and deranged, he lives off snowy insect sugars ("honey-dew," deposited on leaves) and ambrosia, "the milk of Paradise," an oracular nectar of the gods (53–54). Ostracized and entranced, the artist is lost in the hypnotic splendors of his own Xanadu.

SEVENTEEN

WALT WHITMAN

Song of Myself

I

I celebrate myself, and sing myself,
And what I assume you shall assume,
For every atom belonging to me as good belongs to you.

I loafe and invite my soul,
I lean and loafe at my ease observing a spear of summer grass.   5

My tongue, every atom of my blood, form'd from this soil,
   this air,
Born here of parents born here from parents the same, and
   their parents the same,
I, now thirty-seven years old in perfect health begin,
Hoping to cease not till death.

Creeds and schools in abeyance,   10
Retiring back a while sufficed at what they are, but never
   forgotten,
I harbor for good or bad, I permit to speak at every hazard,
Nature without check with original energy.

24

Walt Whitman, a kosmos, of Manhattan the son,
Turbulent, fleshy, sensual, eating, drinking and breeding,   15
No sentimentalist, no stander above men and women or
   apart from them,
No more modest than immodest.

Unscrew the locks from the doors!
Unscrew the doors themselves from their jambs!

Whoever degrades another degrades me,   20
And whatever is done or said returns at last to me.
Through me the afflatus surging and surging, through me the
     current and index.

I speak the pass-word primeval, I give the sign of democracy,
By God! I will accept nothing which all cannot have their
     counterpart of on the same terms.

Through me many long dumb voices,   25
Voices of the interminable generations of prisoners and slaves,
Voices of the diseas'd and despairing and of thieves and
     dwarfs,
Voices of cycles of preparation and accretion,
And of the threads that connect the stars, and of wombs and
     of the father-stuff,
And of the rights of them the others are down upon,   30
Of the deform'd, trivial, flat, foolish, despised,
Fog in the air, beetles rolling balls of dung.

Through me forbidden voices,
Voices of sexes and lusts, voices veil'd and I remove the veil,
Voices indecent by me clarified and transfigur'd.   35

I do not press my fingers across my mouth,
I keep as delicate around the bowels as around the head and
     heart,
Copulation is no more rank to me than death is.

I believe in the flesh and the appetites,
Seeing, hearing, feeling, are miracles, and each part and tag   40
     of me is a miracle.

Infamous and lionized, Walt Whitman was the supreme poet of American Romanticism, Wordsworth's heir as a celebrator of nature. Through impudent experiments with tone and form, he also radically advanced the modernization of poetic language begun by Wordsworth. From the slangy to the rhapsodic, Whitman's poetry is in constant, restless change: his long lines pour out like a torrent or skitter in playful zigzags.

Whitman's *Leaves of Grass* was published in 1855 as a collection of twelve poems that would undergo heavy revision and expansion in eight editions over the next three decades. *Song of Myself* was always the centerpiece, though that title dates from the 1881 edition, where 1,346 lines are grouped in fifty-two sections, like weeks of the year. (Only Part 1 and the first half of Part 24 are discussed here.) In ambition and scale, *Leaves of Grass* is an epic, encompassing politics, nature, and the divine, as Whitman understood it. But the heroic narrative centers on himself—or rather the inflated superself of the Romantic poet, isolated and rapacious. That the first word of *Song of Myself* is an unmannerly "I" illustrates the American genius for self-advertisement, which has characterized our commercial life as well as our political history.

"I celebrate myself, and sing myself": the epic starts not with a humble invocation to an immortal Muse but with a hymn to the bard himself in the fallibly human present. There is no Muse—or rather she has been absorbed by the strutting poet, who will explore the full spectrum of male and female emotional states. In Part 1, she is the "soul" whom Whitman invites to dally with him (4). The collapsing of bard into Muse comes with a fusion of bard with audience: "What I assume you shall assume" (2). By sheer force of will, the poet will invade our minds and make his premises and burdens our own. "For every atom belonging to me as good belongs to you": in Whitman's dream of communality, sharing means interpenetration; we're locked to him in a mystical shotgun wedding (3).

The epic theme of *Song of Myself* is not war or moral struggle but expansion of consciousness. "I lean and loafe at my ease observing a spear of summer grass": like Wordsworth rejoicing in a field of wild daffodils, Whitman finds meaning in the random and commonplace (5). By endorsing a lifestyle of leaning and loafing (a then daring colloquialism), he is also twitting the American work ethic in a go-go era of industrialization. Blades of grass—the only spears or weapons in Whitman's ideal world—draw his rapt contemplation. The book of nature is written in swaying green pages, the main title's "leaves" of grass. As a text, the poem itself is organic, budding and spreading and being pruned like vegetation through its many editions.

"My tongue, every atom of my blood, form'd from this soil, this air": Whitman's American vernacular—eager, forthright, sometimes bumptious—was born in an alchemical melding of earth and air (6). His "tongue," or drive to speak, pokes or erupts from the soil like a plant shoot. Nature, not Old World tradition, gives him his voice. Whitman responds to Emerson's call for American cultural self-reliance by proudly rooting four generations of his family in the land: "born here of parents born here from parents the same, and their parents the same" (7). American writers have shed the distant past. The freshness of American "air" is Whitman's exhilarating inspiration (a word meaning "breathing into"). "I, now thirty-seven years old in perfect health begin, / Hoping to cease not till death": like Dante waking up at midlife to start the *Divine Comedy,* Whitman reinvents himself as a bard (8–9). His "hoping to cease not" is a commitment vow, a prayer addressed to nature rather than God: he asks simply for continued vitality to make poetry. He and his poem are symbiotic and coterminous: it's as if he lives only to serve it. The poem will use him up for our pleasure.

The final stanza of Part 1 is a whorl of lapping, eddying phrases; conventional syntax dissolves toward incomprehensibility (10–13). Such passages struck the more fastidious of Whitman's contemporaries as sloppy or inept but may not trouble modern readers schooled on free verse and improvisatory jazz. Whitman is calling for suspension ("abeyance") of all a priori belief systems—the "creeds and schools" of organized religion, universities, art academies, and any intellectual movement that substitutes abstractions or dogma for free thought (10). There was a time ("retiring back a while") when formal codes nourished human development, but their lingering, subliminal effect is ambivalent ("I harbor for good or bad"; 11–12). Hence Whitman vows to speak spontaneously ("at every hazard"), reacting to chance sensation and impulse. Rules of grammar and etiquette will be broken, he warns, when nature floods into him "without check" or hindrance (13). He makes himself a conduit for nature's "original energy," the primal, procreative power of the universe endowing the poet with raw originality (never a governing principle in art making before Romanticism). Deployed on the page, the blazing last line of Part 1 seems to drive the poem forward and launch it into open white space.

Part 24 begins with a trumpetlike proclamation: "Walt Whitman, a kosmos, of Manhattan the son, / Turbulent, fleshy, sensual, eating, drinking and breeding" (14–15). Syntax implodes again: the entire first stanza is merely a string of adjectives and appositions, as in an epitaph or an inscription on a pedestal. Whitman names himself as the protagonist of his poem. The boastful tone echoes that of Homer's champions proclaiming their epithets on the battlefield. Whitman as "kosmos" is a world unto himself: he, or rather his quasi-autobiographical poem, incorporates all beings and experiences. He flings his arms wide, like Blake's exuberant Universal Man, microcosm mirroring macrocosm.

By declaring himself "of Manhattan the son," Whitman now in effect denies his human parentage and implies he is autochthonous, sprung directly from native soil. He was actually born in rural Long Island and was raised there and in Brooklyn. By Manhattan (or elsewhere "Mannahatta") he means not the island borough but the general region once inhabited by the Manahatta, a small Algonquin tribe displaced by the Dutch in the seventeenth century. For Whitman, the North American Indian, like Wordsworth's prehistoric Briton on Salisbury Plain, represents mankind living in harmony with nature.

Whitman's heraldic self-portrait flaunts not singular, epic feats of valor but our basic metabolic functions: "fleshy, sensual, eating, drinking and breeding" (15). Mundane naturalism of this kind in lit-erature is usually deflected onto comic sidekicks like Cervantes's Sancho Panza or Shakespeare's Falstaff, who are scolded, curbed, or expelled. Throughout Part 24 (twice as long as the excerpt here), Whitman calls for an end to false shame, rooted in Judeo-Christian sexual repression. Even more boldly, he links sexual shame to social injustice and bigotry. Mind must accept and forgive body, he argues, if we are ever to reconnect with nature.

The rollicking, "turbulent," swashbuckling persona projected by the poet is certainly hyperbolic, in the Byronic way (15). In real life, Whitman was mild-mannered, diffident, and erotically drawn to men, though, like Leonardo da Vinci and Michelangelo, he may have been mainly celibate. Despite the propaganda he tirelessly fostered, Whit-man sired no illegitimate children, biracial or otherwise. His over-bearing pose of red-blooded virility serves a rhetorical purpose in the poem. When he says he is "no sentimentalist, no stander above men and women or apart from them," he is using our "fleshy, sensual" physicality against the nineteenth century's genteel cult of sentiment with its pretty, precious verse, a dilution of High Romanticism (15–16). Propriety and respectability will not sweeten or soften his language. Neither should an authentic poet be "above . . . or apart from" ordinary folk: he's a comrade, not a snob, prig, or parson.

Whitman's principles of solidarity and egalitarianism extend to his own body. "No more modest than immodest": if everything is holy, then distinctions between modesty and immodesty are prudish and pointless (17). There is a sudden shift into urgent imperatives, as the poet assaults the barriers: "Unscrew the locks from the doors! / Unscrew the doors themselves from their jambs!" (18–19). It's a call to arms, as if we are being incited to revolution. Whitman wants to end covertness about sex as well as division and suspicion over money and property. He identifies privacy with greed and fear and presents nature as a vista of green mansions shared by the family of man. The unscrewed doors are the frames of Western logic and knowledge, rigid geometries that Whitman will transform via fluid emotion and na-ture's organic curves. The door metaphor is psychologically charged: citizen-inmates languish in isolation in society's Bastille, the tightened screws conveying their mental pressure and tension. Whitman's father was a carpenter and house builder: did the poet suffer from a masculine father's intimidating expectations and judgments? When the doors burst open, we too feel a great gust of relief, as we breathe free. Locked doors recall the gates of Eden: to break through them *(in* here rather than *out)* means to reclaim paradise lost and regain its primal innocence and nakedness.

In Whitman's restructured world without doors, fellow feeling blows in with the bracing breeze: "Whoever degrades another degrades me, / And whatever is done or said returns at last to me" (20–21). Imagination enlarges identity: we each bear moral responsibility for all forms of degradation—repression, coercion, exploitation, prejudice—wherever they occur. This passage would have been understood at the time as a protest against slavery and racial discrimination. The phrasing is perhaps pretentiously Christlike: the poet shoulders the heavy cross of the world's sins. But the notion of cyclic return comes from Hinduism through Emerson: the ever-turning wheel of karma operates by the threefold law of retribution. It's as if negativity creates an imbalance in nature, which automatically rights itself to restore equilibrium.

What goes around comes around: the karmic momentum starts a chain of chanting or drumming rhythms (continued in the second half of Part 24). "Through me the afflatus surging and surging, through me the current and index": Whitman ecstatically opens himself to divine inspiration, which blasts like Shelley's west wind through the poem (22). By magic, the wind turns into pounding, purifying breakers—the thunderous surf that was surely one of Whitman's earliest memories (re-created in his operatic lullaby "Out of the Cradle Endlessly Rocking"). Wind and sea become a river or tide, a "current" bearing a motley wealth of freight—the rest of the section's creatures and things. The galvanizing "afflatus" makes *Song of Myself* an "index"—a pointer like a weather vane or the forefinger (index finger) on a directional sign. An index is also a compendium, like the epic catalogs mimicked by Whitman's sprawling lists.

"I speak the pass-word primeval, I give the sign of democracy": liberated language—the poem itself—is the "pass-word" that permits free passage between enemy camps, the jealous enclaves of posses-sions and power in which people are trapped (23). Whitman wants to defeat habit and arouse a sense of the collective. By linking the "primeval" to modern "democracy," he suggests that the intervening period was an epoch of oppressive hierarchies, when the social classes were at perpetual war. Poetry, the great unifier, is a secret word or sign (as in Freemasonry) welcoming initiates to nature's pagan mys-teries. "By God! I will accept nothing which all cannot have their counterpart of on the same terms": Whitman rejects materialism and swears to remove authority-imposed limitations on understanding (24). Enlightened vision is a universal human right.

The outcast and abandoned now step forward, pressing on the poem like the swarm of greedy ghosts fed blood by Odysseus in the underworld. Whitman volunteers himself as their spokesman and emissary. The "many long dumb voices" ("dumb" as in mute) chan-nel through him and burst out in a clamoring chorus (25). They are the silenced of history: "voices of the interminable generations of prisoners and slaves, / Voices of the diseas'd and despairing and of thieves and dwarfs, / . . . Of the deform'd, trivial, flat, foolish, de-spised" (26–27, 31). There is a huge buzz of energy as the poet, like Dante touring hell, takes testimony from the damned.

The hypnotic litany ("voices . . . voices . . . voices") resembles that of a Roman Catholic novena in which Whitman peculiarly takes the role of Mary, the tender intercessor who deflects the masculine wrath of divine judgment. In ministering to lepers and losers, Whitman fol-lows Christ's example. But when he saved the adulteress from ston-ing, Christ bade her sin no more. Whitman sees nothing to forgive: "Through me forbidden voices, / Voices of sexes and lusts, voices veil'd and I remove the veil, / Voices indecent by me clarified and transfigur'd" (33–35). The voices of illicit "lusts," including homo-sexuality as well as adultery, are "veil'd" because externally sup-pressed or prudently lowered through euphemism and innuendo. To "remove the veil," as Whitman claims to do, is to destroy the old dis-pensation. The veil recalls the curtain concealing the Holy of Holies, Blake's symbol for Judeo-Christianity's ambivalence about the geni-tals. (An earthquake tore the Temple veil at the moment of Jesus'

death.) Whitman has "clarified and transfigur'd" his "voices inde-
cent" by exposing them to nature's pristine air and light. It's as if the
voices are emanations or vibrations of the body, made seraphically
transparent. The concept of sin has been banished: there is nothing
obscene in Whitman's poetry except failure of empathy.

Among the liberated voices are sounds of nature: "voices of cycles
of preparation and accretion, / And of the threads that connect the
stars, and of wombs and of the father-stuff" (28–29). The cosmic me-
chanics of creation are revealed. The poet hears a music of the spheres,
as if the constellations were strung like a harp. Geology seems to be an
echo of ultraslow celestial sound waves. Perhaps Whitman's medita-
tion on "cycles of preparation and accretion"—the incessant processes
of deposit and erosion in land formation—was partly inspired by his
having grown up near a shifting, sandy shoreline annually buffeted
by ferocious storms (nor'easters). He would have seen the relation-
ship between earth and water as visibly dynamic. Hence there are
no firm borderlines in Whitman's liberal worldview—as opposed to
those of the militant doctrine of states' rights, which helped trigger
the Civil War. The universe of *Song of Myself* is not the Newtonian
armory of hard, glittering objects but a plush matrix or webwork of
gummy secretions ("of wombs and of the father-stuff"), oozing saps
identified in myth with androgynous Dionysus. Semen becomes pro-
toplasm or even (because it is eerily vocal) ectoplasm.

Making an epic sweep from stars to soil, the stanza ends obliquely
in a grammatically detached phrase: "fog in the air, beetles rolling
balls of dung" (32). This amazing line can be read two ways. At its
most negative, it shows humanity clouded in illusion and trapped in
futility: the highest endeavors, from politics to art and science, are
idle, sullied pursuits. But in ancient Egypt the scarab, an industrious
beetle that infested heaps of manure, was a sacred symbol of meta-
morphosis and resurrection. The dung beetle is Whitman's homely
role model, capturing his practice as a poet. He too gathers the re-
jected and discarded and compacts them into new forms—the perfect
circle that for Egyptians represented the divine solar disc. That dung
disgusts and yet fertilizes is a paradox Whitman applies to himself: "I
keep as delicate around the bowels as around the head and heart"

(37). He asks for a radical readjustment of perspective: no organ or faculty deserves primacy over any other. Religion and convention divide us against ourselves by teaching revulsion from the body's natural operations. Whitman gives the gut the sensitivity of "head and heart" and makes excretion a biological correlate to earth's "accretion." By attributing delicacy—cleanliness and refinement—to the bowels, he counsels an attitude of uncritical acceptance like the heroic stoicism of monks, nuns, and nurses caring for the squalidly ill and dying, as Whitman himself was to do in military hospitals during the Civil War.

The sex theme persists: "Copulation is no more rank to me than death is" (38). "Rank" is Shakespeare's word of choice in *Hamlet* for the gross and putrid, the inevitability of decay. The concrete facts of both sex and death were being systematically edited out of mid-nineteenth-century Anglo-American literature. Hence Whitman says, "I do not press my fingers across my mouth" (36). He will not be hushed; he and his poem will consume and say everything. This passage is among other things an implicit defense of sodomy, oral and anal. However, the superiority of Whitman's Romantic system to that of modern queer theory is that his blistering critique of social injustice is integrated with a reverent celebration of nature (whose objective existence poststructuralism denies). He defends homosexuality by making it simply another expression of free energy in the organic realm: there can be nothing unnatural in nature.

Whitman's polemic takes religious form, as in the Nicene Creed: "I believe in the flesh and the appetites, / Seeing, hearing, feeling, are miracles, and each part and tag of me is a miracle" (39–40). The body is not the soul's foul cage but a charismatic spirit entity in its own right. Whitman's miracle worker is not Christ but nature operating daily in our five senses. To relieve guilt and anxiety, sex is redefined as one of many hearty "appetites." The penis is just a "tag," a knob or shred of flesh like an ear, nose, or finger. The poet's argument is as much with himself as with puritan censors. Body and soul are not so easily reconciled: it takes an epic for Whitman to wrestle them together and pin them down.

EIGHTEEN

EMILY DICKINSON

Because I Could Not Stop for Death

Because I could not stop for Death –
He kindly stopped for me –
The Carriage held but just Ourselves –
And Immortality.

We slowly drove – He knew no haste   5
And I had put away
My labor and my leisure too,
For His Civility –

We passed the School, where Children strove
At Recess – in the Ring –   10
We passed the Fields of Gazing Grain –
We passed the Setting Sun –

Or rather – He passed Us –
The Dews drew quivering and chill –
For only Gossamer, my Gown –   15
My Tippet – only Tulle –

We paused before a House that seemed
A Swelling of the Ground –
The Roof was scarcely visible –
The Cornice – in the Ground –   20

Since then – 'tis Centuries – and yet
Feels shorter than the Day
I first surmised the Horses' Heads
Were toward Eternity –

In this ingenious allegory, as compactly visualized as a screenplay, a proper, respectable lady is courted and then kidnapped and murdered by a smooth gentleman caller. The "I" of the poem is obviously not Emily Dickinson but a coy role she is toying with, a persona (mask) as intricate as the one created by William Blake for his exploited chimney sweep. Dickinson's protagonist shares the sweep's dangerous naivete: both are cheerful, chatty innocents who meet but never comprehend the dark forces at work in the world.

"Because I could not stop for Death – / He kindly stopped for me": the poem begins with the singsong rhythms and perfect rhyme that Dickinson uses to signal a character's childlike confidence in life's benevolence, sometimes symbolized by imagery of springtime beauty. We too are sucked into a receptive mood by the pat social formulas. The trusting speaker fails to see that her suitor's good manners ("Civility" 8) are a ruse. He is a seducer and cad, a trickster or confidence man—a common archetype in nineteenth-century American folklore and literature. A pleasant ride in the country will end in horror.

The first stanza's punning wordplay was inspired by seventeenth-century Metaphysical poetry, a then-unfashionable style that Dickinson deeply admired. On the literal level, the mysterious visitor has "kindly stopped" by to give the lady a lift because she's too engrossed to take a break from her busy workday (2). On the symbolic level, things are more disturbing: her reluctance to "stop" is peremptorily overriden by his superior force. Death comes, in other words, when we least expect it. His "kindly" behavior is merely natural for man*kind* in its *kin*ship of mortality. (Puns on "kin"/"kind" are a staple of seventeenth-century literature; for example, *Hamlet* I.ii.65.) "The Carriage held but just Ourselves – / And Immortality": the lady is lured from home by the promise of "Immortality," who acts in the allegory as a prim, spectral chaperone (3–4). Their carriage is a hearse (perhaps borrowed from Blake's "London") with just one destination. "We slowly drove – He knew no haste": Death's courtly consideration is really the solemn pace of a funeral procession (5). The speaker is automatically, unthinkingly gracious, deferring her own pressing schedule: "And I had put away / My labor and my leisure too, / For His Civility" (6–8). Dickinson's genius for concision and economy is illustrated in the great line "My labor and my leisure too," which movingly sums up all of human life with its strains and satisfactions.

Stanzas three and four track Death and the maiden on their village tour. At first crisp and specific, the images blur as the speaker's senses weaken and contract. "We passed the School, where Children strove / At Recess – in the Ring": the lively scene, seemingly so simple and innocuous, is contemplated over a melancholy distance of space and time (9–10). This passage shows how Dickinson's archaic, Anglo-Saxon capitalizations (which, along with her innovative, syncopated dashes, were condescendingly "corrected" and removed in the first posthumous collections of her work) give her nouns concreteness as well as philosophical breadth. In literal terms, the school is just a school, like those that introduced the poet to the larger world. Symbolically, however, the school is society itself, indoctrinating the masses and erecting its frail barrier against implacable reality. Thus the "Children" are all of humanity, who crave verities or absolutes in order to survive. Their lack of independence (as seen by the fiercely agnostic Dickinson) keeps them in a juvenile condition. The prior stanza's "labor" and "leisure" are reprised in the way the students oddly "strive" at recess. Work and achievement are child's play in the eyes of the gods; honors and wealth evaporate at death's arrival. The "Ring" is the competitive arena of earthly life, a gated paddock where men are schooled like horses. It's also a communal circle dance, like the one ending Coleridge's "Kubla Khan," suggesting order and regularity on the one hand but conformity and entrapment on the other.

"We passed the Fields of Gazing Grain": an eerie army of mute bystanders stretches out on every side (11). Arrayed by the millions, the wheat stalks with their eyelike heads become human beings waiting for gathering by the Grim Reaper or Christ himself, who wields a sickle on doomsday (Revelation 14.14–16.) Are they staring patiently toward heaven, or accusingly at her? If the latter, the lady recalls Marie

Antoinette in her tumbril, rattling through mobbed streets toward the scaffold. (Metaphors about the luckless Bourbons occur elsewhere in Dickinson.) The carriage's path is methodically charted by the tripled phrase "We passed," which also counts off dwindling time (9, 11, 12). Progression becomes regression as the carriage leaves civilization: we follow the travelers from house to school to farmland (agriculture = nature ordered), until we reach pure, unreconstructed nature, the ominous "Setting Sun," where the lady and her escorts seem to drop off the end of the earth (12).

At the poem's exact midpoint, there is a hesitation or stutter ("Or rather –"), as the personified Sun obliviously vanishes ("He passed Us") and the lady's mental powers start to dim (13). Movement slows, and the imagery shifts downward from the sharply visual to the numbly tactile: "The Dews grew quivering and chill" (14). The lady suddenly finds herself underdressed, disastrously unprepared for nightfall: her pretty "Gossamer" gown is stitched of wispy cobwebs, and her tulle "Tippet" (shawl) is light as chiffon (tulle is fine netting for veils and ballet costumes; 15–16). She's decked out for a wedding that will never happen: the soul as bride of Christ is clad in filmy illusions, a false optimism about salvation and resurrection. The inescapable reality is the cold, damp grave, where she is abandoned. By metonymy (rhetorical displacement), "quivering" actually describes not the dews, of course, but the fearful lady herself, who no longer recognizes her body as her own.

A "pause" turns full stop: the end of the parade is "a House that seemed / A Swelling of the Ground"—like a cozy, thatched honeymoon cottage covered with vines (17–18). But "the Roof was scarcely visible – / The Cornice [a wall's molded upper rim] – in the Ground": we're suddenly in a Gothic novel, with its gloomy, decaying, haunted mansion (19–20). The indecipherable roof is probably a cemetery mound—just a heap of slowly subsiding dirt. The word "Ground," ending two lines in the same stanza, brings the rhyme scheme to a grinding halt (18, 20). After the first stanza's carefree regularity, the rest of the poem uses unsettling, daringly modern off rhymes to hint at the speaker's loss of control as well as the gradual breakdown of meaning ("away"/"Civility"; "Ring"/"Sun"; "chill"/"Tulle"). The insistent repetition of "Ground" (its very sound conveying grungy nondifferentiation and obscurity) dramatizes the return of all earthly things to dust. As in Shelley's "Ozymandias," we are left amid ruins in a barren landscape.

"Since then – 'tis Centuries": the happy patter opening the poem seems eons away (21). Yet because of the atrophy of the lady's faculties, elapsed time "feels shorter than the Day" of her fateful journey (22). History is over for her but not through a Second Coming; on the contrary, it was Christ's rosy offer of an afterlife that cruelly duped and defrauded her. God himself is the suave kidnapper. That the carriage's apocalyptic "Horses' Heads" are steering "toward Eternity," however, raises the question of whether God is the driver or the driven, himself a victim of larger, impersonal forces (23–24). The lady is Everyman: males too don the gauzy, feminine gown of sentimentality and self-delusion. The speaker's hazy recollection of when she "first surmised" she was booked on a one-way trip to the underworld lets us fleetingly share her moment of terror. But it's the last thing she or we can think, as the poem ends in extinction of consciousness.

NINETEEN

EMILY DICKINSON

Safe in Their Alabaster Chambers

Safe in their Alabaster Chambers –
Untouched by Morning –
And untouched by Noon –
Lie the meek members of the Resurrection –
Rafter of Satin – and Roof of Stone!   5

Grand go the Years – in the Crescent – above them –
Worlds scoop their Arcs –
And Firmaments – row –
Diadems – drop – and Doges – surrender –
Soundless as dots – on a Disc of Snow –   10

Immense in scale and oratorical in tone, this amazing short poem departs from Dickinson's usual four-line stanza format, based on sturdy Protestant hymn measure. The first five-line stanza rolls out in a single, thrilling sentence, delivered in the magisterial public voice of a sermon or eulogy. It's as if the poem's disturbing theme—the dead and their defeated hopes—can barely be contained by traditional structure.

Suspense and momentum are produced by Dickinson's dramatic postponement of the sentence subject ("meek members") to the fourth line. We are half hypnotized by a sonorous litany of parallel phrases, their triple adjectives ringing like a church bell: "Safe in their Alabaster Chambers – / Untouched by Morning – / And untouched by Noon" (1–3). The crucial subject recedes even further through a Latinate inversion of syntax, typical of John Milton's *Paradise Lost* but rare in Dickinson's work: "lie the meek members of the Resurrection" (4). The verb surprisingly precedes rather than follows its subject, as would be normal in English.

If this stanza is viewed purely as graphic design, as in the wittily shaped or patterned poems of George Herbert (one of the Metaphysicals whom Dickinson revered), it becomes a mordant pun: the first three lines are stacked like cordwood, crushing the hapless human figures stretched flat in the oozingly elongated fourth line. These rhetorical tricks embody Dickinson's meaning: all of religion's beautiful, stirring words will not save humanity. Trusting themselves to what they think is suspended animation, believers are betrayed by a godless universe into the eternal grave.

The "Alabaster Chambers" in which the departed repose are tombs of incongruous splendor. "Alabaster" was a Petrarchan honorific for aristocratic ladies' fine white complexions; hence the word may also be describing the pallid corpses themselves, caked with frost. They are as "safe" as in a bedchamber but as locked down as in a prison. They will remain "untouched" by "Morning" or "Noon"—symbolically, childhood and adulthood—because life's opportunities and responsibilities are over. Since light can't penetrate physically or mentally, they are pathetically unable to grasp their condition. These graveyard residents resemble a congregation dutifully waiting for a pastor who never comes. They are "meek" because they were led like sheep in life and have now lost the ability to rebel. "Resurrection" was their lure and grail. In Dickinson's ironic restaging, Christ has craftily kept the promise of his Sermon on the Mount: "Blessed are the meek, for they shall inherit the earth" (Matthew 5.5). Their shocking legacy, however, is darkness and dirt.

"Rafter of Satin – and Roof of Stone!" (5) The citadel seems luxurious as well as imposing. Yet a satin rafter is no solid beam but a fragile festoon like holiday bunting. Satin is the soft, sleek shroud of illusions in which the dead wrapped themselves. The Christian doctrine of salvation and resurrection, as Dickinson portrays it, is architecturally unsound. The satin rafters may be sagging cobwebs—an image she uses elsewhere for the flimsiness of uncritical belief. Though the "Roof of Stone" sounds like an ample vault, it may just be the lid of a plain, wooden coffin sealing up the dead with no chance of escape on Judgment Day. Subliminal sound effects end the stanza in suffocation and terror: as the vowels close down in the dissonant off rhyme "Noon"/"Stone" (reinforced by terminal *n*'s in "Resurrection" and "Satin"), we almost feel the heavy lid being slid into place and secured.

Two versions exist of the second stanza. In Dickinson's first draft, dated three years earlier, nature romps on merrily above the deep freeze of the dead: the breeze "laughs"; a bee "babbles"; "sweet" birds "pipe"—pert, pretty sounds unprocessed by the sluggish cadavers' "stolid Ear." The final version makes a stunning leap forward in power and authority. Pictorial style shifts from a frilly, pastoral rococo to rigorous abstraction, as the charming, summery scene yields to a majestic, inanimate panorama. It is severe moments of epic vision like this that make Dickinson unique among women poets.

The first stanza's earthly clock time ("Morning," "Noon") has run down, and astronomy's slower, vaster metric takes over. "Grand go the Years – in the Crescent – above them": constellations sweep over the dome of the sky, imagined as a moonlike, ruthlessly reaping sickle

(6). "Worlds scoop their Arcs – / And Firmaments – row": the planets, as if self-propelled, gouge their orbits out of a dense or resistant medium, a jellied soup of primal matter (7–8). The effect is sinister yet beguiling: "scoop," a blunt colloquialism, may playfully refer to the Big Dipper. Dickinson makes the firmament (sky) of Genesis unexpectedly plural (presumably on the model of "heavens"): it seems to be multiplying uncontrollably beyond the care or capacity of any demiurge. If the firmaments "row" themselves away, there must be oars—perhaps comet tails or solar rays. The image may have been suggested to Dickinson by the fans of brilliant sunbeams that can break through layers of heavy gray clouds in New England (compare her famous poem, "There's a certain Slant of light, / Winter Afternoons"). This passage is typical of Dickinson's singular style, with its juxtaposition of the awesome or fantastic with the humorous and commonplace.

The closing two lines, with their immense spectacle of history being swallowed up by nature, could stand alone as a poem. "Diadems – drop – and Doges – surrender – / Soundless as dots – on a Disc of Snow – " (9–10). Time surreally speeds up, while the reader's perception slows, thanks to Dickinson's idiosyncratic use of dashes, six in all. These internalized hesitations delay yet implacably prod us toward the muffled ending, with its total sensory deprivation. The dropping diadems are both crowns and royal dynasties, falling like snowflakes. Power melts away, as it did for Shelley's stone pharaoh, guillotined in the desert. Doges represent the color and pomp of Venice, the city of art. They "surrender" because they leave no footprint; all trace of civilization is blanketed and bleached out by eternity. With scientific detachment, the pitiless poet takes a godlike perspective: from a distance, human beings are mere specks, "dots" drifting down and vanishing into a "Disc of Snow," our green globe turned glacial. Dickinson's apocalyptic tableau of earthly devastation against an infinite skyscape prefigures the genre of intergalactic science fiction.

"Safe in Their Alabaster Chambers" is like an aria in its operatic manipulation of sound: it begins with high, ornate vocal projection and fades to numbed silence. The stark, mysteriously evocative "Disc of Snow" that ends the poem anticipates dreamlike French Symbolist imagery of the 1880s. I wonder whether the disc was suggested by a sundial or birdbath buried by snow in Dickinson's garden, overseen from that second-story room where she was so often in seclusion. Certainly, the last line's disorienting whiteout (a blinding feature of northern blizzards) would have few parallels in art until the white-on-white experiments of geometric modern design.

Metaphorically, Dickinson's "Disc of Snow" is a clock face stripped bare. It has been reduced to zero—the "O without a figure" that Shakespeare identifies with nothingness and loss of meaning (*King Lear* I.iv.198–99). A flurry of alliterations makes us hear the clock winding down: in the last two lines, nine *d*'s tick off time, while nine *s*'s create a hush and elicit our exhalation. The breath goes out of the poem as it did from the dead. The "Disc of Snow" is ultimately the mechanical perfection of a clockwork universe indifferent to human identity and pain.

TWENTY

EMILY DICKINSON

The Soul Selects Her Own Society

The Soul selects her own Society –
Then – shuts the Door –
To her divine Majority –
Present no more –

Unmoved – she notes the Chariots – pausing –   5
At her low Gate –
Unmoved – an Emperor be kneeling
Upon her Mat –

I've known her – from an ample nation –
Choose One –   10
Then – close the Valves of her attention –
Like Stone –

This is Emily Dickinson's declaration of independence, a manifesto of artistic vocation and mission. It is stern, flat, and implacable. Yet its emotions are intense and stretched to the limit. In conception and execution, the poem is polar opposite to the sweepingly expansive "Safe in Their Alabaster Chambers," where the poet is invisible—simply an eye observing and a mind judging. Here, in contrast, she shrinks her base and sets herself front and center, carving a sharp line between her terrain and the rest of reality.

"The Soul selects her own Society": Dickinson identifies herself with her vital, inner world, not with the homely face and shy personality seen by others (1). Her companions (the original meaning of "society") are her own thoughts, with which she densely populates her work. Her tone is peremptory, her attitude extreme: when she brusquely "shuts the Door" (a curt colloquialism), she exercises the prerogative of queens or sibyls (2). Since the "Door" is mental, shutting it is an act of discipline, concentrating energy and perception. Its inspiration was probably not the front door of Dickinson's house but that of her treasured bedroom, to which she withdrew from family too (though their affluence made her privacy possible).

Dickinson absents herself from communal experience: "to her divine Majority – / Present no more" (3–4). This "Majority" is her coming of age as a Christian on earth and in heaven—an identity she categorically rejects. Second, it is the local congregation with whom she refuses to worship, at some social cost in a small, provincial town of the mid–nineteenth century. They are the "Majority" in every sense—homogeneous, self-satisfied, and repressive. The poet defiantly embraces Emerson's doctrine of "self-reliance." She cannot be bribed by love, wealth, fame, or power. As in George Herbert's "The Quip," the poet is hailed by a steady stream of tempters. She hardens her heart, woman's legendary point of vulnerability: "unmoved," she rebuffs emissaries, suitors, and finally the "Emperor," God himself, who comes courting like Cinderella's prince and kneels to beg her hand in sacred marriage (5–8).

The "low Gate" where the splendid "Chariots" pause marks a humble cottage; it's like the servants' entrance for the snubbed fairy-tale heroine with her broom and pail of ashes. The entry boasts a monastic straw "Mat" rather than a fine rug or red carpet rolled out for potentates (8). It's as if the poet is bedding in a stable, while pilgrim magi arrive bearing tribute. As usual with the macabre Dickinson, her dwelling also resembles a tomb: the parading chariots mimic a funeral procession pulling up to the "low Gate" of an open grave. The mat where kneeling visitors pray is the trodden grass patch of a cemetery plot.

"I've known her," Dickinson casually notes of her soul as if from a schizophrenic distance, "from an ample nation – / Choose One" (9–10). Early readers misread these lines as a confession of disappointed love and feverishly wondered what shadowy man made Amherst's lady poet withdraw from the world. Since we now have access to the whole of Dickinson's work as well as to much of her correspondence, we can clearly see that the "One" Dickinson chose was herself. In this poem, she marries herself for her art and constructs a life as circumscribed as a nun's. Her feminine but imperial soul, like Shakespeare's suicidal Cleopatra retiring to her tomb, acts dictatorially to "close the Valves of her attention – / Like Stone" (11–12). The sensation of a seal being tightened is reproduced for us in the hard, constricting consonants of "choose," "close," and "Stone."

In his Holy Sonnets, Donne appeals to God to "batter" and "break" his "iron heart." But Dickinson wants to make that fortress even more impregnable. Her mental "Valves" (a metaphor of Metaphysical incongruity, conflating cardiology with hydromechanics) are where distractions and trivial demands leak in. Tenderness or compassion would compromise her artistic integrity and endanger her enterprise. At the end, the poet does not surrender her selfhood with the melting bliss of Herbert's "Love," nor does she dance in the open like Coleridge's ecstatic seer in "Kubla Khan." No, with militant resolve, she negates the entire world to preserve her small, proud kingdom of art.

TWENTY-ONE

WILLIAM BUTLER YEATS

The Second Coming

Turning and turning in the widening gyre
The falcon cannot hear the falconer;
Things fall apart; the center cannot hold;
Mere anarchy is loosed upon the world,
The blood-dimmed tide is loosed, and everywhere   5
The ceremony of innocence is drowned;
The best lack all conviction, while the worst
Are full of passionate intensity.
Surely some revelation is at hand;
Surely the Second Coming is at hand.   10
The Second Coming! Hardly are those words out
When a vast image out of *Spiritus Mundi*
Troubles my sight: somewhere in sands of the desert
A shape with lion body and the head of a man,
A gaze blank and pitiless as the sun,   15
Is moving its slow thighs, while all about it
Reel shadows of the indignant desert birds.
The darkness drops again; but now I know
That twenty centuries of stony sleep
Were vexed to nightmare by a rocking cradle,   20
And what rough beast, its hour come round at last,
Slouches toward Bethlehem to be born?

History is a maelstrom in "The Second Coming." The poem was written at a time when Europe was recovering from the cataclysm of World War I and when Yeats's Ireland, torn by religious sectarianism, was in turmoil after a failed rebellion against Great Britain in 1916. The poet imagines the eras of Western culture as spinning, overlapping vortices, which he calls gyres. It's as if history is a brutal, mechanical force more vital than the human beings caught up in it. This poem, which begins with the formality of a lament, speaks with special eloquence to anyone who has ever put faith in politics and then lost it.

"Turning and turning in the widening gyre / The falcon cannot hear the falconer": floating on a column of air, a fierce raptor slowly spirals up and away from its earthbound master (1–2). Symbolically, the falcon (a royal hunting bird) represents events escaping human control. The falconer's distant, fading voice stands for moral reasoning, the spiritual and intellectual faculties on which civilization depends. Left to its own devices, the predatory bird embodies pure appetite and aggressive will, our most primitive instincts. "Things fall apart; the center cannot hold": the collapsing center is stable government or solidarity among the citizenry; it's also a shared ideal, common cause, or sustaining tradition (3). Yeats's metaphor of the weak or failing falconer recalls that of the false king as negligent gardener in *Hamlet,* where the usurped realm has fallen into crime and decay.

"Mere anarchy is loosed upon the world": chaos, unleashed like the rogue falcon, erupts from some obscure, malevolent, or even satanic source (4). ("Mere" means absolute.) "The blood-dimmed tide is loosed, and everywhere / The ceremony of innocence is drowned": the repetition of "loosed" in consecutive lines smoothly shifts the nature imagery from animal (the falcon) to elemental (5–6). The "tide" is the ebbing and flowing waters of life, reliable until a flood tide (produced by torrential rain or a storm surge under a full moon) overflows or crumbles the embankments. Those obliterated borderlines signify the social contract, the codes that curb and channel impulse and emotion.

"Blood-dimmed" waters are profaned and poisoned by carnage. They recall the Nile turned to blood in God's first plague upon arrogant Egypt, which Yeats is implicitly equating with imperial England or self-maddened Europe in its recent bloodbath. Vision too is "dimmed"; clarity of purpose is lost. The "ceremony of innocence" that has been "drowned" along with the wicked (as in Noah's flood) includes all the rituals, sacraments, conventions, and daily routines that structure life and give it meaning, from birth and schooling through courtship and marriage. In crisis, "innocence" itself—trust, hope, joy—is aborted by cynicism, just as the newborn infants (the Innocents) were slaughtered by tyrant Herod.

"The best lack all conviction, while the worst / Are full of passionate intensity": these famous lines are Yeats's anguished formulation of what seems to be an eternal principle of politics (7–8). When "the center cannot hold," neither consensus nor compromise is possible. Public debate shifts to the extremes or is overtaken by violence, which blocks incremental movement toward reciprocity and conciliation. Moderate views are "drowned" out (as by the bloody tide) in strident partisanship or fanaticism. The phrase "passionate intensity" suggests that, for the late Romantic Yeats, eros diverted from the personal to the political turns into a distorted lust for power.

The second stanza opens in doubt and confusion: "Surely some revelation is at hand; / Surely the Second Coming is at hand. / The Second Coming!" (9–11). We are hearing either one voice echoing its own shocked phrases or many voices in public tumult. The book of Revelation lists the dreadful omens heralding doomsday, when Jesus will return and unlock the secrets of history. But in Yeats's poem, Christ's promised glory is overshadowed by a monstrous apparition from antiquity. The poet is seized by an electrifying vision: "a vast image out of *Spiritus Mundi* / Troubles my sight." It's a collective memory, crystallizing from the repository of world myths (12–13). (*"Spiritus Mundi"* is Yeats's mystical term for "soul of the universe.") We witness the resurrection of the pagan era, whose barbarism mirrors that of the war-torn twentieth century. Yeats sees no evidence of moral evolution over two millennia of Christianity.

We are transported to the blazing "sands of the desert"—the barren Egypt of Shelley's "Ozymandias" (13). But the abandoned stone sculptures are coming alive: "A shape with lion body and the head of a man, / A gaze blank and pitiless as the sun, / Is moving its slow thighs" (14–16). Revelation's Antichrist appears as a sphinx, whose hybrid body, like that of the Greek centaur, symbolizes mankind's divided nature (compare the falcon/falconer). Its "blank and pitiless" gaze (like the unblinking African sun) suggests, first, the cruelty and oppression of the autocracies of the ancient Near East and, second, the universal savagery of war, inspired by the desire for revenge or conquest.

As the sphinx unearths itself and stalks languidly across the desert, "all about it / Reel shadows of the indignant desert birds" (16–17). The effect is as cinematic as a silent film: we see but don't hear the diving, looping birds, surely screeching as they harass the interloper disturbing their calm. Actually, we see only their swirling "shadows," a hyperkinetic pattern of checks and dashes. These birds are not noble falcons but probably scavengers, like vultures: as faceless and irrational as a mob, they correspond to the first stanza's noisy ideologues of "passionate intensity." The scene is tremendous: the sphinx's steady, impassive march has a near-robotic grandeur, while the birds furiously buzz and bank like biplanes over an armored tank.

"The darkness drops again": the hallucination vanishes with the fall of a theater curtain (18). From the masquelike tableau, the oracular poet has somehow intuited what is not there: "but now I know / That twenty centuries of stony sleep / Were vexed to nightmare by a rocking cradle" (18–20). A two-thousand-year cycle (astrology's standard span of ages) has ended. The hibernating sphinx was tormented by something paradoxically very mild, a rocking cradle. Baby Jesus proved as potent as the infant Hercules, who strangled serpents in his cradle. Though Christ came as a proponent of love, he bequeathed, in Yeats's view, new hatreds, wars, and atrocities. We oddly see the cradle but not its occupant, as if the latter's essence or even existence is in question. The cradle may be rocking from the baby's agitation or demonic invasion or the invisible hand of history. Its oscillation mirrors society's buffeting by polarized political and cultural forces, which end in stalemate. Each victory spawns a reaction and eventual reversal, as in the clash of opposites in William Blake's poetry (which Yeats edited). The sphinx's long nightmare is the grisly chronicle of Western history.

The poem ends with a question, a couplet like a riddle: "And what rough beast, its hour come round at last, / Slouches toward Bethlehem to be born?" (21–22). The transitional witching hour approaches, but it is not a humanitarian Age of Aquarius that dawns. Uncouth and amoral, the "rough beast" slouching toward its rendezvous is basic human nature, exposed when the masks of civilization are stripped off. Despite its "stony" obliviousness to the suffering of others, it will make its debut in Bethlehem, where Jesus was born in a stable. As if by repetition compulsion, each era begins in Bethlehem under a guiding star of good intentions. Will the beast destroy the village and eradicate all trace of the tender babe? Or will it, more craftily, compress and conceal itself in infant form to infiltrate and menace the world?

Yeats's "The Second Coming" has gained in prophetic power with each decade of the twentieth and now twenty-first century, from the rise of fascism and nuclear warfare to the proliferation of international terrorism. It expresses the melancholy realization that man, yearningly drawn to the divine, will never fully escape his bestial ancestry. The poem is modernistically unrhymed, though the first stanza plays with shadowy off rhymes: "gyre"/"falconer"/"everywhere"; "hold"/"world"/"drowned." It is structured instead by dramatic visuals and emblematic choreography. There are two main movements: a huge, expanding circle (the ascending falcon) and an arrowlike, linear track (the beast bound for Bethlehem). Then two smaller ones: a pendulum arc (the rocking cradle) and an exploding pinwheel (the reeling desert birds). Ideas have become design, starkly juxtaposed with the murky turbulence of elemental forces—storm, flood, drought. Hence the poem, with its horror movie finale, is as hybrid as the sphinx, who represents our buried impulses, vestiges of a past that keeps turning into the future.

TWENTY-TWO

WILLIAM BUTLER YEATS

Leda and the Swan

A sudden blow: the great wings beating still
Above the staggering girl, her thighs caressed
By the dark webs, her nape caught in his bill,
He holds her helpless breast upon his breast.

How can those terrified vague fingers push   5
The feathered glory from her loosening thighs?
And how can body, laid in that white rush,
But feel the strange heart beating where it lies?

A shudder in the loins engenders there
The broken wall, the burning roof and tower   10
And Agamemnon dead.
                                        Being so caught up,
So mastered by the brute blood of the air,
Did she put on his knowledge with his power
Before the indifferent beak could let her drop?   15

The theme of "Leda and the Swan," as of "The Second Coming," is the tragedy of history. Once again, a Yeats poem opens with a predatory bird, which now turns its violence against the human. In form, "Leda" is a rhyming sonnet that seems to have been physically traumatized. The first two quatrains float free, while the third section is cleft crosswise, its final segment dangling precariously, like Leda just before the swan drops her.

"A sudden blow": Zeus, the amorous king of the gods, swoops down in disguise from Olympus to take his pleasure, but the girl he targets experiences his desire as assault and battery. The poem begins with Metaphysical abruptness and rapidly unfolds in the present tense, drawing us into the scene. Like Leda, we are disoriented by a welter of sensory impressions, conveyed by multiplying participles ("beating," "staggering," "caressed," "caught") before we reach the clarifying subject ("He") in the fourth line. The myth of Leda and the swan was a popular romantic theme in Renaissance art (Leonardo and Michelangelo painted it), but the tale was treated as a charming, pastoral idyll and rarely if ever shown from the victim's point of view. In Yeats's version, womanizing is not a titillating sport but a ruthless expression of the will to power.

Despite their decorative association with delicacy and grace, swans are fierce and formidable creatures, as Yeats surely observed (he titled a 1919 book of poems *The Wild Swans at Coole*). The swan overwhelms and immobilizes Leda, "helpless" amid a grotesque profusion of wings and paddled feet (4). The swan seems both spidery ("dark webs") and serpentine, as he twists his long neck around to clamp her nape in his bill and pin their bodies together (3). "How can those terrified vague fingers push / The feathered glory from her loosening thighs?" (5–6). She is weak, confused, and perhaps blinded by a burst of divine light ("glory"). The phrase "loosening thighs" is ambiguous and provocative: have her strained muscles gone slack, or is there awakening complicity on her part? As with the earlier "caressed," a gentle stroking amid the commotion, the reader too is being seduced—toward voyeurism and away from honor and ethical judgment.

Nearly everything in the first half of the poem is tactile, including Leda's alarming sensation of the swan's "strange heart beating" next to hers (8). God is an alien beyond human emotions. The "white rush" in which Leda's body is "laid" (nestled in fluffy down as well as sexually conquered) is the bird's first strike as it forces past her feeble resistance, but it also describes Zeus's ecstatic ejaculation (7). While male swans (cobs) do have a small retractable penis, the coitus here seems to be of a god in incomplete metamorphosis: his own penis may remain magically intact.

But this is only one episode in an epic saga. Zeus has a purpose, and Leda is his instrument: "A shudder in the loins engenders there / The broken wall, the burning roof and tower / And Agamemnon dead" (9–11). The "shudder in the loins" is his pleasure and her fear. Impregnated, she will give birth to the entire classical era. From Leda's egg will hatch Helen and Clytemnestra, the sister femmes fatales. Faithless Helen will trigger the ten-year Trojan War, inspiring Homer's *Iliad* and *Odyssey*. Clytemnestra will slaughter her husband, Agamemnon, commander in chief of the Greek forces, and be murdered in turn by their vengeful son, Orestes. Aeschylus's trilogy about these events, the *Oresteia,* was the first great work of Western drama.

Yeats portrays Western culture as inseminated with treachery and violence from the start. The rape of Leda begins a chain of disasters that will continue to his own day. "The broken wall, the burning roof and tower" apply to all wars but show ravaged Troy in flames as well as the victorious Greek signal fires leaping from peak to peak to Argos (the first scene in the *Oresteia*). The burning tower also suggests Zeus's raging phallic aggression, just as the "broken wall" is Leda's violation and defloration. (Though she was already married to a king, Yeats treats Leda as a virginal, undefended maiden.)

The poem roots the constructions of civilization in the convulsive "loins," the gut or viscera from which surge driving, irrational ambitions and great achievements. But Yeats shows the latter only in decline and fall: "Agamemnon dead" is an emblem of annihilated male authority and pride. While Troy still burns, we eerily see him, as if by time-lapse photography, already slain on the day of his triumphant homecoming. He lies toppled like Shelley's pharaoh. In the time frame of the sonnet's composition, "Agamemnon dead" also refers to the failure of state and military leadership in World War I, with its strategic blunders and massive waste of life. The age of heroes is over.

Because of its vast historical vision and agonizing pantomime of passion and conflict, "Leda and the Swan" can justifiably be considered the greatest poem of the twentieth century. It reflects the disillusion of European and North American artists and intellectuals with the West, whose buoyant confidence in its own moral superiority and technological progress had been shattered by the Great War, as it was then called. The "sudden blow" that opens the poem reproduces the shock of events, numbing and destabilizing. The poet wonders whether Leda, "being so caught up" in her brief, bruising encounter with God, gained "knowledge" of the meaning of history (12–14). Did her penetration by Zeus's "power" give her mental penetration? Or was she, like us, mired in earthly limitation? She says nothing.

Neither Zeus nor Leda is named in the text itself, so that the scene becomes archetypal: the poem records a pivotal moment of contact between humanity and divinity. The exchange is painfully one-sided but revelatory: "mastered by the brute blood of the air," Leda sees God for what he is—a sadistic marauder, as tarnished as a fallen angel (13). Sated, the swan lets her "drop" from his "indifferent beak," a curt phrase that accentuates her cumbersome materiality, her reduction to a thing and trophy, as well as his cavalier disrespect for his own creation (15). Losing interest, God callously discards his toys.

By implication, the poem refers to another commandeering of a virgin by a bird-god—the impregnation of a startled Mary by the Holy Spirit, depicted as a beam of light or white dove. (Yeats makes the Mary parallel explicit in "Two Songs from a Play.") God plays a game of hit-and-run—infusing each declining age with ferocious new energy, then disappearing again for two thousand years. A fellow Irish writer, Samuel Beckett, borrowed Yeats's theme of a capriciously self-withholding God for *Waiting for Godot,* where vagabonds scrabble beneath the blank sky.

The last section of "Leda and the Swan" has a split-level structure, mirroring its content. The irregular gash produced by a broken line mimics the modern breakdown in religious and cultural traditions— the mournful subject of T. S. Eliot's *The Waste Land* (1922), with its fallen idols and disconnected allusions. From this point of view, "Agamemnon dead" would be the failure even to recognize the name "Agamemnon": classical culture has receded and no longer feeds and informs the present. Visually, the last stanza's jagged pattern resembles a thunderbolt, Zeus's emblem. Yeats has projected himself into Leda's story: he wrote elsewhere, "We who are poets and artists . . . live but for the moment when vision comes to our weariness like terrible lightning, in the humility of the brutes" *(Per Amica Silentia Lunae)*. Illumination is sporadic, partial, and costly. Knowledge is not cumulative but subject to periodic destruction and loss, necessitating recovery and revival. Like "The Second Coming," "Leda and the Swan" ends with a question. There is no resolution. All human beings, like Leda, are caught up moment by moment in the "white rush" of experience. For Yeats, the only salvation is the shapeliness and stillness of art.

TWENTY-THREE

WALLACE STEVENS

Disillusionment of Ten O'Clock

The houses are haunted
By white night-gowns.
None are green,
Or purple with green rings,
Or green with yellow rings,   5
Or yellow with blue rings.
None of them are strange,
With socks of lace
And beaded ceintures.
People are not going   10
To dream of baboons and periwinkles.
Only, here and there, an old sailor,
Drunk and asleep in his boots,
Catches tigers
In red weather.   15

It's bedtime, and the genteel streets of Hartford, Connecticut, are as hushed as a graveyard. Wallace Stevens, by day the affluent executive of an insurance company, contemplates the split in his mental life. The title's "disillusionment" is partly his own, lulled and dulled as he is by schedule and routine. But in a larger sense, it refers to the prim evasions of a utilitarian society whose bland burghers have divested themselves of the beautiful illusions of imagination and art.

"The houses are haunted / By white night-gowns": we could be in a shuttered department store in the twilight zone (1–2). The only things visible in the dark halls and empty rooms are swaths of fluttery fabric. These nightgowns are apparitions from the past (when men wore nightgowns too) as well as the uninspiring present. There is a sense of sexual repression or reserve, a puritan heritage. The poet seems poignantly isolated: his wife (who appears in Stevens's great poem "Sunday Morning") is remote or already asleep. He is simply a hovering observer, as ghostly as the nightgowns themselves, standing guard like sexless angels.

Hartford's sober citizens have so bonded with their social roles that their warm flesh has evaporated and, even after hours, only their uniforms remain. There is little space for self-expression or eccentricity: the "strange" is exotic, unseemly (7). The white nightgowns are like hollow, bleached seashells: "None are green, / Or purple with green rings, / Or green with yellow rings, / Or yellow with blue rings" (3–6). Such garish patterns would have been inconceivable and preposterous at the time, above all in Protestant New England. They belong to the sun-drenched tropics, with their florid hues and razor-sharp contrasts. Stevens, in private an aesthete and art connoisseur, may be thinking of Gauguin's paintings of the South Pacific or Matisse's of North Africa. For later readers, the passage engagingly prefigures the psychedelic flamboyance of Pop Art.

But parochial local standards rule: there can't be capricious lace socks or "beaded ceintures [belts]"—the ornate luxury of a Byzantine emperor or empress (8–9). Appeals to the eye are frivolous and superficial in an orderly, practical world whose values are conformism and respectability. In the interests of social harmony and equilibrium, the imagination has been flattened and censored: "People are not going / To dream of baboons and periwinkles" (10–11). Sleepers in this landlocked Northern town are insulated from the dangerous energy and baffling mysteries of primal nature. Baboons suggest the rowdy, lusty, and loutish in men—everything Stevens wasn't—while periwinkles (sea snails), with their flirty, winking name, hint at enticing intricacies of female genitalia.

The few dissidents from the oppressive norm are derelicts and outcasts: "Only, here and there, an old sailor, / Drunk and asleep in his boots, / Catches tigers / In red weather" (12–15). The marooned sailor, Stevens's surrogate, is a daring dreamer. He has wandered the world (like Coleridge's Ancient Mariner) and perhaps seen too much, so that he can never be reincorporated into safe, sane society. Oafish and unkempt, he may have staggered from a disreputable tavern, a refuge from the tranquilized comforts of family life. No nightgowns for him: he has collapsed in his battered, fetid voyager's boots, which any prudent wife would irately strip off and discard. But his inner life remains vibrant and dynamic. "Red skies at night, sailors' delight," goes an old saw about tomorrow's weather. The old sailor is already under weigh: in sleep, he roams free, escaping female control and questing for a vanished heroic manhood. Sailors may chase mythic white whales, of course, but rarely tigers. Stevens's big cat comes from William Blake's menagerie ("Tyger Tyger, burning bright, / In the forests of the night"). Blake's gaudy tiger is a symbol of emotional intensity and uncompromising ferocity of imagination. The "red weather" of Stevens's sailor is a mental space, inflamed by passion and fantasy.

"Disillusionment of Ten O'Clock" captures a mood, a sinking melancholy that the poet talks himself out of with a series of teasing, comic images. Except for the first and last sentences, the bulk of the poem is cast in burdensome negatives ("none . . . none . . . not"), obstructions and cancellations that show the power of convention and social pressure (3, 7, 10). With its short lines and unexpected turns, the poem is simply a riff—like a Chopin prelude or a quizzical piano piece by Erik Satie. The poem has the whimsy of children's nonsense verse. Stevens is indeed implying that art is child's play, flexible, spontaneous, and indifferent to the goal-oriented world of commerce and politics. It's telling that the sailor's "red weather" resembles Gauguin seascapes, with their undulating bands of mauve and magenta, for Gauguin made the jailbreak from business and family (whom he coldly abandoned) that Stevens never did. For Stevens, as for most of us, Tahiti is only a state of mind. Under enchantment by imagination, space and time expand, melt, and cease to exist. Hence art, with its mercurial, all-encompassing climate, is Stevens's escape from the tyranny of ten o'clock.

TWENTY-FOUR

WALLACE STEVENS

Anecdote of the Jar

I placed a jar in Tennessee,
And round it was, upon a hill.
It made the slovenly wilderness
Surround that hill.

The wilderness rose up to it,   5
And sprawled around, no longer wild.
The jar was round upon the ground
And tall and of a port in air.

It took dominion everywhere.
The jar was gray and bare.   10
It did not give of bird or bush,
Like nothing else in Tennessee.

This cryptic poem is about art making. It has three characters, introduced in the first line, "I placed a jar in Tennessee": the artist, the artwork, and nature. All are equally alive and in a dynamic process of collaboration or conflict. There are no people after the initial "I." We are looking directly into the artist's mind, a Spartan arena offering few comforts or protections to the audience.

"Anecdote of the Jar" is a parody of John Keats's "Ode on a Grecian Urn," a creed of High Romantic aesthetics. Encircled with pastoral scenes, Keats's precious Greek vase is a symbol of art's conquest of time. The ode's famous climax: " 'Beauty is truth, truth beauty,— that is all / Ye know on earth, and all ye need to know.' " For modernists like Stevens, however, art no longer necessarily represents either beauty or truth, whose definitions are relative to period and culture. Art for Stevens is simply order, no matter how transient. Without human framing, nature remains a "slovenly wilderness," a primeval chaos (3).

Unlike Keats's exquisitely decorated urn, Stevens's jar is "gray and bare," stripped to its essentials (10). It is pure form, as compact and minimalist as the coarse farmhouse bowls and pitchers in paintings by Cézanne or Picasso. Stevens's realm of art is not Arcadia and Thessaly (site of Keats's Tempe) or Coleridge's opulent Xanadu but backwoods Tennessee, with its hardscrabble mountain ridges, coves, and hollers (hollows). Similarly, this poem is not an exalted, rhapsodic ode but merely an "anecdote"—a colloquial yarn to spin over a fence rail. It makes no appeal to emotion, eloquence, or mythology. It shows art making as unpretentious and craftsmanlike.

Stevens's artist retains Romantic authority but systematically transfers it to the work. After the opening "I," the poem's pronouns shift to "it," a displacement complete by the last stanza, which begins, "It took dominion everywhere" (9). As the artwork gains independent existence, its creator recedes and disappears. The artist's personal turmoil and travails, intrinsic to Romanticism, become irrelevant. There are biblical intonations to "dominion"—the word in the King James translation for mankind's command over the animal realm (Genesis 1.26). The poet as jar maker or deliveryman recalls Jehovah as potter god, shaping Adam out of a handful of clay ("the dust of the ground," Genesis 2.7). For Stevens the skeptic and nonbeliever, however, human artifacts alone produce meaning. Without our perception and concepts, nature would remain a roiling morass. "Dominion" also suggests art's precedence over other ways of knowing, including science. The master principle of all the arts, in Stevens's view, is poetry: elsewhere he claims, "Poetry is the supreme fiction" ("A High-Toned Old Christian Woman").

The jar has a proud separateness (it is "of a port in air"—stately), making the world legible but also transcending it (8). The poet's sole action is placement: by setting the jar on the hill, like an Impressionist painter choosing a spot for his easel, he automatically creates a point of reference or perspective. Modernist art typically juggles or juxtaposes multiple points of view, as Stevens does in the poem "Thirteen Ways of Looking at a Blackbird." In "Anecdote of the Jar," however, the central point remains firm and still, while nature is in flux: the wilderness rises and "sprawl[s]" around the hill like a heaving sea or a woman in labor (5–6). "Round upon the ground," the jar makes a circular impression, mapping a circuit of the eye (7). (Ralph Waldo Emerson's essay "Circles" begins, "The eye is the first circle; the horizon which it forms is the second.") The artwork is open to everything; yet, as an object defined by a boundary line, it is closed in on itself. Stevens is not a realist, holding a mirror up to nature. On the contrary, like the Cubists, he believes art transforms reality, sometimes unrecognizably. "Things as they are / Are changed upon the blue guitar," says a character in another Stevens poem ("The Man with the Blue Guitar").

In style, the jar more resembles a rustic earthenware pot than a polished vase on a pedestal. It rejects the elite standards of uniqueness and perfection of the European "masterpiece." Stevens was born and raised in Reading in Pennsylvania Dutch country, where home produce was "put up" in ceramic crocks or glass canning jars and where farmers' markets still abound. The region borders on West Virginia, just over the Mason-Dixon Line, through which the Appalachian mountain chain drops to Kentucky and Tennessee. Hence Stevens's Tennessee jar, with its dollops of canned or sampled nature, may also be a jug for moonshine (fiery corn whiskey), that staple of the Southern underground economy. Moonlight represents imagination for Stevens: a grouchy naysayer in one of his poems cries, "I have wiped away moonlight like mud" ("Mrs. Alfred Uruguay"). Behind his respectable facade in Hartford, perhaps Stevens in his secluded hours of poetry thought of himself as running a secret still on his own mount of the Muses.

Thus the jar as artwork both preserves and intoxicates. Yet despite his often extravagant imagery, Stevens always keeps a steady, methodical pace: he shuns the rush of afflatus (inspiration), symbolized by the "wild ecstasy" on Keats's urn, with its "mad pursuit" of maidens fleeing randy "men or gods." Though he savors natural beauty, Stevens rejects the transport and abandonment of the Romantic cult of nature, typified by Emerson's "Bacchus" or Emily Dickinson's "I Taste a Liquor Never Brewed" ("Inebriate of Air – am I – / And Debauchee of Dew"). The flat language in "Anecdote of the Jar" matches the jar's plainness. The poem is a bit stilted or disjointed, as if the lines were slowly working themselves out. After the singsong opening, Stevens avoids catchy rhythms and peels away poetry's glossy surface to focus our attention on his tentative exploration of thought.

By the finale, with its awkward double negatives, the poem becomes as inscrutable and intractable as the jar: "It did not give of bird or bush, / Like nothing else in Tennessee" (11–12). The artwork is stubbornly ungiving; it has no obligation to be understood. As a human fabrication, the jar is inorganic, unnatural, and infertile amidst the overgrown, grossly teeming landscape. The jar is as ordinary and taciturn as its nameless, generic hill, just as the poem itself remains oblique.

But language has its own fertility: the emblematic name "Tennessee," which ends the first and last lines, is a splash of proliferating letters, as if consonants and vowels were giddily self-replicating. As the poem's farewell, "Tennessee" has a refreshing effervescence. Its terminal syllable also contains a coded message: "see," the purpose of all art.

TWENTY-FIVE

WILLIAM CARLOS WILLIAMS

The Red Wheelbarrow

so much depends
upon

a red wheel
barrow

glazed with rain   5
water

beside the white
chickens

S implicity is the hallmark of William Carlos Williams's most origi-
nal work, which never loses its mysterious freshness. Like Words-
worth, Williams sought a common language to close the gap between
poetry and everyday experience. "The Red Wheelbarrow" invites us
to cast off habit and look at life again with childlike wonder. The
poem is an extension of Imagism, a modernist Anglo-American move-
ment influenced by unrhymed Asian poetry (such as haiku and tanka)
that strictly limits the number of lines and syllables. In Imagist poetry,
sharp physical details are presented but not explained: the images
must speak for themselves.

The red wheelbarrow carries a heavy load of meaning ("so much
depends / upon"), but what that might be is left unsaid (1–2). Or per-
haps it is inexpressible: language, as an emanation of the human
brain, can never fully reach the stubbornly concrete world. To under-
stand his own riveted reaction, Williams analyzes the scene into its vi-
sual elements and lays them out in small, spare units, unpunctuated
to induce our contemplativeness. As an ordinary, functional, worka-
day object, the wheelbarrow wouldn't rate a second glance from
most passersby. But the poem sees it as potentially as beautiful and
significant as any high symbol of art or culture. Another artist of
Williams's generation, the Dadaist Marcel Duchamp (whom Williams
knew), performed a similar alchemy on coal shovels and urinals. But
by putting his "readymades" on exhibit in art shows, Duchamp al-
tered their context. Williams honors the wheelbarrow's natural envi-
ronment and makes us feel its harmony.

Though no people are visible, the wheelbarrow is their mark or
signature, evidence of human industry and ingenuity. This robust tri-
pod with its warm, festive color presides over the barnyard in a tran-
quil scene resembling a Dutch genre painting. It represents a stable
agrarian society that was already slipping away when the poem was
written. Time seems frozen in a moment of heightened perception.
"Glazed with rain / water," the wheelbarrow gleams as if sprinkled
with diamonds or iced like a cake in a fairy tale (5–6).

The rain may have stopped, but we still feel its soft fall in Williams's spilling lines. The poem is a single sentence consisting of a series of prepositional phrases that dangle from the verb "depends" in the first line. The root meaning of "depend" is to hang down: hence the poem seems to rappel down the page on a smooth chain of words. Movement slows, then speeds up again at the surprise split of "wheelbarrow" in two: when "barrow" drops to the next line (cleverly sliding off "wheel"), we must pause and take breath (3–4). Conglomerations of language are being teased apart for inspection by the appraising eye.

At the very end, "white / chickens" bring a hint of bustling energy to the otherwise inanimate tableau (7–8). They suggest purity, guilelessness, and inquisitive openness. Though chickens lack the romance of Aphrodite's doves or the proud spirit of Yeats's falcon, Williams is unembarrassed to make them his dramatis personae. Chickens are half-comical beings who long ago renounced flight to become man's unassuming servants, domesticated citizens of the peaceable kingdom. Chickens may faint in a fight, but they are active, gregarious, and productive.

As an object, Williams's sparkling wheelbarrow is both surface and structure. Hence, like Wallace Stevens's Tennessee jar, it can be seen as an analogue to the poem itself. Indeed, each of Williams's neat, tiny stanzas has a recessive wheelbarrow shape: the first line is the wheelbarrow's long handles, while the daringly terse, one-word second line mimics the sloping cart. The poem's title, like a novelty cookie cutter, seems to be busily stamping out pointy stanzas from the sludgy batter of language.

If the wheelbarrow is the artwork, then the milling chickens are perhaps partly a cartoon version of art's restless, hungry audience with its pecking questions and complaints and short attention span. At the finale of Coleridge's "Kubla Khan," the suspicious, uncomprehending audience does a hostile circle dance. In Williams's poem, however, the audience loiters in neighborly coexistence with the steady, charitable artist. Solid and sturdy, the wheelbarrow represents Williams's practical view of poetry: the artwork collects and transports material reality, but we do the sorting. In a democratic age of universal literacy, the artist is neither king nor outcast but the reader's companion and equal partner. The leveling of hierarchies is also suggested by the poem's humbling avoidance of capital letters.

What "depends / upon" the wheelbarrow? For Williams, it is the act of *focus,* the effort to see clearly. Within its frame, art establishes relationships, even if the result of chance. The red wheelbarrow is merely "beside" the chickens, momentarily juxtaposed (7). But silvered with rain, it seems to glow with the numinous, as if the object world were sanctified by consciousness.

TWENTY-SIX

WILLIAM CARLOS WILLIAMS

This Is Just to Say

I have eaten
the plums
that were in
the icebox

and which   5
you were probably
saving
for breakfast

Forgive me
they were delicious   10
so sweet
and so cold

With its offhand title, "This Is Just to Say" pretends to be no more than a memo, jotted in haste on a scrap of paper. But it is a highly original love poem whose casualness is a deft tribute and token of intimacy and respect. The note has been left in a kitchen, female space usually ignored by major literature. The poet knows that he is an intruder, a vandal disrupting the orderly center of life. His palpable sense of trespass turns the kitchen into Eden and the pilfered plums into forbidden fruit.

In genre, the poem is a mock confession and appeal for absolution. By confiscating the plums, the poet has preempted tomorrow morning's meal and sabotaged his wife's good housekeeping. "Forgive me," the poet pleads, as if his wife were not only Eve with her seductive apple but the garden's angry deity to be propitiated (9). She commands this realm even in her absence. At one level, the succulent, fleshy fruit is a makeshift proxy for the opulent female form. The poet feels naughty and childlike yet also smugly triumphant, like a hero spiriting away a fabulous treasure (compare Jason and the Golden Fleece). But his trophy is merely a simple pleasure and summer staple, a sun-ripened, royal purple gift of nature.

The note was evidently written overnight, while the rest of the family was asleep. Perhaps Williams, a physician by profession, returned from a house call or was working late at his desk and went foraging for a snack. The chilled plums, with their burst of multiple sensations, bring true refreshment, bracing and restorative after mental tension and fatigue. Hence the poem offers homage to the provisioner of this happy oasis. Women have been honored in poetry as lovers and (from the Renaissance on) as faithful wives, but rarely have they appeared as homemakers, queens of their own domain. Williams asks for no wider world than this. The disdainful frigidity of the Petrarchan lady takes amusing new form: the omnipotent mistress now rules the icebox, which has supplanted the blazing hearth as the vital center of the modern kitchen. The poem's narrow shape actually resembles an icebox, a two-tiered fortress (block ice above, perishables below) that was transformed during Williams's lifetime into the streamlined electric refrigerator. Opening like a vault, the icebox is analogous to a book or poem, which stores up reshaped experience for future pleasure.

Despite its deceptive plainness, "This Is Just to Say" triggers deep associations in the reader by playing on mythic patterns of sin and desire; female secrecy and fertility; and male aggression and violation. The fragmentary, nondescript title—just a sentence sliver—is self-referential in the modernist way, yet the poem's brimming emotion is too rich for irony. Paced by short, halting lines, the rhythms are bewitchingly slow, evoking the reassuring stability of domestic routine. The poem's condensed time scheme is surprisingly complex. The first stanza takes us backward into the dark recesses of the icebox, where the plums nest like eggs. The second stanza leaps forward to the wife's projected enjoyment of the now-aborted breakfast. The third stanza returns to the past—to the poet's gluttonous indulgence, vividly re-created through universal, primary properties ("so sweet / and so cold") that make us shiver with delight (11–12).

Hovering over the poem is an invisible figure similar to the one in John Donne's "The Flea"—a strong, silent female companion whose favor is begged and whose judgment is comically feared. Williams exaggerates his apprehension and psychological distance to set the stage for reconciliation. His poem is an offering and bribe to convert his wife's disapproval to forgiveness—turning her, in other words, from "cold" to "sweet." Hence the "delicious" fruitiness of the final images has the tactile lushness of a kiss.

TWENTY-SEVEN

JEAN TOOMER

Georgia Dusk

The sky, lazily disdaining to pursue
  The setting sun, too indolent to hold
  A lengthened tournament for flashing gold,
Passively darkens for night's barbecue,

A feast of moon and men and barking hounds,   5
  An orgy for some genius of the South
  With blood-hot eyes and cane-lipped scented mouth,
Surprised in making folk songs from soul-sounds.

The sawmill blows its whistle, buzz saws stop,
  And silence breaks the bud of knoll and hill,   10
  Soft settling pollen where plowed lands fulfill
Their early promise of a bumper crop.

Smoke from the pyramidal sawdust pile
  Curls up, blue ghosts of trees, tarrying low
  Where only chips and stumps are left to show   15
The solid proof of former domicile.

Meanwhile, the men, with vestiges of pomp,
  Race memories of king and caravan,
  High priests, an ostrich, and a juju-man,
Go singing through the footpaths of the swamp.   20

Their voices rise . . . the pine trees are guitars,
   Strumming, pine needles fall like sheets of rain . . .
   Their voices rise . . . the chorus of the cane
Is caroling a vesper to the stars . . .

O singers, resinous and soft your songs   25
   Above the sacred whisper of the pines,
   Give virgin lips to cornfield concubines,
Bring dreams of Christ to dusky cane-lipped throngs.

The scene is the Deep South in the early twentieth century. The Civil War has receded in time, but its painful legacy remains. Black Americans, now emancipated day laborers, are making their way through an uncertain and still-dangerous world. The "Georgia dusk" of Toomer's title is a moral twilight: fantasies and delusions linger from the antebellum Old South with its genteel, chivalric dreams (compare the sun's "tournament for flashing gold," 3). But the tranquil rural routine is marred by bursts of brutality and barbarism: "a feast of moon and men and barking hounds" (5). Dogs once tracking escaped slaves have become jeering mobs who burn and lynch for sport. It's a holiday "orgy," a sadistic mass entertainment (6). But darkness brings terror for those who are not guests but ritual victims, the main course at the "night's barbecue" (4).

In the background, nature serenely glows, indifferent to human injustice. As if paralyzed by the heavy heat, the sky (and by implication the Christian heaven) "lazily," "passively" watches the saga of crime unfold (1, 4). The sun is setting on Southern culture. Yet in this land of stark dualities and incoherent contrasts, boiling hatreds ("blood-hot eyes") are strangely wed to sugared lyricism ("cane-lipped scented mouth," 7). "Some genius of the South"—a pagan spirit of place (genius loci)—magically transforms ugliness into art (6). Taken by surprise at balmy nightfall, it is "making folk songs from soul-sounds," as if by a dreamy process of creativity organic to the region (8). The blues and Negro spirituals capture an infernal symphony of "soul-sounds"—the cries and longings of the suffering and exploited but also, paradoxically, the deadly silent moral evasions of their oppressors.

The local sawmill is a symbol of Reconstruction, when the South struggled to rebuild after the Civil War's devastation—particularly severe in Georgia after General Sherman's scorched-earth march from Atlanta to the sea. Despite underdevelopment of mineral resources and industry, the state was rich in lumber, notably pine. Toomer's mill owners, presumably white, are as remote as the recessive God of the first stanza: thus the sawmill "blows its whistle" as if by impersonal, mechanical impulse (9). The "buzz saws stop" as the laborers quit, but those spinning, shrieking, jag-toothed blades, ferocious as the earlier "barking hounds," convey the relentless daily pressure of economic need. "Silence breaks the bud of knoll and hill": Georgia's rolling topography blossoms of its own accord (10). Life regenerates at day's end, as the slow agrarian routine resumes.

The fertility of these lands, fulfilling "their early promise of a bumper crop," is dramatically juxtaposed with the sterility of the society that has battened on it (11–12). A misty shower of "soft settling pollen," activating the eternal cycle of germination and harvest, parallels the plumes of smoke curling up from the mill's "pyramidal sawdust pile" (11, 13). Those tendrils are, in Toomer's beautiful image, the "blue ghosts of trees," a tapering mirage of what is gone (14). "Tarrying low" like fog, the spreading smoke becomes a blue veil over standing trees. The ghosts are ultimately melancholy apparitions of paradise lost in Africa. That "former domicile," the unknown homeland, stretches from the lush rain forests of the Atlantic coast to the eastern desert with its pharaonic pyramids and temples (compare the mill's "pyramidal" sawdust pile; 16, 13). "Chips and stumps" left by loggers in the Georgia woods suggest the rags and remnants of a civilization truncated, of African identity stunted and manhood maimed (15).

But the reaction of Southern blacks to humiliation and loss is not despair or surrender but dignity under duress: "Meanwhile, the men, with vestiges of pomp, / Race memories of king and caravan, / High priests, an ostrich, and a juju-man, / Go singing through the footpaths of the swamp (17–20). "Meanwhile" is the pivot turning the poem from bleak circumstance to incandescent imagination. "Meanwhile" also expresses the fluidity and continuity of time, felt here as a mythic river carrying the mill workers back to ancient origins and defeating the brutal cultural break of slavery. The men's proud carriage and unhurried pace evoke stately tribal ceremonies. Their narrow footpaths (possibly trails blazed by Indians) recall the "caravan" routes through savanna and mountain range that interconnected the far-flung peoples of Africa. "Race memories," whether genetically or culturally encoded, release more ghosts—of king, high priest, and shaman ("juju-man"), ancestral images escorted by that uniquely African creature the earthbound ostrich, with its speed, power, and fabulous prized plumes.

Filing along in impromptu procession, the workers break into song: they, like their voices, "rise" above the limitations and frustrations of the present (21, 23). Music, their medium of community and solidarity, is how they find their way through the "swamp," a metaphor for hostile American society with its hidden barriers and murky entrapments. Swamps also symbolize spiritual inertness and negativity, as in the "Slough of Despond," a depressing bog in John Bunyan's allegorical *Pilgrim's Progress* (1678). Through music, Toomer seems to say, American blacks have chosen the road of aspiration and affirmation and shunned the wallow of self-pity. Everything else was taken from the kidnapped and transported Africans—home, kinship, possessions, name. What remains, passed down the generations by oral tradition, is the thing that could not be stolen—the music. Power of voice, linking blacks to the distant land from which their forebears were ripped, is for Toomer supreme power, hope-giving and redemptive.

Because the impoverished laborers lack musical instruments, nature acts as their accomplice and collaborator: "the pine trees are guitars, / Strumming, pine needles fall like sheets of rain" (21–22). Like the Aeolian lyres of High Romantic poetry, the trees are played upon by the wind that lifts the men's voices. The pine needles, softly falling through nature's strumming, resemble the myriad individuals swept away by the African diaspora. The metaphorical "sheets of rain" suggest nature's ability to cleanse and purge. More musical accompaniment comes from "the chorus of the cane," rustling reeds "caroling a vesper [an evening hymn] to the stars" (23–24). The song is no Christmas carol to newborn Jesus but an ode to the stars and planets themselves, sailing above earth's strife. Like the sun and moon of the opening stanzas, the glittering stars are universal guides, transcending race and nation. Heading home, the workers see over Georgia what their forebears did over Africa or the magi over Judaea.

The main body of "Georgia Dusk" is neatly structured in three groups of linked stanzas. In the first pair of stanzas, the panorama of nature "darkens" and contracts to ominous intimations of passion and confusion (4). The second pair is set at the sawmill; the third, in the swamp. The concluding stanza is a valediction or blessing, like the climax of Wordsworth's "Tintern Abbey" ("Therefore let the moon / Shine on thee in thy solitary walk," 134–35). In formal apostrophe, Toomer hails the singers as fellow creators and workers of juju. Those in bondage understandably long for a savior, but as the poet ambiguously puts it, the spirituals' "dreams of Christ" may remain just that—a dream (28). With its "sacred whisper of the pines," the poem shows divinity immanent in nature, as in the African cults of pre-Islamic animism (26). Infused with pagan natural power, the singers confer or restore purity: "Give virgin lips to cornfield concubines," secret lovers finding intimacy and pleasure in the open air (27).

The men's songs are felt as well as heard: their vibrant harmonies are "resinous and soft," with the sticky suppleness of oily pine sap (compare the rosin used for violin bows; 25). Music is a healing balm or holy anointing for those who make it or receive it. In the poem's last line, "dusky cane-lipped throngs" (a racial reference) are enveloped by the Georgia dusk but also transform it. They are "cane-lipped" because, having absorbed the sugarcane's chorus, they refuse to internalize the bitterness of experience. These dusky throngs include the underworld shadows of those who came before and whose names are lost.

The voice of Toomer's rueful pastoral is itself a victory over grim reality. After the unsettling opening stanzas, with their hallucinatory assault on the senses, the mood is one of hushed relaxation. The easy, regular rhythms (helped along by the sixth stanza's swatches of expansive dots) gradually slow our pulse until we attain a meditative serenity. Like Blake's "London," "Georgia Dusk" sets anonymous members of the working class against an epic sweep of nature and history. But it exorcises resentment: Toomer will not rage or condemn. As they break for the night, his singers enter an enchanted mental zone where spirit and sensuality commingle. With its strict rhyme scheme and courtly, flowery diction, "Georgia Dusk" more resembles Victorian than modernist poetry. Its style too is enticingly "cane-lipped," meshing with the spontaneous music making of its stoical, questing characters.

TWENTY-EIGHT

LANGSTON HUGHES

Jazzonia

Oh, silver tree!
Oh, shining rivers of the soul.

In a Harlem cabaret
Six long-headed jazzers play.
A dancing girl whose eyes are bold   5
Lifts high a dress of silken gold.

Oh, singing tree!
Oh, shining rivers of the soul!

Were Eve's eyes
In the first garden   10
Just a bit too bold?
Was Cleopatra gorgeous
In a gown of gold?

Oh, shining tree!
Oh, silver rivers of the soul!   15

In a whirling cabaret
Six long-headed jazzers play.

In the same decade that T. S. Eliot's *The Waste Land* proclaimed the disintegration of Western culture and set the despairing tone for modernist literature for the rest of the century, popular culture was exploding in Hollywood and in Harlem, the district in northern Manhattan to which hundreds of thousands of blacks had recently migrated to escape poverty and oppression in the rural South. Langston Hughes's "Jazzonia," published in a magazine in 1923 (a year after *The Waste Land*), is an ode, luminous and rhapsodic. Racial injustice and economic struggle, themes normally prominent in Hughes's writing, aren't felt here. But "Jazzonia" remains oppositional nonetheless through its celebration of a taboo-breaking counterculture, seen in the process of giving birth to a revolutionary mode of art making.

"Jazzonia" presents Harlem as a thriving nation unto itself. The snappy sobriquet (coined by Hughes) echoes Babylonia, whose grandiose capital became the Bible's prototypical city of sin. Like Coleridge's Xanadu, Jazzonia is a realm of art: music and dance are its pagan religion and modus vivendi. The poem's "Harlem cabaret" is certainly not the famous, elegant Cotton Club but one of the small nightclubs where singers and sometimes scantily clad dancers performed with a house band. (Aaron Siskind's 1937 photographs of a Harlem cabaret show tables of white patrons viewing strip and dance routines, backed by a formally dressed ensemble of black musicians on a low stage.) Jazz—originally "jass," a risqué slang term—was a folk music just emerging from its shady past in New Orleans's redlight district, but Hughes hails it as a galvanizing life force. Though he also admired "the weary blues" (the title of his first book), he sees jazz as energy, beauty, and joy, liberating black culture from the heavy burden and unspeakable sufferings of the past.

Like Wordsworth on Westminster Bridge at dawn, Hughes is overwhelmed by a complex spectacle for which he struggles to find words. The poem proceeds by bursts of sensation and emotion that sweep us into its world. Structurally, it alternates between mystic invocation and dramatic description, divided by three sets of exclamatory couplets. The jazz is played but not described, the poem functioning instead, through mood and syncopation, as a transposition of the music. "Oh, silver tree! / Oh, shining rivers of the soul": the awed opening makes us think we are in church and being impelled toward prayer. The metaphors of river and tree sound biblical, recalling the Jordan's baptismal waters or Eden's Tree of Life, identified with Christ's cross. But we are in exuberantly secular, commercial space.

The six "jazzers" are called "long-headed" (shrewd, wise, prescient) because, for Hughes, there's more to jazz than meets the ear (4). Then evolving from ragtime through swing toward bop, jazz was often dismissed as vulgar, ephemeral entertainment, or it was reductively labeled "jungle music," primitive and lewd. But Hughes (here and elsewhere) insists that jazz is a vehicle of ideas and that it must be taken as seriously as European classical music, the genre of a long-haired elite. His jazzers are "long-headed" because they also have a long memory, as they draw from a repository of melody, rhythm, and phrasing to improvise, embellish, and advance the art form. Finally, "long-headed" may be a visual motif: the dynamic musicians are in a blur of motion, like double exposures in an action photo or like streaks in a streamlined Futurist painting.

The "dancing girl" lifting her dress "high" is driven and inspired by the music (5–6). She is a sensuous vision of "silken gold" (probably yellow satin shimmering under the lights) who makes the poet think of "gorgeous" fabled queens and enchantresses like Cleopatra (12–13). Yet the dancer is also an authentically modern woman, her eyes "bold" from frank sexuality. This daughter of Eve rejects original sin and flaunts her carnality (9–11). She may be doing the Charleston, the wild Roaring Twenties dance fad that, like the naughty cancan in nineteenth-century Parisian music halls, helped break the code of respectability governing female behavior. From our distant vantage point, she resembles Josephine Baker, a line dancer at the Cotton Club in 1923 before she worked on Broadway and then left the United States in 1925 to conquer France.

By the end, the cabaret, engulfed by music, is "whirling" in Dionysian delirium (16). Perhaps everyone is dancing, or it may be the poet's own mind that has become "a whirling cabaret" of flashing images. He is in a state of spiritual intoxication enabling him to intuit ancient glories pressing on the moment. The feverish immediacy of music and dance cancels out the hostile outside world of law and politics, implicitly linked in the poem's mythic scheme to Jehovah and Caesar, whom Eve and Cleopatra defied. In the heart of Jazzonia, performing artists, whatever their marginal social status, reign supreme.

Language turns iridescent to capture the fluidity of the music: the "silver tree" becomes a "singing tree" and finally a "shining tree" (1, 7, 14). Similarly, the "shining rivers" become "silver rivers" (2, 8, 15). The tree represents the genealogy or family tree of black music, while the shining river is the emotional continuity or soul power of black culture. It gleams and sparkles because, for Hughes, Jazzonia's eroticism, as embodied in the flirtatious dancer, is essentially pure, redeemed and sanctified by nature. When the tree itself sings, it's as if nature is drawing music from the instrument of the human form. As in African tribal practice, performance is an ecstatic ritual in which the community coalesces and body and soul are wed.

"Jazzonia" appears to be Hughes's own riff on a psalm in which the enslaved Hebrews lament their fate in the imperial city of hanging gardens:

> By the rivers of Babylon, there we sat down, yea, we wept, when
>   we remembered Zion.
> We hung our harps upon the willows in the midst thereof.
> For there they that carried us away captive required of us a song;
>   and they that wasted us required of us mirth, saying, Sing us
>   one of the songs of Zion.
> How shall we sing the Lord's song in a foreign land?
>   Psalm 137.1–4

Beyond minstrelsy: in Harlem, Hughes implies, the descendants of African captives, once forced to make music for their masters, have transformed Babylon into their promised land. Jazz is the "Lord's song" in a modern key, hopped up and revamped. Anywhere, anytime, the silver river of music is the route to Jazzonia, the paradise garden.

That the poem has turned New York's branching Hudson and

Harlem Rivers into Babylonia's Tigris and Euphrates is corroborated by a line in another Hughes poem: "I bathed in the Euphrates when dawns were young" ("The Negro Speaks of Rivers"). There Hughes also connects Mesopotamia (the legendary locale of Eden) to tropical and arid Africa and to New Orleans, the birthplace of jazz ("the Congo . . . the Nile . . . the Mississippi")—all of which the poem militantly identifies as black civilizations. Even the "silver tree" of "Jazzonia" may be biblically coded: the botanical name of the weeping willows on which the Hebrews hung their harps is *Salix babylonica,* after this very psalm. The willow's trunk is gray, as is the underside of its leaves, glimpsed when stirred by the wind. Shakespeare evokes the silvery willow at Ophelia's drowning in a brook: her supporting bough breaks off a willow whose "hoar [silver-gray] leaves" are mirrored from below in "the glassy stream" (*Hamlet* IV.vii.167).

Enchanting and exhilarating, "Jazzonia" as a poem seems to burst the walls of the cabaret. We sway between the riveting sights and sounds of the performance and a rushingly expansive panorama of trees and rivers—at one point unveiled by the dancer lifting her dress. Seduction and revelation are combined. So intense is the poet's delighted contemplation that the audience falls away. No witnesses remain but him—and us as his shadowy guests. The poem itself seems spun out by the jazzers as they play. What they are creating—the only American art form not born in Europe—will spread across the world over the next century in triumphant fulfillment of Hughes's prophecy.

TWENTY-NINE

THEODORE ROETHKE

Cuttings

Sticks-in-a-drowse droop over sugary loam,
Their intricate stem-fur dries;
But still the delicate slips keep coaxing up water;
The small cells bulge;

One nub of growth   5
Nudges a sand-crumb loose,
Pokes through a musty sheath
Its pale tendrilous horn.

The son of a German immigrant grower who was himself the son of a forester, Theodore Roethke spent his youth amid gardens and greenhouses in Michigan. His love of nature is in the Romantic main line. The tender attentiveness shown here to cuttings (stems sheared and reset to generate a new plant) resembles Wordsworth's celebration of his field of "dancing" daffodils: people disappear or rather are transformed into and reabsorbed by the organic tableau.

But Roethke's portraits of nature are often eerie or unsettling. While Wordsworth's creative myth was suffused with his melancholy memory of a lost, nurturing mother (she died when he was eight), natural process for Roethke is more ambivalent and mechanical, charged with the blind ruthlessness of a godlike father. Like the dead king in *Hamlet,* the elder Roethke is honored (or overestimated) as the earthly realm's omnipotent master gardener. In real life, his Prussian drive for order, efficiency, and perfection cowed his shy, sickly son, who came to identify with the manipulated plants. Roethke's poetry often projects subtle psychological disturbances into the plant world, which seems afflicted by modern conflicts and anxieties as well as a sexual primitivism suggesting less High Romantic lyricism than late Romantic decadence (as in Baudelaire and Huysmans). Roethke combines a cool, scientific eye with a sense of inner pressure or turmoil. Tall and powerfully built as an adult, he was painfully conscious of the disparity between his lumbering bulk and his hypersensitivity and vulnerability. "Cuttings" exquisitely embodies that disjunction, drawing us down in all our clumsiness to a hushed, colorless, microscopic dimension where life bubbles and stirs by its own mysterious law.

We seem to be witnessing the first steps of evolution itself as it struggles from the mineral to the vegetable realm and onward toward the animal. The enforced intimacy of our scrutiny can be unnerving, partly because Roethke's imagery evokes vaguely human analogies. "Sticks-in-a-drowse" (a fairy-tale-like portmanteau word cleverly mimicking a compound German noun) describes embryonic beings half emerged from the tacky mother-stuff, a silty "sugary loam" that isn't truly sustaining (1). The transplanted stems, wilting from partial evaporation, "droop"; their fragile frames can barely support them. But "droop" also has a depressive connotation: the cuttings seem apprehensive and daunted by separation, the birth trauma. Their "intricate stem-fur" (another invented hybrid word) makes them half plant, half beast (2). Their barely visible fuzz, like the down of a chick or newborn infant, invites our pity and care. Identity begins and coheres as the "delicate slips" suck in water, life's basic element: it's an uneven process of "coaxing," which may imply that a nursing baby is not only dependent on but suppliant for parental sustenance and approval (3). The stalks' limp fibers steadily gain resilience and confidence: replenished, "the small cells bulge," like brain cells assimilating raw data and preparing to replicate (4).

In the second stanza, we move from potentiality to action: "one nub of growth" pushes into virgin territory and disarranges it—new order beginning as disorder (5–6). The nub merely "nudges a sand-crumb loose," an infinitesimal movement. The hindering "sand-crumb" (yet another striking compound noun) is the merest fleck, as if earth's dust were leavings scattered from a banquet of the gods. Yet it seems big as a boulder to the aspiring shoot reaching for light. The cutting's once-protective "musty sheath" is now rank and confining: it represents the cocoon of the past—family stock that is life-giving but ultimately entrapping (7–8). The "pale tendrilous horn" that "pokes" through is both bold and defenseless. It's as if sex and consciousness were simultaneously awakening. If the damp "sheath" can be understood as a prepuce ("poke" is sexual slang), then the horn is the nascent phallic power of a timid boy craving freedom from overbearing authority. It also suggests the first, feeble voice of one who will blow his own horn as a poet (compare the "wreathèd horn" sounded by Wordsworth's orgiastic Triton).

"Cuttings" captures the uncertainty yet compulsive drive of the vital principle and its subset, the sex urge, operating impersonally in physical space. The poem shows life as a gamble, search, and act of hope—a risk from conception on. Male sexuality specifically is portrayed as isolated and tentative as it makes its incremental way toward exposure and assertion. Everything, no matter how minute, has its drama: the poem obeys William Blake's visionary command "to see a World in a Grain of Sand." Roethke's humble images and mild verbs ("droop," "dries," "bulge," "nudges") slow time down and take us to a point where matter and spirit are indistinguishable. Concreteness of language is intensified by his punchy, monosyllabic word choices ("sticks," "loam," "stem," "slips," "nub," "crumb," "sheath," "horn"), which are mainly drawn from the Anglo-Saxon and Old High German (as opposed to Norman and Greco-Roman) roots of English. With its horticultural setting and medieval etymology, "Cuttings" is a regrounding of modern English poetry in lost agrarian universals. Botany is a fertile paradigm, for poems too are cuttings from the ancestral tree of art.

THIRTY

THEODORE ROETHKE

Root Cellar

Nothing would sleep in that cellar, dank as a ditch,
Bulbs broke out of boxes hunting for chinks in the dark,
Shoots dangled and drooped,
Lolling obscenely from mildewed crates,
Hung down long yellow evil necks, like tropical snakes.   5
And what a congress of stinks!—
Roots ripe as old bait,
Pulpy stems, rank, silo-rich,
Leaf-mold, manure, lime, piled against slippery planks.
Nothing would give up life: 10
Even the dirt kept breathing a small breath.

While "Cuttings" is a nursery poem showing the fragility and pathos of newborn life, "Root Cellar" is a leap into the grave. It's as if we've gone from the hope of early spring to midwinter lockdown. "Root Cellar" forces us to contemplate the grisly, melting borderline between life and death. The influence of seventeenth-century Metaphysical poetry on Roethke can be felt in the theme of universal decay (also signaled by that key *Hamlet* word "rank," 8). But a relentless energy erupts from the teeming, twisting forms, which defy human notions of beauty, proportion, or propriety. Vegetation has an animal urgency, spreading and colonizing with gross sexual power.

Root cellars were standard equipment in villages and farms before electricity. For cold storage of fruits and vegetables, a pit or trench was cut near the house, or a cave dug in a hillside and vaulted with stone. Root crops like beets, turnips, potatoes, and onions were laid up in wooden boxes and blanketed with moist dirt, sand, straw, or moss. Roethke's poem depicts the harvested vegetables tumultuously refusing to "sleep," to go inert in the "dank" earth (1). The "mildewed crates," with their dungeonlike "chinks [slits] in the dark," seem like makeshift coffins from which the dead, with vampiric vitality, constantly try to escape (2, 4). Are the tubers looking for spiritual light as they grope toward freedom, or do they want to drag humanity back to the primeval?

The rebellious, erupting "bulbs" and clumps of sprawling sprouts seem alien, monstrous (2). The shoots passively "dangle and droop," but their "long yellow evil necks, like tropical snakes," are literally creepy and vaguely menacing (3, 5). "Evil" is certainly the poet's projection, registering our unease with boneless beings even more regressive than the reptilian. Their facelessness makes them hard to anthropomorphize or adapt to fairy tales. Without light to activate chlorophyll, we get no pleasant, reassuring, pastoral green. This is an infernally sulfurous jungle, a "slippery," unstable, directionless morass (9). It's the realm of cloying moisture where life incubates and where, on the human level, sex occurs. "What a congress of stinks!"

(6). "Root Cellar" assaults the sense of smell, our most primitive faculty, predating the intellectual, discriminating eye. "Congress" means sexual intercourse as well as communal congregation, here a fractious governing body whose unanimous law is decay. Roethke's imagery is coarse and repellent yet comic and trollish, as if just beneath earth's sunny surface, nature is cavorting with Rabelaisian prankishness. The crude word "stinks" (used as an unusual collective noun) pungently captures nature's slap-down of human pretensions.

Ripening and rotting are interlinked in the perennial growth cycle, which indifferently converts plant wilt and animal tissue to "leaf-mold," compost, and "manure" (9). Death is merely nature's agent. (The piled-up "lime" was used to dry out manure, neutralize acid soil, and aid decomposition in the cellar's malodorous cousin, the outhouse.) Like the restless roots, we too are "pulpy stems"—the trunks of our fleshy bodies as well as our cherished family trees (8). Our graves or scattered ashes restock the "silo-rich" earth, with its heavy, winey stench. "Lolling obscenely" and gelling like "ripe . . . old bait" (a pail of stale fishing worms but also Eden orchard's ancient temptations), the serpentine shoots resemble vagrant genitalia, just as the slimy "ditch" is both womb and tomb (4, 7, 1). At poem's end, the dirt itself stirs, "breathing a small breath," suggesting the imperceptible churn of microorganisms (11). The effect is touching but macabre, forcing us cleanly, genteel readers into a premature burial out of Edgar Allan Poe: we snuff the humid dust from which we rose and to which we will return.

Though seemingly devoid of people, "Root Cellar" is a dark mirror of our spiritual and physical life. The poem's nonstop single stanza, with its hammering, Donne-like rhythms and lurid listing of tumbling sense impressions, is as relentless as what it represents. Hit by the putrid gases, poet and reader have no time to pause or take breath. (Is it relevant that from childhood Roethke was an asthmatic?) In psychological terms, the poem shows unseemly desires and impulses seething beneath rational control. It is also an allegory of creative consciousness: in the prolific tangle of insinuating roots, inchoate ideas push and strain toward verbal form, while poetic lines work themselves out toward visual clarity.

Roethke's root cellar is an untidy vault of memory: the family nest is both cradle and prison, engendering strangling entrapments from which each generation must slash itself free. Each shoot, like a running vine, is a new tongue seeking its own voice. Like "Cuttings," the poem shows life as an agonizing struggle for independence. But natural cycle, properly seen, contains both redemption and resurrection. "Root Cellar" is a descent to the underworld and a mesmerized standoff with snaky Medusa—the labyrinthine snarl of sex and procreation from which the poet escapes, still awed but with mind and mission intact.

THIRTY-ONE

THEODORE ROETHKE

The Visitant

1

A cloud moved close. The bulk of the wind shifted.
A tree swayed over water.
A voice said:
Stay. Stay by the slip-ooze. Stay.

Dearest tree, I said, may I rest here?   5
A ripple made a soft reply.
I waited, alert as a dog.
The leech clinging to a stone waited;
And the crab, the quiet breather.

2

Slow, slow as a fish she came,   10
Slow as a fish coming forward,
Swaying in a long wave;
Her skirts not touching a leaf,
Her white arms reaching towards me.

She came without sound,   15
Without brushing the wet stones,
In the soft dark of early evening,
She came,
The wind in her hair,
The moon beginning.   20

3

I woke in the first of morning.
Staring at a tree, I felt the pulse of a stone.
Where's she now, I kept saying.
Where's she now, the mountain's downy girl?

But the bright day had no answer.   25
A wind stirred in a web of appleworms;
The tree, the close willow, swayed.

The poet meets his Muse. She comes as a "visitant," a messenger from the spirit world (a dimension coexistent with ours in nineteenth-century spiritualism). The poem is structured like a dream play. In the first part, a traveler tarries by a mountain lake. In the second, an apparition emerges from the mist and floats toward him. In the third, he awakes alone and desolate the next morning. One act is missing—the night encounter, left mysteriously blank.

The nine classical Muses were daughters of Zeus and Mnemosyne (Memory) who brought creative inspiration as well as energy and endurance for art making. Carl Jung interpreted the Muse as a projection or emanation of the anima—the repressed female part of a man's psyche, experienced by the artist as an outside force conveying startling new ideas. Roethke's Muse resembles the numinous "white goddess" of Celtic myth who is identified with the moon and the willow. In this poem, with its hint of Druidic ritualism, she is conflated with High Romantic enchantresses like Coleridge's white-robed vampire Geraldine, who stalks the maiden Christabel in "the midnight wood."

With its quiet, hypnotic language and incantatory rhythms, "The Visitant" puts us too under a spell. In the very first phrase, "A cloud moved close," space contracts, as a ghostly, gathering fog makes heaven seem to touch the earth. The shifting "bulk of the wind" is felt as a subtle pressure to which the swaying tree also responds. Time is suspended; it's like the charged, prickly moment before a storm. Is the voice with its cryptic command to "stay by the slip-ooze" internal or external? (3–4). The mud zone at the lake edge recalls our biological origins in the womb or primal sea.

Nature is cordial yet inscrutable. "Dearest tree, I said, may I rest here?" (5). The weary wayfarer feels Walt Whitman's tender intimacy with nature. But the tree is mute; only a ripple makes an ambiguous "soft reply"—perhaps the lapping of a fish breaking surface (6). Rest, in any case (as Emily Dickinson's naive protagonists discover), might be impossible before extinction. To stay by the "slip-ooze" could mean stagnation and infantile regression. "Alert as a dog"—scaled down to raw animal readiness—the poet accepts his passive state of waiting, shared by a leech and a crab (7–9). Again like Whitman, he bonds with nature's humblest creatures. There are possible bodily referents: the wily leech is visceral or penile, while the shy crab, "the quiet breather," may be the poet's own rib cage as it starts to swell and settle in sleep. Psychologically, a "leech clinging to a stone" is a shadowy symbol of emotional starvation—of an insecure child's parasitic attachment to a remote, frigid parent.

"The Visitant" charts the genesis of poetry from a spontaneous moment of heightened perception and sensory awareness to the birth of rhythm in the regular breathing and lowered heart rate of sleep. In Part 2, the poet is entranced or dreaming. "Slow, slow as a fish she came, / Slow as a fish coming forward, / Swaying in a long wave": with steady, measured pulses, the Muse gradually materializes from the dusk's "soft dark," liquid and luxuriously tactile (10–13, 17). Her approach is all silent, cinematic visuals as she eerily hovers "without brushing the wet stones" (16). (The swaying fish may signal his arousal.) It's a divine epiphany, resembling the descent of the moon goddess Selene to seduce Endymion, a beautiful shepherd sleeping in a mountain cave. With "the wind in her hair" (does she bring the wind or merely ride it?), Roethke's Muse has glamour in its original sense—an atmospheric sorcery (19). As "the moon beginning," she could be the auspicious new moon or the waxing crescent whose bow or blade shape is linked to pitiless goddesses (20). "Her white arms reaching towards me": will she embrace, or choke and drown, him? (14). And is his response ecstasy or terror?

Something unexplained happens in the time lapse between Parts 2 and 3 (a plot device possibly borrowed from Donne's "The Flea"), forcing us to presume or speculate. The poet wakes disoriented in the "bright" dawn light: "Staring at a tree, I felt the pulse of a stone" (21–22, 25). The spell is broken: the tree that sheltered him is now unrecognizable, and he is in shock, as if stunned by a queen bee. Reabsorbed into nature, the vanished visitant (bride or succubus) has become "the mountain's downy girl" again, nymphlike and fresh as a peach (24). It's as if her virginity has been renewed—a motif found in goddess legends. (Hera annually recovered her virginity by bathing in a magic mountain spring on Crete.)

Did the rendezvous with the Muse lead to an artistic breakthrough? If so, this poem is its result and record. In the bleak postmortem, the depleted poet resembles the hapless suitors of Blake's "The Crystal Cabinet" and Keats's "La Belle Dame Sans Merci," who are bewitched and abandoned by demure femmes fatales. By the close of "The Visitant," nature gives "no answer" whatever to the poet's plaintive cries (25). But a trace of afflatus remains: "A wind stirred in a web of appleworms" (a treetop nest of caterpillars; 26). This brilliant metaphor unites sex with aesthetics: the web, mythically associated with entrapping female power, is the mazy weaving of words in poetry. All nature-loving Romantic art is "a web of appleworms," a morally ambivalent manifesto of "the Devil's party" (in Blake's phrase about Milton), issued from Eden with its tainted fruit and traumatic revelations of nakedness and mortality.

With its archetypal universals of cloud, wind, tree, and water, "The Visitant" dramatizes the taunting unpredictability of artistic inspiration, infatuating when it comes but cruel when it goes. The poet is transfigured, then dropped. Has the Muse migrated into the swaying "close willow" (27)? The poem ends with an aching sense of men's incompletion, their anguished separation from the maternal body, to which they vainly try to reconnect through the deceptive medium of sex. The uncanny is the flip side of the all too familiar. Haunted by indistinct memory, the outcast poet quests for knowledge and, through the eyes of art, briefly glimpses the elusive spirit presences of pagan nature.

THIRTY-TWO

ROBERT LOWELL

Man and Wife

Tamed by *Miltown,* we lie on Mother's bed;
the rising sun in war paint dyes us red;
in broad daylight her gilded bed-posts shine,
abandoned, almost Dionysian.
At last the trees are green on Marlborough Street,   5
blossoms on our magnolia ignite
the morning with their murderous five days' white.
All night I've held your hand,
as if you had
a fourth time faced the kingdom of the mad—   10
its hackneyed speech, its homicidal eye—
and dragged me home alive. . . . Oh my *Petite,*
clearest of all God's creatures, still all air and nerve:
you were in your twenties, and I,
once hand on glass   15
and heart in mouth,
outdrank the Rahvs in the heat
of Greenwich Village, fainting at your feet—
too boiled and shy
and poker-faced to make a pass,   20
while the shrill verve
of your invective scorched the traditional South.

Now twelve years later, you turn your back.
Sleepless, you hold

your pillow to your hollows like a child;   25
your old-fashioned tirade—
loving, rapid, merciless—
breaks like the Atlantic Ocean on my head.

In this poem about decline and fall, the poet himself takes a tumble. Evolving American history is condensed to a triad of cryptic snapshots. The waning of New England's illustrious Lowell family into the mundane present is juxtaposed with the recalibration of modern sex roles: emancipated women are revving up, while men, uneasy and abashed, fall silent. Elsewhere in *Life Studies,* the autobiographical 1959 collection from which this poem is drawn, Robert Lowell traces the lost opportunities for masculine adventure and heroism suffered by his forebears, notably his father, who began his naval career on a gunboat in China.

The title "Man and Wife" makes us reexamine those two terms in an uncertain period of colliding career ambitions when divorce, once unthinkable, has become common. (This poem features Lowell's second wife, the literary critic Elizabeth Hardwick; his first wife, Jean Stafford, was also a writer.) Marriage as a social institution has dissolved into a fluid "relationship" whose emotional temperature the poet mordantly takes. Man and wife are laid out on the ancestral bed as at a wake. They seem paralyzed by dynastic tradition and specifically by "Mother"—as genteel yet oppressive a sepulchral presence as the matriarch haunting Alfred Hitchcock's *Psycho.*

Bed is for rest or sex, but neither is happening here. The "sleepless" couple lie numbly side by side, "tamed by *Miltown,*" a common tranquilizer (24, 1). The brand name evokes American commercialism—not only the delusive instant panacea offered by a pill but the declining mill towns (such as Lowell, Massachusetts) which at the peak of industrialism shook the hegemony of the Boston Brahmins. The "rising sun" that should promise a fresh start is disturbingly bedecked in "war paint" (presumably streaky clouds) whose ruddy glow "dyes" them red, as if they were colonial settlers menaced or butchered by Indians (2). They are their own worst enemies, caged like snarling animals. The shiny bars are formal, stockadelike "gilded bed-posts," luxury artifacts of a vanished age and style (3). The gilding suggests family status but also deception and hypocrisy. This bed is presumably the one where the poet's snobbish, domineering mother (a Winslow and a *Mayflower* descendant) brooded apart from his passive father. The bedposts are "abandoned" in two senses: they are desolate symbols of a secretly broken marriage (their baroque red and gold recalling Vergil's color scheme for Dido and Aeneas's doomed love affair, which ends with a burning bed) but also mimic priapic ("Dionysian") maypoles, taunting the poet with the sturdy virility he lacks (4). Can he ever be the "man" of the house?

Nature has revived ("At last the trees are green") but can't transmit its energy to the pair locked in stalemate (5). The glaringly white magnolia blossoms that "ignite / the morning" seem "murderous" because their festive burst intensifies the spouses' acute sense of stagnation and sterility (6–7). "All night I've held your hand": the chivalrous protectiveness is surprisingly hers (8). He clings to her as a foster mother who has daringly rescued him three times before from "the kingdom of the mad"—the psychiatric wards where he was treated during his many mental breakdowns (Lowell was manic-depressive; 9–12). The mythic roles are reversed: Eurydice now leads her poet husband, Orpheus, from hell, where the worst torture is a deadening of language. "Hackneyed speech" describes the rote euphemisms of doctors and nurses as well as the unbearably trite sound of his own words when he is ill. The "homicidal eye" from which she saves him is his own self-destructive aggression, judgmentalism, and despair.

A drift into memory is signaled by a row of drowsy dots (12). We are transported a dozen years back to what may have been the couple's first encounter, when she was also in full verbal flight while he was equally tongue-tied and immobilized. The social disaster of the drunken scene in bohemian Greenwich Village comes as a comic relief from the poem's purgatorial claustrophobia. Clutching his glass like a life preserver, the poet nervously or competitively "outdrank the Rahvs"—their literati hosts (15–17). Philip Rahv, coeditor of *Partisan Review,* epitomized the leftist, mainly Jewish New York intellectuals, prominent from the late 1930s to early 1960s, who were upstart challengers to the inbred WASP establishment still controlling academe, media, big business, and national politics in America.

In the party's three-way culture clash, the fainting guest is not the tiny, vivacious Southern belle but the tall, laconic, "poker-faced" New Englander (18–20). He's the one who can't hold his liquor and is too "shy" or intimidated to show sexual interest ("make a pass," originally fencing parlance)—all of which seems to have attracted her. His falling at her feet is a clumsy parody of wooing rituals. The atmosphere is dizzyingly superheated from the torrid weather, his stifled lust and intoxication (he's as "boiled" and embryonic as an egg), and her relentless talking, which "scorched the traditional South" (21–22). The latter could mean she's denouncing Jim Crow segregation and racial injustice, or perhaps it's simply that her boldly opinionated manner flouts the stereotype of gracious Southern womanhood. "The shrill verve / of your invective" is a splendid phrase whose cutting reverberation makes us hear and almost see her. She slashes and burns her way through her heritage like Sherman marching through Georgia. The poet, meanwhile, surrenders and collapses, as if the North were capitulating to the South without a shot.

When the poem returns to the present, her "old-fashioned tirade" seems never to have stopped, as if we're trapped in a tape loop (26). Her body language is emblematic of frozen protest: turning her back, she glumly clutches her pillow to her "hollows" like a child (25). The consoling pillow, displaced from her head consumed with charging thoughts, is proxy for her unresponsive husband as well as their recently born child (a daughter), whom they had hoped would unite them. But her emptiness or spiritual starvation continues, partly because he stubbornly remains her neediest child. Here as before, he processes her strident, martial speech not as separate words but as timbre, rhythm, and volume. "Loving, rapid, merciless," she lashes him as if scolding alone could shatter his brittle, lifelong barriers (27). He feels the pulsations of her rhetoric—regular as a pounding headache—like waves breaking from the Atlantic Ocean, the key to New England's history and prosperity (28). The sea seems to be flooding Boston to reclaim or obliterate it. Its encroachment parallels the way that the new in American culture—the New York avant-garde and slangy Beat poetry as well as the immigrant ethnicity and adversarial stance of the Rahvs and their circle—is triumphing, while the old guard of social prestige and refined good taste is fading. Even the Lowells' address on no longer fashionable Marlborough Street (in the declining Beacon Hill neighborhood where he grew up) has an archaic ring, touting the British roots of Massachusetts's fabled first colonists (5).

Written in the present tense, "Man and Wife" has a wonderful you-are-there quality. We're intruders at a primal scene of marital intimacy. Has the poet violated his wife's privacy and revealed too much? The "confessional" school of poetry led by Lowell promoted a method of ruthless exposure. At its best, it could turn humiliation and squalor into nimble arpeggios of defiant wit. As a courtly homage to his wife's birdlike energy, persistence, and speed ("Oh my *Petite*, / clearest of all God's creatures, still all air and nerve"), this is a classic love poem that demonstrates the survival of tenderness through bitterness and alienation (12–13). After the magisterial opening with its grand, Neoclassic couplets, the rhyme disintegrates, and line lengths fray, capturing the jagged randomness of everyday life. But despite the overall mood of harrowing exhaustion, the ending, thanks to its imagery of cold, purifying seawater, is oddly invigorating. What ultimately braces us is the poet's own modest, graceful articulateness. The poem speaks what he can't in real life. Its steady unfurling of supple syntax is a threading of the maze, a victory of humor and lucidity over madness.

THIRTY-THREE

SYLVIA PLATH

Daddy

You do not do, you do not do
Any more, black shoe
In which I have lived like a foot
For thirty years, poor and white,
Barely daring to breathe or Achoo.   5

Daddy, I have had to kill you.
You died before I had time—
Marble-heavy, a bag full of God,
Ghastly statue with one grey toe
Big as a Frisco seal   10

And a head in the freakish Atlantic
Where it pours bean green over blue
In the waters off beautiful Nauset.
I used to pray to recover you.
Ach, du.   15

In the German tongue, in the Polish town
Scraped flat by the roller
Of wars, wars, wars.
But the name of the town is common.
My Polack friend   20

Says there are a dozen or two.
So I never could tell where you

Put your foot, your root,
I never could talk to you.
The tongue stuck in my jaw.   25

It stuck in a barb wire snare
Ich, ich, ich, ich,
I could hardly speak.
I thought every German was you.
And the language obscene   30

An engine, an engine
Chuffing me off like a Jew.
A Jew to Dachau, Auschwitz, Belsen.
I began to talk like a Jew.
I think I may well be a Jew.   35

The snows of the Tyrol, the clear beer of Vienna
Are not very pure or true.
With my gypsy ancestress and my weird luck
And my Taroc pack and my Taroc pack
I may be a bit of a Jew.   40

I have always been scared of *you*,
With your Luftwaffe, your gobbledygoo.
And your neat moustache
And your Aryan eye, bright blue.
Panzer-man, panzer-man, O You—   45

Not God but a swastika
So black no sky could squeak through.
Every woman adores a Fascist,
The boot in the face, the brute
Brute heart of a brute like you.   50

You stand at the blackboard, daddy,
In the picture I have of you,

A cleft in your chin instead of your foot
But no less a devil for that, no not
Any less the black man who   55

Bit my pretty red heart in two.
I was ten when they buried you.
At twenty I tried to die
And get back, back, back to you.
I thought even the bones would do.   60

But they pulled me out of the sack,
And they stuck me together with glue.
And then I knew what to do.
I made a model of you,
A man in black with a Meinkampf look   65

And a love of the rack and the screw.
And I said I do, I do.
So daddy, I'm finally through.
The black telephone's off at the root,
The voices just can't worm through.   70

If I've killed one man, I've killed two—
The vampire who said he was you
And drank my blood for a year,
Seven years, if you want to know.
Daddy, you can lie back now.   75

There's a stake in your fat black heart
And the villagers never liked you.
They are dancing and stamping on you.
They always *knew* it was you.
Daddy, daddy, you bastard, I'm through.   80

Garish, sarcastic, and profane, "Daddy" is one of the strongest poems ever written by a woman. With driving power of voice, it marries the personal to the political against the violent backdrop of modern history. Like Emily Dickinson, another shy New Englander, Sylvia Plath challenges masculine institutions and satirizes outmoded sexual assumptions. But the energies aroused by "Daddy" ultimately become self-devouring. The poem is so extreme that nothing can be built upon it. Plath has had many imitators, but she may have exhausted her style in creating it.

"Daddy" is a rollicking nursery rhyme recast as a horror movie. Its arguable premise, simplistically read, is that women are kept in a state of perpetual childhood by domineering fathers and husbands. Hence *Ariel*, the 1965 book where this poem appeared two years after Plath's suicide at thirty in London, became a manifesto of the resurgent women's movement. Her claims seemed to have special force because she had paid for them with her life. But Plath's canonization as a feminist martyr has been a two-edged sword: on the one hand, it gave her near-mythic fame; on the other, it has driven away some readers and stunted literary criticism of her work. Plath's erudite engagement with canonical male writers, for example, has too often been minimized or suppressed.

Plath repeatedly acknowledged her debt to Robert Lowell's *Life Studies,* the pivotal book of the "confessional" school of poetry that documented lacerating private traumas. (Lowell wrote the foreword to the first American edition of *Ariel.*) In the last months of her life, when she was separated from her husband, the poet Ted Hughes, and struggling to care for two small children, Plath's work gained a furious intensity. She was absorbing the heedlessness of Beat poetry with its cheeky raunch and casual expletives, though she never abandoned structure and symmetry. "Daddy," for example, uses an unusual five-line stanza that, in running over traditional four-line ballad form, subliminally strains and unsettles the reader. The poem itself seems to be having a nervous breakdown.

As a ferocious saga of sexual sadomasochism, "Daddy" recalls

William Blake's "The Mental Traveller," which has the same cyclic pattern and hurtling velocity. Plath revamps Blake's tyrant god, Nobodaddy, "silent & invisible / Father of Jealousy" ("To Nobodaddy"). She may also be parodying the impious effrontery of Donne's Holy Sonnet "Batter My Heart, Three-Person'd God," with its theme of erotic bondage and its town invaded and "usurp'd" by evil. From Dickinson, Plath learned how to construct hallucinatory, apocalyptic metaphors of lightninglike speed. Dickinson's deft notations of nature made a great impact on her, as did Theodore Roethke's weirdly suggestive greenhouse poems.

Plath so revered Yeats that she rented the flat where she died because he had lived in that house. In its nightmarish panorama of European history, "Daddy" should be viewed as Plath's response to Yeats's "The Second Coming" and "Leda and the Swan," which she updates with the horrors of Nazism and World War II. Plath called "Daddy" an "allegory": its wounded sexual players are as symbolic of their era as Kafka's human cockroach trapped in a bedroom or Samuel Beckett's bickering tramps, enslaved by a cruelly absent God. Taking in far more than the festering female condition, "Daddy" is a tragicomedy of the isolated modern self. The public structures of creed and nation have failed, and emotion has become blindingly all-consuming in the seething crucible of the nuclear family.

"Daddy" is a sensational exercise in rhetoric, using a disarming rocking-horse cadence for its implacable bill of indictment. "You" is scathingly flung out twenty-one times by Plath toward her long-dead father. Thirty other words rhyme with "you," so that the whole poem seems to hoot and whoop, catching us up in its frenzy. There's a bratty *nyah-nyah-nyah* air of school yard taunting: the poet is sticking her tongue out and giving her father and all sexists the finger. The childish persona and singsong rhythm have surely come from Dickinson, who turns her naive, exploited maidens into unmaskers of male authority. But the overall effect of "Daddy" is closer to the poisonous cynicism of German Expressionism, as in the corruption-exposing caricatures of George Grosz or the distorted carnival sets of *The Cabinet of Dr. Caligari*. Although it's a long poem (eighty lines), "Daddy" seems to dart and skip along with barely a pause, partly because twelve of its sixteen stanzas are syntactically linked. The poet sweeps us into her stream of memories and associations, smoothly shifting from the United States to Europe and back. The airless family bubble is cracked open by flashing glimpses of the vastness of history and geography.

"Daddy" opens with the rebellion of a docile fairy-tale maiden against her evil captor, the father as a crimping "black shoe" in which she has "lived like a foot / For thirty years" (2–4). The shoe, representing deforming social pressure, evokes archetypes like Cinderella's rigid glass slipper and the ramshackle shoe house of the old woman maddened by family drudgery. The poet is like a Chinese princess hobbled by foot binding. Since the shoe can't grow with her, it functions like a tight-laced corset constricting her lung power ("barely daring to breathe or Achoo"), hampering her ability to speak and write or even admit pain (5). If the shoe is kicked off—as the first line promises—she should be able to walk and run. But by the end, the poem declares her too crippled to live.

To escape, the girl-woman must somehow commit patricide—difficult against a spectral image that was fixed in childhood. The Freudian dynamics of "Daddy," showing the ambivalent intertwining of love with hostility in family and marital relationships, are already prefigured in Blake's "arts of Love & Hate" ("The Mental Traveller"). Plath may have felt that psychoanalytic self-consciousness had exacerbated her distress: fed by melting snow, "the clear beer of Vienna" (Freud's city) is "not very pure or true" (36–37). "Daddy" sharpens memory without purging it: there's no catharsis. Plath said that the speaker of the poem suffers from an "Electra complex," which would make her want to kill her mother and marry her father. Indeed, the mother is oddly invisible here. But when the female principle is erased, all that's left is a death camp—an extermination factory symbolized by Plath's real-life asphyxiation (she laid her head in an unlit gas oven). Only one other woman is permitted in the poem: a remote, hypothetical "gypsy ancestress" who is the poet's role model as nomad and sibyl (and who may have bequeathed an ambiguous skin tone—Plath tanned darkly from infancy; 38).

The father now becomes a fallen colossus, a "ghastly statue" blanketing and suffocating the continent (9). Its head is in the "freakish Atlantic" (that ocean's notorious unpredictability suggesting the fa-

ther's frightening moodiness), and its toes come up as the rocky out-
croppings where seals gather in San Francisco Bay (10–11). The head
rests "off beautiful Nauset," the eastern edge of Cape Cod, where the
warm Gulf Stream mixes with frigid Arctic currents: that the luminous
waters pour "bean green over blue" puns on a frugal regional dish
identified with Boston (Beantown)—molasses-brown baked beans,
here uncooked and indigestible (12–13). The immigrant Otto Plath
(whose death following diabetic gangrene is glossed in the statue's
"grey toe") merges with New England's puritan forefathers. He's
"marble-heavy, a bag full of God": even reduced to rubble, the stern
patriarchs burden the present (8). The guilt-laden bag implies that
Judeo-Christianity is a jumble and that it's bound for the trash heap
of history. As a death sack (once just a sewn-up shroud), the bulging
bag will recur in Plath's account of her first suicide attempt ("they
pulled me out of the sack," 61). The passage recalls the opening of
John Keats's *Hyperion,* with its solemn tableau of Titans overthrown
by a new generation of gods: "gray-haired Saturn, quiet as a stone,"
sits stunned, his right hand lying "nerveless, listless, dead."

The first German words in the poem—"Ach, du" (Oh, you), mim-
icking the prayers Plath offered as a child for her father's return from
the grave—bring with them the inky cloud of European history (15).
We are suddenly on the plains of Eastern Europe, where national bor-
derlines are fluid. The Polish villages routinely "scraped flat by the
roller / Of wars, wars, wars" correspond on the poem's psychological
level to children bullied by exacting parents (16–18). Otto Plath's ori-
gins are unsettlingly obscure, as in hero legends (19–23). His native
German seems to have thwarted his daughter's English: "I never
could talk to you. / The tongue stuck in my jaw. / It stuck in a barb
wire snare" (24–26). German culpability for two world wars and the
Holocaust is prefigured in German typography, the bristling spikes
and tendrils of medieval black letter. Plath's real-life frustrations in
trying to learn German are expressed by the protagonist of her novel,
The Bell Jar: "Each time I picked up a German dictionary or German
book, the very sight of those dense, black, barbed-wire letters made
my mind shut like a clam." German is convoluted with contradic-
tions and defensiveness. "Ich, ich, ich, ich, / I could hardly speak":

"I" in German sounds like "icky" in English; it's as if German identity, distantly forming her own, is innately afflicted with disgust and self-doubt (27–28). The stuttering repetitions show her inability to formulate her selfhood or escape it. Sex too is blighted: "I thought every German was you. / And the language obscene" (29–30). German's guttural consonants become four-letter words lewdly grunted by her dead father, vampirically replicating himself through language.

What Plath calls German's "chuffing" engine—its robust assertiveness and pragmatic efficiency—feels mechanical, like a train carrying her to a concentration camp (31–33). This is a huge emotional leap. To what degree is it justified for Plath, with her comfortable middle-class upbringing and privileged education, to appropriate the unspeakable annals of "Dachau, Auschwitz, Belsen"? She claims empathetic solidarity with victims of oppression: "I began to talk like a Jew. / I think I may well be a Jew" (34–35). Plath may have had some Jewish lineage, obscured by Austrian émigrés to England on her mother's side. But what atrocities did she suffer? European bloodlines, symbolized by the tainted Tyrolean "snows," have so mixed over time that the Nazi crusade for racial purity was futile from the start (36–37). Miscegenation, muddled identity, is the rule. How does her "weird luck" (she regularly won prizes and honors) make Plath "a bit of a Jew"—one of the chosen people (38–40)? The occult cards ("Taroc pack") that she deals as Gypsy fortune-teller (Romany Gypsies were also persecuted by the Nazis) may be pages of poetry, her own and others'. They're inscrutable and doom-ridden, but she reads them like holy writ.

Plath's facile association of her father with Hitler is equally problematic. He commands heaven and earth with his air force ("Luftwaffe") and tanks ("Panzer-man, panzer-man"; 42–45). He intimidates by "gobbledygoo," as if Sinai's speechifying demiurge were babbling the nonsense verse of "Jabberwocky." Otto Plath has Hitler's "neat moustache" and "Aryan eye, bright blue," coldly rational and disdainful of lesser minds. His high parental and professional standards weigh like a thundercloud: "Not God but a swastika / So black no sky could squeak through" (46–47). The Nazi symbol becomes a soaring crucifix of life-as-it-is: power, not morality, is the law of the universe. The blackened sky, possibly conveying Plath's recurrent depressions, is reminiscent of an eerie Roethke poem, "Night Crow": "a tremendous bird" rises up "over the gulfs of dream" and flies "into a moonless black, / Deep in the brain, far back."

The looming menace produces a dubious generalization: "Every woman adores a Fascist" (48). Is Plath saying that nature, for procreative reasons, implants in women a hormonal attraction to dominating men? Is the sex drive inherently demeaning? Or does Plath believe that women are socially conditioned for subservience? She seems to conflate emotional manipulation with physical violence ("the boot in the face"). Her bizarrely amusing tone implicates the reader: "the brute / Brute heart of a brute like you"—the punchy monosyllables bouncing like a rubber ball in a game we suddenly find ourselves playing (49–50). What are Plath's grounds for calling her father a "brute"? Did he physically abuse her? Or did his strong personality simply eclipse hers? This stanza, which begins with a swooping swastika and ends with the hammering of "brute," succinctly illustrates the poem's reinterpretation of Yeats, whose Leda is ambushed by a swan-god and "mastered by the brute blood of the air."

Fantasy momentarily recedes as a concrete object is set before us— a picture embedded in the text (51–52). This family photo of Otto Plath in his classroom was published by Aurelia Plath in a 1975 collection of her daughter's letters. Within the poem, however, it is used as the devil card in a Tarot pack (53–54). Standing at a blackboard (compare Moses' stone tablets), Otto is a glamorous "devil" or ladykiller with a Byronic "cleft" in his chin instead of his foot (the medieval devil's telltale goat's hoof, signifying lust). As a "black man" burnt by hellfire, he's the king of Hades who abducts Persephone and makes her queen of the dead—a role Plath covets (55). He sadistically "bit my pretty red heart in two"—Persephone's ruby pomegranate reimagined as a bloody Valentine (56). The father's tearing teeth marks branded her heart and made her what she is—divided, irresolute, dissatisfied.

Now thirty, the poet posts her revolutionary manifesto. Each decade's end brings a crisis point. She does simple arithmetic ("two . . . ten . . . twenty") but, like a careless student, gets it wrong (56–58).

Plath was eight, not ten, when her teacher father died. (She says "buried" rather than died, since he survives in her obsessed imagination.) She claims her first suicide attempt at twenty was a grisly anniversary gift to her father: she wanted to get "back, back, back" to him—the drumming repetitions miming the eager beating of her heart as well as the clock now running out on her third decade (59). "I thought even the bones would do": are these his bones or hers? (60). Either she ghoulishly embraces a corpse or anorectically skeletizes herself as her passport to the underworld.

But "they" intervened. "They" rescued her against her will (61). Who are "they"? The poet dissolves her patient, cultivated mother (who warmly supported her daughter's literary endeavors) into the general pack of do-gooders and busybodies who don't understand her and thwart her deepest desires. She threw herself and her promise away, hiding in the "sack" (a mental cul-de-sac) from which they had to pull her. (Plath crawled under her mother's porch and took an overdose of pills; she was found comatose two days later.) "They stuck me together with glue": she had gone to pieces, like a broken marionette (62). Their attention and care—the "glue"—are represented as a weak mass of sugary sentiment. Her doctors foolishly reconstructed her as a whole person, she complains, despite her lack of a coherent self. "I have no face," she says in another *Ariel* poem ("Tulips").

Her unwanted rehabilitation inspired her next strategy of evasion and sabotage: "I made a model of you" (64). The sorceress crafts a voodoo doll, a husband molded (as in Freudian family romance) in her father's image. The miniaturized toy husband is her creation—which is why partisan feminist readings of this poem can go so astray. In a conformist era of the corporate man in the gray flannel suit, Plath chooses "a man in black with a Meinkampf look" (65). (*Mein Kampf,* the title of Hitler's autobiography, means "My Struggle.") It's not just his dress but his spirit that's black, with a pagan lust for mastery. Plath found a soul mate who similarly understood life and sex as a bruising battle, as in the self-annihilating union of Gerald Crich and Gudrun Brangwen in D. H. Lawrence's *Women in Love.* Like an agent of the Spanish Inquisition, Plath's glowering mate has "a love of the rack and the screw" (66). These authentic torture devices become a risqué metaphor for intercourse: the rack is the bed, and the screw is a bulldozing husband who uses his penis for conquest. But this excites her: "I said I do, I do," her girlish squeals of pleasure-pain trilling through the wedding ceremony (67).

If she had hoped to exorcise her father's ghost by marrying, the effort has failed. For all his vaunted power, she cuttingly implies, her husband isn't man enough to supplant her father's towering image. "So daddy, I'm finally through": she's fed up with relationships, ambition, and even personhood (68). "The black telephone's off at the root, / The voices just can't worm through": this stunning metaphor, regressively fusing the modern with the archaic, portrays miscommunication and a dying family tree as technology on the blink (69–70). We normally say a phone is "off the hook," not "off at the root"; the wire, slithering into the ground like a snaky vine, has been cut. (Furious at her straying husband, Plath once tore the telephone out of the wall.) The voices trying to "worm through" are harbingers of decay, like the phallic borers in Andrew Marvell. If "worm" refers to the primordial serpent, all language and knowledge are tainted "at the root"; we can't get back to Eden. Finally, the line of transmission is broken with Plath's literary forebears, including Yeats, honored yet dreaded because of the massiveness of his achievement. The poem says she will make no more poems.

The climax is a barbaric orgy with the poet as avenging Maenad. She boasts of killing not one man but two—that is, her father and her husband, "the vampire who said he was you" and drank her blood for seven years (71–74). She is accusing Hughes of draining her creative energy—when in fact her work flourished during their partnership. The paradox of killing two in one echoes Donne's "The Flea," where a parasite swollen with "one blood made of two" is archly crushed by a masterful lady. The joke is that Plath has shrunk her formidable husband to a louse brushed indifferently away. And by turning that blunt, proud Yorkshireman into Dracula, the fiend of Transylvania, she gives him as shady a lineage as her father's.

The reign of terror is over. Her father can no longer live through her by usurping her consciousness: "There's a stake in your fat black heart," encrusted with vice and mold yet still throbbing with her stolen blood (76). What is the phallic stake (the legendary way to kill vampires)? Plath has driven it home: it's the poem itself, with its pointed tone and long, linear format. "Daddy" is devastating, *nailing* her father forever and getting her husband too—since Hughes would have to defend himself for the rest of his life against his dead wife's charges. The liberated "villagers" take to the streets to desecrate the corpse of their oppressor (77–78). Who are these jubilant citizens? Otto Plath's family? Neighbors who "never liked" him, perhaps because he was German? Or is it a comic uprising of his students, as in medieval goliardic verse? "They"—perhaps all of the above— "always *knew* it was you" (79). What did they know? That he was a spy? A carrier of plague? Satan incarnate? The vengeful gathering of the community resembles the lynch mob in *Frankenstein* as well as the spooked audience ostracizing the oracular poet at the end of Coleridge's "Kubla Khan." But the heroine who has saved the town takes no bows. Like Dickinson, Plath rejects all alliances and chooses exile.

"Daddy, daddy, you bastard, I'm through": in this searing and blasphemous last line, Plath perversely defeats her readers' hopes for her deliverance (80). We expect her to say "I'm free," not "I'm through." It must be remembered that swearwords like "bastard" were not yet used publicly by respectable middle-class women. It's shock theater, defiling the poem and even coarsely questioning her father's legitimacy. Plath ends up like Ibsen's headstrong, father-fixated Hedda Gabler, who plays wild piano music before shooting herself. Plath's "I'm through" means the poem and performance are over. It also makes her life coterminous with the poem. She leaps into white space after the last words as if she were Sappho, the first great woman poet, who was (mistakenly) said to have jumped off a cliff into the sea for unrequited love. Everything in the last line—from the diminutives and contraction to the cursing and slang—conveys the collapse of poetic discourse and tradition. The mundane has triumphed—as it did when Plath killed herself in a kitchen.

By foregrounding the rancor of sex war, *Ariel* has been enormously influential in women's writing, but it has yet to inspire poetry of equal weight. A taboo can be broken only so many times. Some Plath disciples seem to think that a litany of grievances, accompanied by sullen mutterings about patriarchy, is enough to make a poem. They fail to recognize Plath's enormous respect for great male writers as well as her studious approach to writing: her beloved thesaurus was her equivalent to Dickinson's bible, Webster's dictionary. Because Plath had so profoundly absorbed major literature, it came flowing out of her in crisis, reforming itself into dazzling metaphors, mercurial allusions, and macabre witticisms. Read aloud—as Plath stipulated her late poems should be—"Daddy" is hilariously funny.

If Plath has had no major literary successors, she certainly has her peers—but they are in popular music. I nominate Sylvia Plath as the first female rocker. "Daddy" was written just before rock 'n' roll morphed from teenagers' good-time tunes to content-heavy social protest. This poem has the sneering sardonicism and piercing propulsiveness of Bob Dylan's 1965 blockbuster single, "Like a Rolling Stone." It looks forward to rock classics by women performers of the mid-seventies to early eighties: the Delphic posturing of Patti Smith's haunted *Horses,* the foulmouthed brashness of Chrissie Hynde's *Pretenders* and Marianne Faithfull's *Broken English,* and the strutting sexual confrontationalism of Pat Benatar's hit songs "Heartbreaker," "Hit Me with Your Best Shot," and "Love Is a Battlefield." The nihilistic wipeout of the last line of "Daddy" is also in the fractious rock spirit: it parallels the smashing or burning of guitars by the Yardbirds, the Who, and Jimi Hendrix, the peak of expressiveness being a destruction of the instrument—in this case the poet herself.

Ironically, the last line of "Daddy," where the poet is at her boldest, is swamped by her father. In her dispute for mental territory with him, "I" appears thirty times in the poem (in English and German). But her exit line proclaiming victory grants him even more space: he appears there three times to her one. He has survived, even with a stake in his heart. She has built his funeral monument: her best poem belongs to him. Father and daughter are locked together in psychic struggle for eternity.

THIRTY-FOUR

FRANK O'HARA

A Mexican Guitar

Actors with their variety of voices
and nuns, those arch campaign-managers,
were pacing the campo in contrasting colors
as Jane and I muttered a red fandango.

A cloud flung Jane's skirt in my face   5
and the neighborhood boys saw such sights
as mortal eyes are usually denied. Arabian day!
she clicked her rhinestone heels! vistas of lace!

Our shouting knocked over a couple of palm trees
and the gaping sky seemed to reel at our mistakes,   10
such purple flashing insteps and careers!
which bit with lavish envy the northern soldiers.

Then loud startling deliberation! Violet peered,
hung with silver trinkets, from an adobe slit,
escorted by a famished movie star, beau idéal!   15
crooning that dejected ballad, "Anne the Strip."

"Give me back my mink!" our Violet cried
"and cut out the heroics! I'm from Boston, remember."
Jane and I plotz! what a mysteriosabelle!
the fandango died on our lips, a wintry fan.   20

And all that evening eating peanut paste and onions
we chattered, sad, of films and the film industry
and how ballet is dying. And our feet ached. Violet
burst into tears first, she is always in the nick of time.

Poems work their magic over time even when they survive only as fragments (as with early Greek lyric) or when their local context has been lost. A good example is Frank O'Hara's "A Mexican Guitar," a coterie poem with a private frame of reference and cast of characters that needs as many marginal glosses as a Neoclassical satire by Alexander Pope. Though it may never be completely decoded, O'Hara's poem nonetheless delights and rewards the reader with its vivacious imagery, waves of excitement, and unexpected emotional turns. Indeed, our bafflement may replicate the poet-protagonist's sense of overwhelmed imagination, his striving for meaning and reassurance and for a place in the world.

The title echoes that of Wallace Stevens's "The Man with the Blue Guitar," an allusion to Picasso's pre-Cubist Blue Period. The guitar represents art as a mediating instrument that shapes life's flux into transient form. Like Stevens, O'Hara was deeply knowledgeable about modern painting: he fraternized with the New York Abstract Expressionist and Action painters and became a curator at the Museum of Modern Art. But unlike Stevens with his genteel reserve, the gregarious O'Hara recklessly plunged into direct experience. His swift, surreal poetry was a diary of his brooding longings and sophisticated, febrile life. O'Hara's Mexican guitar plays not the mournful blues but a "red fandango," a flamboyant, triple-time Spanish dance (4).

This poem is about the movies. It dates from a period when the grittily realistic, socially conscious Actors Studio was in the ascendant and when gay men were virtually alone in taking seriously the splashy kitsch and brazen glamour of entertainment-oriented, studio-era Hollywood. They collected vintage movie posters and publicity stills, traded trivia about obscure B-pictures, and peppered their speech with extravagant one-liners from favorite divas. Their studious connoisseurship, with its satirical, campy edge, would go mainstream in Andy Warhol's iconic movie star portraits, silk-screened from magazine photos and gaudily colorized. O'Hara was well aware that his passionate response to Hollywood style would seem absurd or fey to most people, especially men. Here he and a woman friend (the painter Jane Freilicher) are seated in a theater and so united in admiration at what they see that they are ecstatically swept into the movie world, with its swirling conflicts and voluptuous seductions.

The big 1950s screen is a "campo"—in Spanish, a fertile landscape as well as a battlefield or drill ground (3). Cinema is a field of vision. What O'Hara sees is factions at war—actors versus nuns. They are costumed "in contrasting colors" because they represent the two parts of his sensibility, whose contradictions tormented him. The dictatorial nuns, the imperious "campaign-managers" of his Irish Catholic youth near Boston, are "pacing" off space, as if ready to duel with the jabbering crowd of actors, whose "variety of voices" flouts the monolithic uniformity of church dogma (1–3). In their holy crusade, the nuns are the censoring shock troops of the Roman Catholic Legion of Decency, which had supported the strict Hays Production Code in the 1930s and, decades later, was still publicly rating and condemning films for the guidance of the faithful. The nuns are in black-and-white—their stark habits expressing their Manichaean morality—while the actors may be in flaming Technicolor.

The red fandango "muttered" by the two moviegoers is a pagan prayer for exuberant carnality, for life redeemed from the dour negations of guilt-ridden religion (particularly burdensome in Irish-American culture; 4). It's also the magic incantation (abracadabra) that electrifies and transforms the poem. A spirit descends—a rogue "cloud" that sweeps them into motion (5). They are dancing (O'Hara and Freilicher loved to jitterbug at parties), but Jane's twirling skirt, symbolic of female power, flies into his face and momentarily blinds or suffocates him. (To the end of his life, O'Hara was in epic battle with his intrusive, strong-willed mother.) It's not the gay poet but the "neighborhood boys" who are granted a vision of paradise, Jane's secret charms ("such sights / as mortal eyes are usually denied," 6–7). These swarming urchins are like the lucky Times Square passersby transfixed by Marilyn Monroe's skirt naughtily ballooning above the subway grate in *The Seven Year Itch*. The boys are also the mocking, casually masculine school yard bullies with whom O'Hara never bonded in agonized adolescence. His platonic confidantes are women, who prize him as a dapper escort and witty conversationalist.

"Arabian day! / she clicked her rhinestone heels! / vistas of lace!" (7–8). This is the poem's light-flooded peak—a dazzling montage of film clips where the magic carpet rides of Scheherazade's *Arabian Nights* (as in *The Thief of Bagdad*) blend with Dorothy's dreamlike adventures in *The Wizard of Oz*. ("Friend of Dorothy" was a tag or password for a gay man.) Jane is clicking Judy Garland's glittery ruby slippers and kicking up her heels like Zsa Zsa Gabor as Jane Avril doing the cancan in *Moulin Rouge*. The dancers are whirling like Fred Astaire and Ginger Rogers or Gene Kelly and Cyd Charisse in the underrated genre of musical comedy—"such purple flashing insteps and careers!" (11). It's the rat-a-tat-tat of the red fandango, the Hollywood rat race as a thundering, synchronized chorus line, beautiful but bruising.

As they careen around, boisterously "shouting" with militant pleasure, they topple the palm trees, which are simply studio props—the tatty but enchanting fabrications of all art (9). The *Oz* tornado is spinning them back to Kansas, with its flatland routine and pinched scarcities. "The gaping sky seemed to reel at our mistakes": the sky gapes because it's staring in disbelief or wonderment at human brio but also because it's empty, godless (10). Heaven is the soaring screen itself, against which the celluloid strip un*reels*. Their "mistake" is to think that life can be like the movies. Who are "the northern soldiers" who watch it all with "lavish envy" (12)? Are they the regimented, authoritarian nuns with their repression and hypocrisy? Or are they other movie characters—the U.S. Cavalry, or the Canadian Mounties, or the military police who arrest Bizet's Carmen between her habanera and seguidilla? Perhaps they are the orderly ranks of the audience, obediently hemmed in in their dark, air-cooled seats while the screen blazes with Mexican fire. California was once a province of Mexico: for O'Hara, then, Hollywood's heady romanticism is a Latin legacy. America remains riven by culture war: the Northern soldiers are frostbitten with New England's residual puritanism.

The reference to the North heralds a Northern visitor—Violet, who materializes like a vengeful deus ex machina in the balcony or opera box, reimagined as the "adobe slit" of a Southwestern mission or fort (13–14). (Violet "Bunny" Lang, another of O'Hara's intimates, was a poet and madcap heiress from Boston.) "Hung with silver trinkets," she is as bedizened as a cantina hussy played by Jane Russell or Katy Jurado. Her escort, the "famished movie star," is so eclipsed by his own pursuit of physical perfection ("beau idéal") that he's as insubstantial as the flickering phantoms projected on-screen (15). Perhaps he's famished because (like hunky Rock Hudson) he's secretly gay and mouthing pretty lies. Here he serenades Violet with an ode to her heretical other life as "Anne the Strip": Lang in actual fact flouted her social-register family by moonlighting as a stripper at a Boston burlesque house (16). The ballad is "dejected" because rejected: it's the life of the red fandango (the anthem of Hollywood's garish, fast-track Sunset Strip) that Violet has now renounced. She peers accusingly from her slit as from a convent or confessional. Indeed, a mud-work slit may suggest walled-up or entombed female sexuality (just as the image of lavishly bitten soldiers is fleetingly homoerotic; 12).

The spell is broken by Violet's epiphany, triggering their "loud startling deliberation" (13). She terminates the delirious energy released by Jane's clicking heels. "I'm from Boston, remember": the superego city is the killjoy that dampens the poem's fiery id (18). But Violet is chiding herself too back to propriety. "Give me back my mink!" she barks, as if reasserting a vanished canon of tradition and class (17). (The line puns on "Take Back Your Mink," a song by a nightclub floozy in *Guys and Dolls*. One winter in New York, Lang and Freilicher exchanged coats, to the outrage of the latter's mother; Lang's signature mink stole wasn't involved.) "Cut out the heroics!" means "Stop your nonsense": your self-transfiguring intervention into art is delusional; Yankee prudence and practicality must prevail. Yet Violet herself is using movie talk—the snappy, hard-bitten lingo of a film noir gun moll played by Ida Lupino.

Chastened, the poet and Jane nevertheless applaud Violet's stentorian imperiousness as yet another performance. The pair's fraternal, near-psychic mental merging (like Gwendolen and Cecily chanting together in Oscar Wilde's *The Importance of Being Earnest*) is shown

in the inimitably effervescent line "Jane and I plotz! what a myste-
riosabelle!" (19). From Freilicher comes earthy, punchy Yiddish (*plotz*
means to burst and collapse in amazement), while O'Hara's flashy
contribution is "mysteriosabelle," a precious neologism, half Italian
and half French, recalling gay men's once fabled cult of grand opera
and its tempestuous bitch queens like Maria Callas. "Plotz" is savored
by the Harvard-educated poet as a delicious exoticism, recalling the
dynamic ethnic history of American show business, rooted in vaude-
ville. This stanza's eruption of the vernacular preserves pre-Stonewall
gay patois, a stylish banter brightly mimicked by Holly Golightly in
Truman Capote's *Breakfast at Tiffany's*.

"The fandango died on our lips, a wintry fan": the air is going out
of the poem with a sigh, a cool breeze from the swish of a flirtatious
Spanish fan (20). Like a commedia dell'arte troupe at the end of the
day, the three huddled characters glumly share a meager meal while
lamenting signs of cultural decline. Their banal food is vestigially col-
ored by the movie they've just seen—perhaps a 1940s "road" picture
starring Dorothy Lamour, like *Road to Singapore* or *Moon over
Burma*—so that their standard American fare, possibly peanut butter
sandwiches on flimsy white bread, has become tangy satay and chut-
ney ("peanut paste and onions," 21). Their feet "ache" because the
red fandango has worn them out; their pilgrimage to Hollywood
wonderland is over (23). They weep after their expulsion from Eden.
Beauty, fantasy, and heightened emotion are no longer ruling values
in "films and the film industry" or in the dance world ("ballet is dy-
ing"): the studio system was then foundering beneath the onslaught
of television, with its family programming, while classical ballet was
being challenged by new dance styles of avant-garde minimalism and
aggressive grubbiness in downtown New York (22–23). That Violet,
who cries first, is "always in the nick of time" (compare her "slit")
suggests not just her instinctive aplomb but her sense of urgency or
martyrdom by time, which gouges us all (24). Bunny Lang was to die
of Hodgkin's disease at age thirty-two in 1956, a loss from which
O'Hara never fully recovered.

The high pitch of the poem—its hectic animation, volatile mood
swings, and erratic exclamation points (ten in all)—is defiantly anti-

masculine. But it's like music: O'Hara was a gifted pianist who had planned to be a composer until he was converted to poetry in college by James Joyce's musicality of language. "A Mexican Guitar" is a capriccio—a free-form, up-tempo jeu d'esprit with the lilt of a dance tune. It has the brilliant attack and shifting opalescence of a Chopin étude. The poem is also a pastiche of American idioms, swanky to slangy, and at times parodies the convolution of formal French syntax, literally translated into English. O'Hara wrote his poems at top speed on his typewriter (as if playing the piano), and he treated them cavalierly, indifferent to their fate. That transience also characterizes the social constellation of "A Mexican Guitar," where Jane and Violet, along with the inquisitive reader, become an impromptu foster family, held together for only so long as it takes us to read the poem.

THIRTY-FIVE

PAUL BLACKBURN

The Once-Over

The tanned blond
                        in the green print sack
in the center of the subway car
                                        standing
tho there are seats   5
                        has had it from
1   teen-age hood
1   lesbian
1   envious housewife
4   men over fifty   10
(& myself),   in short
                        the contents of this half of the car

                        Our notations are :
long legs, long waists, high breasts (no bra), long
neck, the model slump   15
                        the handbag drape & how the skirt
cuts in under a very handsome
                                        set of cheeks
'stirring dull roots with spring rain' , sayeth the preacher

            Only a stolid young man   20
        with a blue business suit and the New York Times
        does not know he is being assaulted

So.
She has us and we her
all the way to downtown Brooklyn   25
Over the tunnel and through the bridge
                    to DeKalb Avenue we go
all very chummy

She stares at the number over the door
                        and gives no sign   30
Yet the sign is on her

This is a hipster's syncopated ode to female sexual power, flaring up like a bewitching hallucination amid workaday banality. Blackburn fuses William Carlos Williams's American colloquialism with Beat impudence, starting with the title's wisecracking slang. The poem's irregular format—jagged indentations, suspended fragments—suggests the disconnection yet hyperstimulation of urban life. The numbered list of anonymous subway riders, on the other hand, is curiously soothing—an orderly résumé of generic types where even the quirky or crude becomes reassuringly familiar (7–12). Cast in the present tense, the poem makes us experience what the characters do, so that the reader enters the scene as a ghostly voyeur. The plot unfolds in medias res (in the middle of things): a lovely young woman, standing at stage center, becomes the focus of collective consciousness shooting at her from crosscutting points of view around a subway car. Out of embarrassment or pretentiousness or both, however, she refuses to acknowledge her impromptu audience.

She represents the peak of fashion and desire, on incongruous display in a gritty commuter train rattling from Manhattan to Brooklyn. As a blonde, she rules the social hierarchy of the 1950s, when this poem was written. Her tan suggests she has the leisure time for vacations or weekends at the beach. Her trendy dress (the waistless Balenciaga "sack" that flopped in the United States) is a fertile green. She brings springtime freshness and possibility into this mechanized, claustrophobic space. Is it modesty, wariness, or snobbery that makes her stand while others sit? (Of course, maybe she doesn't want to crease that dress!) Her superiority comes not from wealth or position but from innate looks and style. She has the hauteur and long legs and neck of a fifties mannequin: her "model slump" (compare the 1920s "debutante slouch") would be angular and chicly blasé (15). Her "handbag drape," as Blackburn calls it, must mean she's carrying a sporty shoulder bag rather than a lady's decorous snap purse (16). Her "high breasts" are those of maiden, not matron (14). That she wears no bra, at a date when brassieres were stiffly structured, is daring, even bohemian, and invites speculation. Though the blousy sack, nipped in at the knees, was notoriously unrevealing, her contrapposto stance accentuates her voluptuous curves: "the skirt / cuts in under a very handsome / set of cheeks" (16–18). Thanks to Blackburn's teasing line breaks, her buttocks seem more expressive than her impassive face. "Set" (compare "rack," slang for big breasts) also implies they are as molded and top-of-the-line as her handbag.

The scattered observers in the poet's half of the car have been scrutinizing and appraising her attributes. She's "had it" from them—that is, gotten "the once-over," a sweeping inspection, appreciative or skeptical (6). Attraction and hostility overlap. The oglers make the precise "notations" of art students sketching a studio nude (13). She's been as minutely dissected as the disdainful mistress in a Petrarchan blazon. There seems to be telepathic agreement about her traits, as if they were primary and essential, but the verdict varies. The leering "teen-age hood" (a street punk; short for "hoodlum") is paired with the presumably butch lesbian since they would have the same reaction to a dishy blonde—frank lust but resignation to being seriously outclassed (7–8). They know she can bag much bigger game. The "envious housewife," no admirer, shrewdly recognizes the market value of what she sees (9). Does a harried homemaker more resent the girl's freedom or her high status as ornament? The "4 men over fifty" are a sad lot, society's stoic dray horses who still respond to a young woman's sex appeal but can't compete for it; their bid could only be bribery (10). The poet adds himself, linked by a generic ampersand and half-hidden in nested parentheses, to this nondescript group (11). He is as unclassifiable a witness as the all-seeing, punning Fool in *King Lear*. In his thirties at the time, Blackburn is midway between the randy teen and the sagging elders: he sees what he was and what he will be.

Against so mundane and mediocre a background, the girl's erotic allure is a kind of sorcery. It brings life out of death-by-boredom: " 'stirring dull roots with spring rain' sayeth the preacher" (19). Her ripeness juices up her male admirers and prods their torpid members, sluggish from duty and routine. Blackburn's "preacher" is T. S. Eliot, the austere parson of pessimistic modernism who begins *The Waste*

Land with Chaucer's April showers (the first line of *The Canterbury Tales*), renewing the earth after winter's hard freeze. (The entire "dull roots" phrase in quotation marks is verbatim from Eliot.) In the urban wasteland, therefore, the mere sight of youthful beauty brings rebirth. The onlookers, sensually aroused, are also spiritually restored, purged of fatigue and despair. Only one passenger is impervious to the girl's flowering charms: the "stolid young man / with a blue business suit and the New York *Times*" (the Gray Lady versus populist tabloids) is effectively blind (20–22). Armored in his frigid uniform, he's trapped in arid mental categories and carries his office jail cell with him. Eyes are the channel of the girl's power. For Blackburn, it's not she but the men who are being "assaulted" or invaded; their longing gaze proves their pitiable weakness, not (as feminism would later claim) their oppressive power. If she is objectified, it's because she has become a symbol of their own failures and dashed dreams.

"So": this wry, flat, one-word line marks the stalemate, the stand-off, between watchers and watched (23). It dramatizes the strange suspension yet expansion of time as the passengers bask in their epiphany, their radiation by inexplicable charisma. "She has us and we her": sexual possession here is a subliminal transaction—which is why only poetry can capture it (24). It's a Wordsworthian "spot of time," a moment of intensified perception. For Blackburn, beauty's surprise provides what Wordsworth, standing on a cliff, calls "glimpses that would make me less forlorn"—rollicking pagan spirits rising from the sea ("The World Is Too Much with Us").

Things blur en route, and sense of direction is lost as the passengers are lulled into drowsy contemplation. We too feel the rocking, jolting ride in Blackburn's eccentric, wide-set typography, with its runs, slides, and drops. At first, "Over the tunnel and through the bridge / to DeKalb Avenue we go" makes no sense (26–27). It should be "through the tunnel and over the bridge," as the train emerges from underground and crosses the double-decked Manhattan Bridge to the main junction of working-class DeKalb Avenue in Brooklyn. Blackburn is parodying the nursery rhyme (originally a Thanksgiving poem by Lydia Maria Child) "Over the river and through the woods / to Grandmother's house we go." The riders, "all very chummy" in enforced intimacy, have bonded as if on family holiday (28). They're like Chaucer's company of twenty-nine pilgrims, "sondry folk, by aventure yfalle / In felaweshipe" ("varied people, fallen by chance into fellowship"), merrily setting out from London (*The Canterbury Tales* I.25–26). Perhaps Blackburn doesn't say "through the tunnel" since the sex is vicarious or displaced—as in Alfred Hitchcock's mischievous last image in *North by Northwest,* where a train suggestively penetrates a tunnel. The title's "once-over" also applies to this voyage over river waters: to travel between boroughs in New York City is to migrate between states of mind.

Whatever the passengers' reflections, the young woman herself is as detached as a goddess. She occupies her own aura, a misty envelope like the one around Homer's Helen, strolling the city walls and still enamoring the war-weary Trojan elders. Blackburn's girl "stares" at the train number over the door as if it were a coded message from a higher realm (29). Has *she* "had it"—reached her limit—with her daily parade of fans (6)? She "gives no sign"—no hint of mood or indication she is aware of her mass apotheosis—"yet the sign is on her" (30–31). The language echoes the book of Revelation, where the number of the Antichrist is 666 and the "sign" is "the mark of the beast," the sore or scar of sin (Revelation 13.18; 16.2). Female beauty brings out the beast in men and makes them revert to pagan idolatry. It's like a *Mad* magazine satire of holy writ: if this adventurous, liberated girl is the Whore of Babylon ("arrayed in purple and scarlet"), then the subway car is the harlot's monstrous chariot, the biblical beast with "seven heads"—corresponding here to the seven passengers (excluding the housewife and self-neutered technocrat) who respond to the girl's erotic magic (Revelation 17.3–4). By absorbing their minds, she has reined them in.

Is her treatment in this poem homage or exploitation? A punitive feminist reading would indict the men for sexual harassment—that is, for sexualizing public space and causing discomfort. But isn't Blackburn's point that the young woman as self-created artifact not only promotes her own theater but is protected by civilization? No one touches or solicits or even flirts with her. On the contrary, we feel the aching pathos of men in groups—stymied, paralyzed, even as they are brought to white heat. They created the structures that make her vivid existence possible. Lonely in her nonchalance, she is a privileged being who daunts her subjects into silence. The poet monitors the archetypal surge of instinct beneath the busy, brittle surface of modern life. He portrays the city as a million strangers in flux who continually cluster and coalesce and break apart again. The poem itself is in process, splintering and consolidating before our eyes.

Like the wanderer Walt Whitman, who wrote "Crossing Brooklyn Ferry," Blackburn finds visionary truth in the random and ordinary. "The Once-Over" deftly catches the tracks and rhythms of modern perception as it struggles under sensory overload. The poem's nervous lines record our darting eye motion, while the neat, embedded list replicates the passengers' coerced patterns of patient queueing through gates and turnstiles. The columnar list also visually parallels the young woman's statuesque figure, studied from every side of the car. She is a found object, an artwork escaped from the museum. No unknown man, however handsome, could excite so broad and elemental a response. Even at her height of artifice, a nubile young woman is a force of nature. Carrying the burden of mystery or mystique, she becomes the poet's transient Muse, turning the prosaic into poetry.

THIRTY-SIX

MAY SWENSON

At East River

Tugboat: A large shoe
shuffles the floor of water,
leaving a bright scrape.

Floating Gulls: Ballet slippers, dirty-white,
walk awkward backward. 5
Bobbing closer: yellow-pointed painted
wooden shoes.

The Bay: Flat, shiny, rustling
like parquet under the bridge's
balustrade of gray garlands. 10

On the Bridge: Slow skates of cars (a distant whisper)
and the long swishing foot of a train.

A Plane: Turns on its elegant heel:
a spark, a click
of steel on blue. 15

That Steamer: The top of a short boot, red and black,
budging deep water wading to the sea.

Brooklyn: A shelf of old shoes,
needing repair,
but clean knots of smoke 20
are being tied and untied.

Like a painter setting up her easel, May Swenson surveys the panorama of gleaming water off lower Manhattan. She is standing somewhere near the old South Street Seaport, where two great suspension bridges cross the East River to Brooklyn. Here the river meets New York Bay, stretching out toward the Narrows, gateway to the open Atlantic. (The Verrazano Narrows Bridge, linking Brooklyn to Staten Island, was not yet built.) The poet makes us share her exhilaration with air, space, and light. She is experiencing Wordsworth's "calm so deep" as he contemplates the sparkling city and gliding river from Westminster Bridge. Both poets are transfixed by the juxtaposition or interconnection of nature and culture. And Swenson's scene, like Wordsworth's, is curiously bare of people: we see their works and hear their motion, but the poet herself seems breezily isolated.

"At East River" is charming and playful but strictly structured, with a ladder shape resembling the abstract grid of a modernist painting or skyscraper. The poem is a seven-part list or index of points of reference on sea, sky, and land. Its split columns, connected by a colon, record two voices, or rather a single voice in two modes. The first proposes a theme by directing our attention to a concrete object, while the second describes and imaginatively transforms that object through analogy and association. The mind's operation on the physical world is demonstrated through the conversion of the left column (what science sees) into the right (what poetry sees). But the laconic left column can also be read vertically as a stark Imagist poem. The overall format, furthermore, mimics a play script, where characters' names preface their dialogue. Thus the nouns on the left seem to be speaking, but only the poet can hear what they say. White space, lavishly built into the page, guides our eye toward the designated sights. There is a dramatic contrast between the poem's vast setting and its abbreviated language, like deft strokes of watercolor.

Solitary though she may be, Swenson affects no avant-garde alienation. Her simple pleasure and sense of wonder recall an earlier literary period but also anticipate the prankish naivete of Pop Art.

"At East River" has the sprightliness of children's verse; it's like a teacher's set of flash cards met by the pupils' whimsical response. Art often takes a child's point of view: humble details overlooked by preoccupied adults suddenly become incandescent. The poet here is beset by metaphor after metaphor, each a comic turn on shoes. They reveal a world on the move, its restlessness signaled by the poem's many participles. Matter is animated or self-propelled. Things are anthropomorphized but without sentimental emotion: it's feet Swenson wryly focuses on, not faces.

Direction is precisely mapped by horizontals and verticals. The poet looks south across the bay, then north toward bridge and sky, and finally down again toward the Brooklyn wharves. The bay's smooth surface is like a fine, waxed "floor" being gouged ("bright scrape") by a passing tugboat (1–3). Swenson calls the stubby tug a "large shoe," like a work boot, because its fate is to haul and shove, to badger its way through life. It "shuffles the floor of water" because it is too busy for good manners. But perhaps the poet is seeing its foaming wake, from the prow's first cut, as a white flash of shuffled playing cards.

Paddling by stops and starts, the "floating gulls" look like "ballet slippers" on feet surreally lopped from legs and wobbling in reverse (4–5). "Dirty-white, / walk awkward backward": the five *w*'s impede pronunciation, as in a child's lisp, and replicate the obstruction. The *w*'s are also quacklike, turning the normally aggressive gulls into placid ducks. They look dirty from afar because their white breasts blur with their gray or black wings. As they come "bobbing closer," however, their now-distinct beaks turn them into "yellow-pointed painted / wooden shoes," quaint rustic clogs (as in a Dutch genre painting) riding the tide like buoys (6–7).

The bridge brings a touch of class. Webbed with arcing steel cables, it resembles a balcony or grand staircase ("balustrade") festooned with "garlands" as if for a party (8–10). But the leaves and blooms have gone ghostly "gray": the Belle Époque that built all four of Manhattan's East River bridges has faded forever. That the water below, as "flat" and "shiny" as a dance floor, is "rustling / like parquet" (intricate, highly varnished boarding) surely means the sea breeze is rippling the water and complicating its architectural reflections. But the poet hears the rustle of ball gowns, silken skirts brushing the parquet in a social whirl.

On the bridge deck, files of cars coast in tandem like "slow skates," their motors a discreet "distant whisper" (11). These must be groove-making ice skates rather than roller skates, which would clatter and thunder. The train, in its blustering rush, is seen and heard as a "long swishing foot," as if it were skidding and sloshing along a wet surface (12). Swenson's lines similarly go long here, a luxurious glissando.

The airplane, banking on takeoff from a Queens airport (La Guardia or Idlewild, now JFK), "turns on its elegant heel" as if disdaining the proletarian outer boroughs below (13). Its angular aluminum tail and fin are as crisp as a buffed riding boot. Air travel was still tony: the plane has the proud panache of an old-school cavalry officer. In its swashbuckling hubris, it seems to strike the sky's enameled blue dome. A refracted sunbeam blazes from the plane's mirrored skin: "a spark, a click / of steel on blue" (14–15). Sight turns to sound (synesthesia), the pace quickened by the clipped monosyllables and short lines. Is the dapper officer clicking his heels?

Indifferent to the plane's dandyism, the steamer, like the tug, just plows ahead, heading purposefully for sea (16–17). So massive it makes the transit channel seem shallow, it seems to trudge along the bay bottom as if it were a giant's kid "wading" puddles for fun. Its fat smokestacks banded with "red and black" (a period style) make it look in silhouette like a greengrocer's "short boot." The phrase "budging deep water" (an unconventional use of a colloquial verb) captures the steamship's sturdy push against the water's weight and resistance.

The poem ends with the comfortable shabbiness of the Brooklyn shoreline, its staggered rows of weathered warehouses and factories like "a shelf of old shoes, / needing repair" at a cobbler's shop (18–19). In contrast to Manhattan's soaring spires, Brooklyn's buildings are homely and unpretentious, but they are sanctified by manual labor. "Clean knots of smoke / are being tied and untied": the chimneys' sooty, curling plumes become shoelaces guided and purified by nature's invisible hand (20–21). There is release and relief in the hint of mental problems ("knots") being worked out through activity and routine. These dissolving smoke signals are the lines of the poem itself, which ends with spiritual "repair"—just as the tug's "bright scrape" will be automatically healed as the water returns to equilibrium.

"At East River" anchors us on terra firma, while our eye roves free. Eye movement is slow and deliberate. Swenson's self-pleasuring language reproduces what it represents (the technique of onomatopoeia), notably in tactile words like "bobbing" and "swishing." The poem evokes New York's singular geology of land and water, its ethos of solidity and change: the rhythmic left column hammers the frame, while the right spurts and eddies with mercurial image clusters in irregular stanzas. Swenson's small epiphanies have a mystic clarity and gentle humor, as in the poetry of George Herbert and Emily Dickinson, with her alertness to birds and weather. Yet Swenson was born only nineteen years before Sylvia Plath. If Swenson is dogged by inner turmoil, we do not feel it. She finds renewal and rebirth in the common and universal. For her, the artist is not a better person but someone who makes us see better. "At East River" demonstrates the poetic gift of discovering or asserting patterns and connectedness (symbolized by the nine bridging colons): everything is alive, and nothing is boring. The poem's mischievously mobile shoes and boots show life as a mazy journey with no goal but itself.

THIRTY-SEVEN

GARY SNYDER

Old Pond

Blue mountain white snow gleam
Through pine bulk and slender needle-sprays;
    little hemlock half in shade,
    ragged rocky skyline,

    single clear flat nuthatch call: 5
    down from the treetrunks

    up through time.

At Five Lakes Basin's
Biggest little lake
    after all day scrambling on the peaks,   10
    a naked bug
    with a white body and brown hair

    dives in the water,

Splash!

Contemplation to action: the two parts of Gary Snyder's "Old Pond" move from admiration of the luminous beauty of a mountain snowscape to the quick impulse and impact of a dive into a glacial lake. The poet (if this is a reimagining of his experience) presents himself as a solitary seeker attuned to nature's subtlest messages. His "all day scrambling on the peaks" resembles the "glad animal movements" that Wordsworth recalls in "Tintern Abbey" from his "boyish days" exploring northwestern England's mountains and lakes (10; "TA," 73–74). Snyder's pond invites comparison to Thoreau's secluded Walden Pond near Boston, but we are in far rawer terrain—northern California's Sierra Nevada. Snyder aims not simply for the freethinking Thoreau's frugal self-reliance, repudiating society's vanity and materialism, but for extreme physical challenge and a radical re-alignment of self to cosmos.

"Blue mountain white snow gleam": with its disorienting lack of punctuation and definite articles, the opening line lets words float dreamily free, re-creating the poet's overwhelmed first impression. Nature's elements are reduced to primary color and essential form, hitting the eye before the mind can organize them logically. It's surely the sky that's blue and not the granite mountain, but everything is uncontrollably shimmering with light. The snowcap is glimpsed through a green screen of "pine bulk and slender needle-sprays," a mouth-filling phrase conveying both the heft and delicacy of the massed trees (2). The spindly "needle-sprays," all fine lines and sharp points, are also metaphorical: over time, the pines are spraying or scattering their needles in the endless cycle of birth and death, where waste and fertility are often indistinguishable.

With their exquisite, economical images and breath-controlled pace, the first two lines of "Old Pond" can be excerpted as a free-standing haiku. The same can be done with the second pair of lines, where a "little hemlock half in shade" (suggesting a frail human figure subject to life's mysterious dualities) is seen beneath a "ragged rocky skyline," like nature's scrawling signature (3–4). Mountains would usually be called "jagged," a ruggedly masculine word. Snyder's "ragged" suggests fraying, as if the sky were cut from slowly unraveling fabric. Only our limited human senses let us see mountains as symbols of strength and permanence, for they too are in flux, like ocean waves.

A sharp, startling sound—a "single clear flat nuthatch call"—makes us realize that in just four graceful lines we have been lulled into a trance of luxurious silence (5). The busy nuthatch (a small, insect-foraging tree climber) is invisible. Is its curt call a warning or a summons to union? It sails "down from the treetrunks / up through time" in a giddy warp of dimensions (6–7). The bird is the unembellished voice of nature itself—Snyder's modest, flutelike substitute for the authoritarian boom of the Judeo-Christian God. The bird's swooping chirp defeats time insofar as the years ringed in tree trunks are, from the geologic perspective, no more than moments.

The pert, elusive bird is the transition to part two, a portrait of the artist as humble acolyte of nature. The mountain scene, which could initially be anywhere from Switzerland to Tibet to Japan, is now specifically located in America—Five Lakes Basin, a field of glacial tarns in the forest above Lake Tahoe (8). Nature sees man as nothing but "a naked bug," prey fit for a nuthatch (11). His "all day scrambling" on the rocky slopes is a child's adventure on all fours as well as a driving escape into the wilderness (10). Here the poet has no name, possessions, social status, or even discernible gender: he is simply a small, scuttling being with "a white body and brown hair" (12). His whiteness suggests his primal innocence (in an Eden curiously without an Eve). It also signifies race: he descends from European migrants, invaders of this land. But his thin-skinned pallor, exposed to high-altitude sunshine, means weakness, not privilege.

The poem ends in palpable refreshment as the weary hiker takes a dip in the "biggest little lake" of the five (9). The detached line "dives in the water" follows the long flash of his body and matches the prior detached line, "up through time" (13, 7). Hence his flight through space is prefigured or inspired by the airborne birdcall. Dropping into the water headfirst, he clears his mind of cobwebs, trivialities, and false ideas. "Splash!"—the joky finale—looks like a comic-book starburst or explosion, rambunctious fun after the poem's Zen-like sobriety of brisk consonants and cool colors (14). The splash (evoking the earlier "needle-sprays") gets on us too. Artworks, when we plunge into them, always make a splash, drenching us before resuming their still surfaces again.

What of the title, "Old Pond"? A phrase from a classic haiku by the Japanese poet Bashō, it's also a metaphor for the ocean-wrapped globe as well as for womblike, percolating creative consciousness. The bottomless pond is archaic, like literature's repository of myths. Snyder revises and extends key precursors: he dunks himself in water, as the fastidious Wordsworth, gazing out to sea, would never do. And though he is as athletic as Byron (who swam the Hellespont), it's for reverent subordination to, rather than conquest of, nature. Snyder asserts the here-and-now salvation of his "naked bug," the powerless human being castigated by the New England Calvinist minister Jonathan Edwards as a repulsive spider dangled by God over the fiery pit of hell. Similarly, in a canonical text of depressive modernism, Kafka turned the self-loathing Gregor Samsa into a helpless cockroach. Snyder honors freedom and energy. Rejecting guilt and fear, he strives to quiet the mind, often pictured in Buddhist teaching as a still pond.

Stripped: "Old Pond" presents the quest for meaning as a process of divestment. The clothing shed by the poet in his travels from the peaks to the depths represents constricting cultural assumptions and emotional baggage. Visually, the poem's two parts resemble beetling cliffs or sturdy trees, while the overall shape is a rough V, like a diving figure. The end is a colloquial exclamation point, a slash of guileless enthusiasm: sensation stills irony. Will the diver emerge from the purifying waters, or has he been swallowed and reabsorbed by nature? The poem itself is evidence of his survival. It speaks for him, since he has playfully hidden in the third person to watch himself in amused detachment. The measured rhythms of "Old Pond" show him testing and weighing words—the one thing he cannot do without.

THIRTY-EIGHT

NORMAN H. RUSSELL

The Tornado

just when he said the tornado
is now located at and moving at miles per hour
the television set went black
black as the sky black as death
black as the hell outside   5
black as the closet we groped into
falling all down with blankets and dresses
clutching each other our hearts pounding
loud as the pounding of the wind on the windows
gasping for breath holding our breath   10
like the wind outside roaring and pausing
then the great chunking of the short thunder
imprisoned in the small black animal
of a cloud rushing among the oak trees
went on east we heard it go we heard it talking   15
to the people in the eastern houses
and we sat still holding each other
still a long time yet in the black closet
slow to come back from the black
from the death in the teeth of the tornado.   20

N ature here is pure brute force, dwarfing the human and even threatening to obliterate it. The long, black column of Norman Russell's poem mirrors that of the tornado itself. There is neither punctuation nor capitalization because the unstoppable twister flattens everything in its path. The poem is safely couched in the past tense until the tornado arrives, bringing a shower of participles that re-create the storm as a present event. Only when the tornado skips on to become history does the past tense return. The poem is delivered from destruction along with its cowering characters.

The family's near-death experience starts with the bland patter of a television newscaster, routine background noise that suddenly takes on a significance so urgent it can barely be absorbed. Missing words (emergency data about the tornado's location and speed) mark traumatic erasures from memory (2). Mathematical coordinates of space and time don't register because man's acculturated ways of knowing break down before elemental nature. When power is knocked out, the TV set, typifying the conveniences and packaging of modern technology, goes "black" (3). The neat, shiny box can't encompass the storm's mammoth reality. The household is terrifyingly isolated, as if abandoned by God and fate to a living "hell" (5). "Black," repeated like a litany eight times in the poem, describes the mental abyss into which the characters plunge.

Sudden darkness triggers primal panic, and sense of direction is lost. Blindly, the family members "grope" their way into a closet as if it were a prehistoric cave (6). With everyone "falling all down" (compare the nursery rhyme "Ashes! Ashes! We all fall down!"), parents regress to childhood, as if they are siblings helplessly "clutching each other our hearts pounding" (7–8). Their entangling possessions ("blankets and dresses"—night swaddlings and daytime finery) are now only debris. It feels like a shipwreck with the wind "pounding" like surf, its blows indistinguishable from their violent heartbeats (9). "Gasping for breath," they seem to be drowning (10). Loss of breath, caused by fear as well as a tornado's eerie drop in air pressure (which can burst the windows), occurs at the poem's exact midpoint and nadir.

The "roaring" subsides as the tornado sweeps on toward the nameless, equally defenseless "people in the eastern houses," to whom it is idly "talking" (11, 15–16). With its "imprisoned" thunder, the jabbering tornado seems like a coarse, penned spirit (as in Shakespeare's *The Tempest*), compulsively driven to communicate by its scribbling swath of destruction (13). Its inky, low-hanging cloud—an amorphous "small black animal" whose tail is the dangling twister—scurries on through the mighty "oak trees," brittle as twigs (14). "The great chunking of the short thunder" is the beast's rumbling growl (12). ("Chunking" mimics a locomotive's chug: witnesses often say a tornado sounds like a freight train.) The thunder is "short"—without roll or reverberation—due to dangerous proximity. Only the passing of time will bring distance and detachment.

Though the crisis is over, the stunned family remains huddled and intertwined in the bunkerlike "black closet" (18). They are "slow to come back from the black" because they've looked directly into the void—the chaos before creation and its division of day from night (19). It's as if they've suffered an episode of hallucination or madness and must recover the most basic sense of self. There is no room yet for concern for or even curiosity about their neighbors. They only know they have somehow escaped "the teeth of the tornado," a man-eating monster like mythic dragons or biblical behemoths (20). Death, like the avenging hand of the Lord, has passed over their house.

"The Tornado" can be classified as a Romantic poem insofar as it confronts raw nature and exposes the frailty of social forms. Its ancestor is Shelley's "Ode to the West Wind," whose "Wild Spirit" the poet hails as "Destroyer and Preserver": "O uncontrollable!" The relentless emotional intensity of "The Tornado" strains language toward the tumultuous dissonance of tone poems like the Witches' Sabbath in Mussorgsky's *Night on Bald Mountain* or the storm movement ("Cloudburst") in Ferde Grofé's *Grand Canyon Suite*. Russell's realm, however, is not the remote or exotic but the domestic, the mundane heart of modern life.

Huge tornadoes develop in the Great Plains of the central United States because of atmospheric instabilities between the cold Rocky Mountains and the subtropical Gulf of Mexico. Enormously destructive tornadoes, sometimes in clusters, can hammer the Midwest and

South and even reach the mid-Atlantic seaboard. Russell's poem is characteristically American: it records an encounter with the American sublime. His tornado resembles Poe's colossal whirlpool ("the terrific funnel") in "A Descent into the Maelstrom," just as the poem's tomblike "black closet" recalls Poe's tales of premature burial. Foreign observers often fail to understand the vast drama of nature in America, where the political will is tested and defined against a catastrophic background of hurricanes, earthquakes, and raging wildfires. Tornadoes are the American version of Yeats's intersecting gyres, which represent the bloody nightmare of European history. Russell's poem invokes major Yeatsian images: his chatty twister borrows the insouciant power of Yeats's sphinxlike "rough beast" slouching toward Bethlehem ("The Second Coming"), while the brusque "rushing" of his black cloud recalls the "sudden blow" and seminal "white rush" of Yeats's divine rapist ("Leda and the Swan"). The tornado comes and goes like a capricious god.

Language reasserts control: the tornado becomes "The Tornado," an artifact giving shape and coherence to an experience that (whether the poet lived or merely imagined it) was all ugly whirl. Words are rescued from cacophony, as the survivors (like Coleridge's dogged Ancient Mariner) begin to tell and retell their harrowing stories. Russell implies that we should look not to journalism or science but to poetry, as a vestige of the sacred, for the deepest truth about such staggering blows to human pride. His veiled theme is theodicy, the paradox of why evil or suffering exists. There is no justice, only chance, in who is trapped or who spared in any disaster, including terrorist attack. The poem's cosmology is close to animism, the world's oldest religion, which saw spirits residing in trees, rocks, and weather. We are led to ponder our need for security—in physical dwellings as well as in consoling systems of belief. From nature's long view, grass hut and wigwam, framed of perishable materials, were shelters only marginally flimsier than our own proud towers of steel and glass.

THIRTY-NINE

CHUCK WACHTEL

A Paragraph Made Up of Seven Sentences Which Have Entered My Memory Via Hearing Them or Reading Them and Have Each Left an Impression There Like the Slender Scar Left by a Salamander in a Piece of Rapidly Cooling Igneous Rock

Gentlemen, which of these three vegetables: tomatoes, pumpkins, or squash, will your wives say most represents the part of their anatomy that has come to sag the most since your wedding night. There was no blood or anything but when I got there she was turning blue. It's forty-eight WABC degrees. We control the horizontal. Bachelor number three is a sales manager who collects Disney memorabilia. Missing coed found slain. All this in Encyclopedia Britannica 111: American Indians, Louis "Satchmo" Armstrong, The Reproductive System, Poisonous Animals and Plants, Atomic Energy, The Circus, Abominable Snowman, Napoleon and More . . .

When they abandoned traditional rhyme and meter, modern poets began to experiment with visual format. Painters from Cubism on used typography as design, partly inspired by commercial posters and newspaper headlines. At first glance, Chuck Wachtel's witty poem looks like a poster: the boldface title is nearly as long as the poem, which is indented like a prose paragraph and laid out flush to the margins. The title's courtly clauses recall bombastic chapter headings in eighteenth-century novels, but its freakish imagery of salamanders incinerated in lava veers toward the tabloid. Consisting of seven unrelated sentences, Wachtel's text is "found" poetry, collected rather than composed. It's a choral compilation of the intrusive media voices that bedevil us.

The massive title, where the author makes his sole appearance, hangs like an ominous, undulating, headachy cloud over the text. Is it approving or resisting what follows? The seven units (a magic number) are ostensibly connected only by the mysterious "impression" they made on the poet's mind. He is not the coiner but the transmitter: by reviving (according to Marshall McLuhan) the pre-Gutenberg oral tradition, mass media have made the poet a bard again, taking dictation from an invisible Muse. Random though they seem, Wachtel's seven sentences mischievously interact to give an unsettling, satiric picture of modern life.

According to the title, the poet's cardinal faculty is "memory" (as it was for Homer). Hyperacute, it takes everything in, the dross with the gold, and experiences stimuli as trauma ("slender scar"). The captured sentences, meanwhile, are like salamanders—slippery, mercurial, amphibious. They are run past the reader like automatons in a museum diorama. Though mythically impervious to fire, the salamanders melt in the poet's boiling brain, from which the poem solidifies. An artwork, in other words, is the fossil of an idea. "Rapidly cooling igneous rock" describes our helter-skelter perceptual system— the heating up and cooling down of attention as well as sensory data's reshaping of the malleable brain. Reality, as Emily Dickinson would say, is Vesuvian—exploding and raining down on us.

The poem is launched by a hearty, overbearing TV host engaged in the humiliation-for-fun of his guests, who are greeted with mock dignity ("Gentlemen"), then cajoled to betray their marital secrets and disappointments (1–4). Their Cinderella brides have turned into fleshy vegetables ("tomatoes, pumpkins, or squash"), and everything's been downhill since the "wedding night." "Sag" is life's universal law— a comic turn on poetry's perennial theme of time and decay. That the paraded husbands may be unnerved by woman's link to teeming nature is signaled by the flat, fatalistic period (instead of a question mark). The engine of procreation, stoked by male animal energy, rolls on.

Next is a crime or accident report from broadcast news (4–5). The discoverer of a woman "turning blue" sounds like an ordinary passerby or neighbor, if we may judge by the slack phrasing and stilted bravado ("There was no blood or anything"). The language is banal since human crisis is so routine. Whether bound for hospital or morgue, the blue woman makes the poem's temperature drop: "It's forty-eight WABC degrees" (5–6). WABC (a major New York radio station) rebrands the elements. The docile audience is trained to hear first, then feel. The garrulous, omniscient announcer is not simply conveying weather news but, godlike, claiming to cause it.

"We control the horizontal": Big Brother or Big Mother (6)? It's the sinister prelude to *The Outer Limits*, a 1960s science-fiction TV series. ("We are controlling transmission. We will control the horizontal. We will control the vertical. For the next hour, we will control all that you see and hear.") Who are these faceless forces—space aliens, government agents, TV producers, or women commanding the horizontal combat zone of sex? Or is "we" the wily, wizardlike artist? Early TV sets' skittish, rolling pattern bands map the earth's new latitude and longitude and correspond to the poem's stacked, wavering architecture.

A quick flick of the dial to another 1960s quiz show, *The Dating Game,* where hidden suitors compete for a night out with a pretty, prospective mate (6–7). Eager "bachelor number three" is oblivious to the vegetable bed that awaits him. Though his sales career is on a fast track, he's childishly stuck on his presexual "Disney memorabilia." Walt Disney cartoons express America's Arcadian spirit, indomitable but overinvested in happy endings. If he's hooked by a gal on this show, the bachelor's treasure stash will surely be swept to the nursery.

Sexual tensions resurface in a newspaper headline: "Missing coed found slain" (7–8). The sentence has the punchy, condensed grammar and titillating moralism of the sex-and-crime populist press. With its deft shorthand, the teaser implies a fruitless search for the girl by desperate family and inept police and lures readers in for voyeuristic details about the corpse. "Coed" once had a provocative ring: it meant a young woman away from home for the first time at a mixed-sex school. Fresh, fun-loving, a bit naive, she became a curvaceous bobby-soxer in peppy B-movies and smutty pulp fiction, where she was ravished by football captains or motorcycle gangs. Here she's succumbed to a real-life marauder, perhaps a disgruntled beau or Jekyll-and-Hyde loner (the regressive Disney dreamer?). Her tragic tale illustrates Wachtel's running theme of disorderly longings and frustrated fantasy.

"All this in Encyclopedia Britannica 111": the final, grab-bag sentence, culled from a magazine ad or junk mail circular, takes in the entire poem (8–12). Its subject headings reinforce or sabotage one another and suggest that categorization cannot fully fathom the primitivism of either man or nature. Ancestor of encyclopedias hawked door to door (our Disneyite's first sales job?), the *Britannica* with its European claims to universal knowledge flutters apart here like falling playing cards.

"American Indians, Louis 'Satchmo' Armstrong, The Reproductive System, Poisonous Animals and Plants, Atomic Energy": embattled cultural traditions drolly jostle with the nature drama of vegetables, predators, and crossed mating signals, while government-sponsored science (as in 1950s horror films) goes very wrong and spawns mutant organisms. "The Circus" forecasts society's total Disneyfication. "Abominable Snowman, Napoleon": are the two interchangeable? Europe's conqueror was defeated by the Russian winter. The Abominable Snowman (the legendary beast of the Himalayas) has stalked through the poem—chilling marriages, turning ladies blue, abducting a coed, and sheathing Napoleon in ice. The stealthy Snowman is an alter ego of the skeptical modern artist, who casts a cold eye and who has, as Wallace Stevens says in his poem "The Snow Man," "a mind of winter."

The writer's intuition and receptivity may be disabling. He has been seared by the fevered imperialism of mass communication (compare the title's scarred rock to Moses' stone tablets). Wachtel's poem ingeniously captures the surreal jump cuts yet seamless streaming of modern media. The seven sentences churn out like confetti strips from a telex machine. The rhetorical distance from grandiose title to goofy text dramatizes the diminution in language over the past two centuries. What place is there, the poem asks, for art or the artist in a world of gaudy entertainment and deafening media buzz?

Language is not versified here but put into hyperstate by the writer's strategic collage. We are invited to decipher the cultural code and supply our own play of associations, to collaborate in the poem's creation. The final trail of periods ("and More . . .") means "to be continued": life and literature have no real resolution. There's only more and more, until our intake valves clog and we ourselves turn blue.

FORTY

ROCHELLE KRAUT

My Makeup

on my cheeks I wear
the flush of two beers

on my eyes I use
the dark circles of sleepless nights
to great advantage   5

for lipstick
I wear my lips

The voice of modern woman: tough, blunt, pragmatic. The feminine veils of modesty, delicacy, and sentiment have been stripped away. Rochelle Kraut's short, robust poem can be read as a sardonic variation on Shakespeare's Sonnet 130, which celebrates a dusky-skinned mistress whose earthy appeal doesn't conform to the alabaster-and-rose idealizations of Petrarchan tradition. Kraut's inventory of "cheeks," "eyes," "lips" recalls the Petrarchan blazon—a pining lover's itemization of his distant lady's glorified attributes. But poet and lady have now merged, and she speaks for herself. We are no longer in the exquisite court world but in a rough-and-tumble cityscape of dark bars and mean streets.

The title cuts two ways: "My Makeup" refers to one's constitution or psychology as well as to cosmetics—what used to be called "paint," a female art. Hence the title puns on soul versus surface, substance versus style. The poet rejects alternate or rusing personae: in life or art, she claims, she has no masks; she is simply herself. Yet the denial of fiction is itself a fictive act. As Oscar Wilde said, "To be natural is such a very difficult pose to keep up." Kraut's impudent naturalism has a bohemian decadence. As a writer, she spurns bourgeois gentility and academicism; as a woman, she trades sheltered innocence for bruising experience, with its loneliness and ennui.

The poem has an open form with irregular, improvised stanzas (of two and three lines, then two again). There is no punctuation or capitalization except for the all-important "I," pugnaciously asserting the poet's self-reliance and search for authenticity. There's no primping or prettifying of text or person: her only rouge is from "the flush of two beers" (1–2). The glowing charm of bashful belles of old has yielded to mannish truculence, a boastful wallowing in the moment. Until fairly recently, beer drinking was not entirely respectable for American women past college, and even today, despite the microbrew trend, mixed drinks are still thought classier, more ladylike. Kraut's point is: I'm no snob; I take life as it comes and can fend for myself. Is her "flush" from booze, rage, sex—or all three? Her brusqueness proclaims she needs no gallant protectors in the urban jungle.

For eyeliner and mascara she uses "the dark circles of sleepless nights" (3–4). She flaunts her bags and shadows as trophies of women's hard-won freedom to roam and loiter, once possible only for social outcasts like beggars and whores. (Compare the tired streetwalkers dourly sipping mugs of beer in Parisian cafés in late-nineteenth-century paintings.) Better harridan than hothouse flower, Kraut seems to say. She is "sleepless" because her eyes are open; she can't be fooled. Is her insomnia the burden of modernist anxiety, or is she trapped in the infernal "dark circles" of private miseries and compulsive thoughts? She can't affect history; she is merely a haggard witness. And who gains "great advantage" from those haunted eyes (5)? Is it she—brushing away illusions or power-tripping her way through erotic encounters—or is it we, the readers, beneficiaries of a poet's flashes of perception?

Her "lipstick" is simply her "lips," which (like the liquored-up "flush") she "wear[s]" like clothing (6–7). But she is also *wearing out* her lips. She won't be shut up, and she accepts fading age. Lips, as poetry's oral instrument, represent her most essential self. Unlike so many female icons (from Marilyn Monroe to Betty Crocker), she offers no deferential or reassuring smiles. There is flirtation—these lips may be for kissing—but not submission. Kraut's "lipstick" is brandished like a club—the tubelike column of the poem itself.

In "My Makeup," the poet confronts her readers head-on while also gazing into the mirror of her own consciousness. She is not defined by others. The "dark circles" of her eyes have a witchy, moonlike remoteness. The poem is like a key light falling starkly on her face: it shows a woman boldly taking stage, appropriating space, and declaring she has no responsibility beyond herself and her voice. As spiritual autobiography, the poem is compressed but rock solid, without the wild, Valkyrie flights of a Sylvia Plath. Kraut avoids masochism and melodrama as well as bills of indictment and blame. Patriarchy is not the bogeyman, a scapegoat for all female ills.

The poem has a Beat flippancy, but its literary ancestry is in the cheeky putdowns of sexual adventurers like Edna St. Vincent Millay ("My candle burns at both ends") or Millay's versifying admirer Dorothy Parker ("One more drink and I'll be under the host"). Kraut's louche defiance descends from the new women of the flapper 1920s who threw respectability to the winds and mimicked the argot of floozy, fishwife, and gun moll. Neither angel nor victim, Kraut accepts the mundane and demands the right to explore it. Like male writers before her, she too can prowl, slumming through the lowlands and gathering tarnished mementos for women's art.

FORTY-ONE

WANDA COLEMAN

Wanda Why Aren't You Dead

wanda when are you gonna wear your hair down
wanda. that's a whore's name
wanda why ain't you rich
wanda you know no man in his right mind want a
      ready-made family
why don't you lose weight   5
wanda why are you so angry
how come your feet are so goddamn big
can't you afford to move out of this hell hole
if i were you were you were you
wanda what is it like being black   10
i hear you don't like black men
tell me you're ac/dc. tell me you're a nympho. tell me you're
      into chains
wanda i don't think you really mean that
you're joking. girl, you crazy
wanda *what* makes you so angry   15
wanda i think you need this
wanda you have no humor in you you too serious
wanda i didn't know i was hurting you
that was an accident
wanda i know what you're thinking   20
wanda i don't think they'll take that off of you

wanda why are you so angry

i'm sorry i didn't remember that that that
that that that was so important to you

wanda you're ALWAYS on the attack   25

wanda wanda wanda i wonder

why ain't you dead

A poem struggles to be born. The poet's mind is invaded by a raucous gang of nags, snoops, gripers, and doomsayers. Wanda Coleman's eponymous protagonist at first seems invisible. But the haranguing voices, with their multiple points of view, gradually sketch her ghost portrait, like a shimmering hologram. Making us share her exasperation and despair, she gains substance and presence until by the end she looms like an avenging Fury, beating off all opponents and willing the poem into existence.

Coleman's vernacular is so alive it practically jumps off the page. The snatches of boisterous conversation, as if overheard on the street or through a window, become hilarious through sheer excess. We get slang and profanity ("ain't," "goddamn") as well as African-American syncopated speech rhythms and idiomatic verb forms (a man "want" rather than "wants"; "girl, you crazy"; "you too serious"; 4, 16, 19). There's a strange effect of claustrophobia yet speed, produced by the absence of stanza breaks and full punctuation. We can't escape the chattering racket. Language is an affliction or epidemic. Eleven questions (including the title) stream by without a question mark because the interrogators don't really want answers. Their loaded questions are acts of hostile encroachment—or at least that's how the poet processes them in her cynicism and fatigue.

Coleman's persona adopts a stoic silence like George Herbert's in "The Quip," where the poet is derided by worldly temptations. Herbert italicizes his inner voice *("But thou shalt answer, Lord, for me")* because it's unheard—or rather heard only by the reader. Coleman too uses italics to signal her inner voice of resistance to materialism and status envy: *"wanda why are you so angry"* (24). But Herbert's serene, priestly detachment is impossible for a single mother with "a ready-made family," deemed by others an obstacle to romance (4–5). She's enmeshed in practical responsibilities.

This poem is a classic drama of an individual pitted against the tyranny of the group. Coleman's protagonist is in transition between generations, races, and social classes. Little solidarity is evident within her home community, which is portrayed as competitive and coercive. Her habits and nascent wishes snake through the grapevine for review and debate by a catty chorus of family, friends, lovers, neighbors, and coworkers. Whatever her aspirations or achievements, she is doggedly judged by her appearance and male attachments. Even well-meaning advice becomes subtly undermining.

Everything about her needs to be fixed—according to the meddlers whose critiques she has dangerously begun to internalize. Her hairdo isn't black or hip enough. She's too fat, and her feet are too big. Her pay's mingy, her apartment's a dump, and despite all that, she should lighten up! Her sex life is under withering scrutiny: she's used goods, with dependents in tow. She's uppity for shunning black men—a cunning provocation, of course, if it comes from a black man trying to seduce her (12). Even her exotic name is reductively redefined ("that's a whore's name"), making her scrabble for every iota of identity (2). She's bullied to embellish: any kinkiness—bisexuality, promiscuity, sadomasochism—would be better than her humdrum self (13–14).

Her tormentors' baiting insinuations mire her in subtext. "I think you need this" is a pusher's tagline coming from an intimate: drinks or drugs are just the elixir to normalize her—or rather to make her receptive to the speaker's hidden agenda (18). Banal or squalid scenes are glimpsed as if by strobe light—episodes of insensitivity, forgetfulness, or bad or careless sex ("i didn't know i was hurting you / that was an accident," 20–21). Medical crises make the body yet another betrayer. "I don't think they'll take that off of you": moles, tumors, and unplanned pregnancies all look the same to an arbitrary, impersonal health system (23).

Strangers patronize: "wanda what is it like being black"—as if she were an anointed spokesman for her race, ready to recite on cue and condense an epic to an anecdote (11). The bystanders' most presumptuous claims—"i know what you're thinking" and "i don't think you really mean that"—evict her from her own mental space (22, 15). The pestering voices are as mechanical as a broken record: "if i were you were you were you"; "that that that / that that that" (10, 25–26). Fill in the blanks. The real "hell hole" is not her shabby flat but the echo chamber of her overwrought brain (9). Words dull and drain or infest with clichés. The poem's refrain is her anger, alleged by third parties. Though we don't hear her responses, the climax—"wanda you're ALWAYS on the attack"—becomes intelligible by increments: anger is her energizer and defensiveness her armor, allowing her to think and write (27).

In the poem's visual design, the dense mass of negative comment rises like a black slab, a Tower of Babel. At the end, escaping lines float free, as if the poem were taking breath. Slowly gaining distance, the poet muses, "wanda wanda wanda i wonder / why ain't you dead" (28–29). The wonder is that she survives and thrives. The poem asserts the life force amid daily wear and tear, small humiliations and frustrations. She endures, a Wonder Woman who can't vanquish enemies but knows how to deflect their bullets off her magic bracelets. Yoked to duty and routine, this Wanda can't wander like Walt Whitman but must hold her ground as she fends off the guilt-trippers, parasites, and con artists. But she turns the painful struggle for selfhood into deliciously quirky comedy. The poem's lashing lines resemble "snaps" in an old African-American game, the "dozens," where duelists trade mock insults ("Yo' mama's so ugly, she'd scare moss off a rock"). It's an exercise in mental toughening: when the worst can be said, reality seems less harsh.

Chanting "wanda" nineteen times, the poem is like an exorcism, banishing impish spirits that grasp and scratch. Who *is* Wanda? The poem answers for her, as she wickedly parodies her detractors' voices. Their yammering stops with the door slam of the last word ("dead")— the line recapitulating the more formal, teacherly title ("aren't" rather than "ain't"). The poet is definitely *not* dead: her salvation is her grit, resilience, and commitment to art making. This poem would be explosive in performance, with the poet's grumpy, sarcastic persona barreling through hindrances, then pausing a beat before bursting free. She has regained control of language and made it hers.

FORTY-TWO

RALPH POMEROY

Corner

The cop slumps alertly on his motorcycle,
Supported by one leg like a leather stork.
His glance accuses me of loitering.
I can see his eyes moving like a fish
In the green depths of his green goggles.   5

His ease is fake. I can tell.
My ease is fake. And he can tell.
The fingers armored by his gloves
Splay and clench, itching to change something.
As if he were my enemy or my death,   10
I just standing there watching.

I spit out my gum which has gone stale.
I knock out a new cigarette—
Which is my bravery.
It is all imperceptible: 15
The way I shift my weight,
The way he creaks in his saddle.

The traffic is specific though constant.
The sun surrounds me, divides the street between us.
His crash helmet is whiter in the shade.   20
It is like a bull ring as they say it is just before the fighting.
I cannot back down. I am there.

Everything holds me back.
I am in danger of disappearing into the sunny dust.
My levis bake and my T shirt sweats.   25

My cigarette makes my eyes burn.
But I don't dare drop it.

Who made him my enemy?
Prince of coolness. King of fear.
Why do I lean here waiting?   30
Why does he lounge there watching?

I am becoming sunlight.
My hair is on fire. My boots run like tar.
I am hung-up by the bright air.

Something breaks through all of a sudden,   35
And he blasts off, quick as a craver,
Smug in his power; watching me watch.

K night, samurai, cowboy, matador: a motorcycle cop stopped at a corner traffic light makes the archetypes of heroic masculinity pass before the poet's eyes. Was this tense scene of street theater based on an actual incident? Irrespective of origin, the poem stands on its own. The setting is probably San Francisco, where Ralph Pomeroy, who began his career as a painter, lived during the city's Beat era. What makes this a poem rather than a letter or short story is its stark, ritualistic structure and incantatory rhythms. The style is hallucinatory realism, interweaving concrete description with oracular revelation of the unseen.

With his white crash helmet and high leather boots, the inscrutable policeman staring the poet down probably belongs to the elite California Highway Patrol, then famous for their signature black leather jackets. This is a pre-Stonewall poem: before the 1969 riots at New York's Stonewall Inn that began the gay liberation movement, municipal antiloitering ordinances aimed at panhandling and prostitution were often arbitrarily enforced against homosexuals in areas notorious for cruising. "Loitering" is explicitly the issue here—penalties for which ranged from a simple if humiliating "Move on" to mass sweeps backed up by paddy wagons (3).

The tale has already begun. Propped on his bike, the policeman spies the poet on the sunny side of the street, where he may simply be taking a cigarette break. (Since the sun "surrounds" him, he is presumably leaning on a lamppost; 19, 30.) Uneasy, then paranoid, the poet feels pinned down and interrogated by the cop's accusing glance. Suddenly on trial, he must summon every ounce of energy to resist an unexpected wave of guilt and shame. Despite the ragged traffic flow, the street seems as empty as a desert. The two men are like knights crossing paths in the woods (the cop's fingers are "armored") or gunslingers facing off in *High Noon* (the cop "creaks in his saddle"; the ground is "sunny dust"; 8, 17, 24). But no weapons are drawn: it's a test of wills, a battle of eyes.

The policeman, "king of fear," is the living law, a judge and enforcer embodying cold authority (29). Yet he is ruggedly half animal, like a centaur. With their murky "green depths," his all-seeing "green goggles" seem disturbingly alien or amphibious (5). His "fish" eyes and "leather stork" leg resemble wildlife emblems on samurai armor (4, 2). Restlessly alternating from claw to fist, his lizardlike gloved fingers "splay and clench, itching to change something": the masculine drive to interfere or dominate, as Pomeroy depicts it, is instinctual and therefore amoral (9). But the poet's hand will prevail, transforming this mute transaction to language—to the poem we are reading.

The confrontation is a tournament of masks. The poet's pose is "prince of coolness"—the young rebel typified by Marlon Brando and James Dean (29). But "my ease is fake," betrayed by his eyes smarting from cigarette smoke (7, 26). He's not so tough. But the cop too is playing a role: "His ease is fake" (6). Buttressed by his official regalia, the cop has merged with function; doubt faintly registers only in the submarine jitter of his eyes. Wedded to his machine, he has the robotic ruthlessness of mounted warriors like iron-jawed condottieri and conquistadors.

Time stops. The poet stubbornly defends his small patch of pavement: "I cannot back down. I am there" (22). It's an existential crisis, as if the cop's disdain could annihilate him. "I am in danger of disappearing": his identity is porous, evanescent, its borders barely maintained by his baking blue jeans and damp T-shirt, sweating like a second skin (24–25). He asserts his "bravery" through minute body language—crudely spitting out his gum ("gone stale" from a nervous dry mouth), tapping out another cigarette (a masculine mannerism), and shifting feet to dig in (12–16). But he's almost swooning in his state of enforced passivity. "Hung-up by the bright air," he feels crucified, shafted by the cop's lacerating stare (34). "I am becoming sunlight. / My hair is on fire. My boots run like tar": stuck in place yet melting like Icarus, he is losing form and gender (32–33). The punning metaphor of hot boots running like tar suggests an infernal cityscape of bubbling asphalt, Sodom in flames.

Reading each other, the two opponents are psychically locked in electric clairvoyance, their hatred indistinguishable from attraction.

Will they split or converge? "Smug in his power," the cop retreats, sparing his victim (37). (He "blasts off, quick as a craver," possibly a misprint for "craker," a crow; 36.) It's a brush with the divine: the stork-god drops his prey like a frog in the street's swift currents. The cop as predatory bird recalls Zeus as Yeats's hit-and-run swan or as the eagle abducting pretty Ganymede. But here the marauder capriciously abandons his boy prize.

"Corner" is a drama of male bonding—or rather of its failure. The inscrutable cop merges with the distant, disapproving father. (Another of Pomeroy's poems, "Between Here and Illinois," relates miscommunications making him miss his father's funeral halfway across the country.) It was at a corner, or crossroads, that Oedipus met and slew his unknown father. The cop's helmet as "bull ring" suggests the father's closed mind and confident virility amid emotional drought (21). But who is the matador, who the bull? The poet's life flashes before his eyes (to be "hung-up" implies hang-ups, neuroses; 34). He recognizes the vulnerability and irresolvable insecurities of manhood. The cop as father figure is the poet's superego shadowing his vagrant id. Their stalemate recalls the one between another prince and king—Hamlet and his father's armored ghost, who rebukes his son for procrastination. Pomeroy's poem is a long hesitation. Is the cop's unspoken charge of "loitering" a vestige of the unhappiness of Pomeroy's father with his artist son's allegedly frivolous or effeminate career?

The leather-clad cop is also a disorienting materialization of fantasy: men in uniform are idealized stereotypes in gay male culture, from artist Tom of Finland's satyr storm troopers to the drill-team personae (cop, biker, soldier) of the Village People, a 1970s pop group whose anthem was "Macho Man." As "my enemy or my death," Pomeroy's cop has the alluring menace of the hell's angels in Jean Cocteau's film *Orphée* (1949), where Death's messengers are swooping motorcyclists who ambush poets (10). This poem, like George Herbert's "Love," parodies sexual mechanics: it "slumps" at the start, then is stiffened by the poet's struggle to get or keep it up—his posture, his resolve, his forbidden desires, and the poem's narrative spine (1). The cop is still "loung[ing]" just before he explodes like a rocket when the light changes (31). The pattern is limpness to ejaculation, excited by voyeurism ("watching me watch," 37). The noise, like a thunderclap ("Something breaks through"), exhausts or discharges the cop's own ambiguous impulses (35).

Written in the present tense, the poem has the methodical intensity of an S&M script, a prompting of arousal. The cop's hand working the throttle, for example, can be read as a castrating caress. Pomeroy is exposing the irrational energies seething beneath waking consciousness: "It is all imperceptible" (15). His dance of intimidation and defiance shows how hard men can be on one another. "Who made him my enemy?": there is a touching longing for reconciliation and mutual forgiveness (28). But the breakthrough ends in disconnection. The entire episode unfolds in less than a minute. Or was it all a dream? The cop is a male Muse—no tender nurse but an antagonist who braces and hardens. He fuels a creative spurt, then vanishes into another realm.

FORTY-THREE

JONI MITCHELL

Woodstock

I came upon a child of God
He was walking along the road
And I asked him, where are you going
And this he told me

I'm going on down to Yasgur's farm   5
I'm going to join in a rock 'n' roll band
I'm going to camp out on the land
And try and get my soul free

We are stardust
We are golden   10
And we've got to get ourselves
Back to the garden

Then can I walk beside you
I have come here to lose the smog
And I feel to be a cog   15
In something turning

Well, maybe it is just the time of year
Or maybe it's the time of man
I don't know who I am
But life is for learning   20

We are stardust
We are golden
And we've got to get ourselves
Back to the garden

By the time we got to Woodstock   25
We were half a million strong
And everywhere there was song
And celebration

And I dreamed I saw the bombers
Riding shotgun in the sky   30
And they were turning into butterflies
Above our nation

We are stardust
    million-year-old carbon
We are golden   35
    caught in the devil's bargain
And we've got to get ourselves
Back to the garden

In the 1960s, young people who might once have become poets took up the guitar and turned troubadour. The best rock lyrics of that decade and the next were based on the ballad tradition, where anonymous songs with universal themes of love and strife had been refined over centuries by the shapely symmetry of the four-line stanza. But few lyrics, stripped of melody, make a successful transition to the printed page. Joni Mitchell's "Woodstock" is a rare exception. This is an important modern poem—possibly the most popular and influential poem composed in English since Sylvia Plath's "Daddy."

"Woodstock" is known worldwide as a lively, hard-driving hit single by Crosby, Stills, Nash and Young (from their 1970 *Déjà Vu* album). This virtuoso rock band, which had actually performed at the Woodstock Music Festival in August 1969, treats Mitchell's lyric uncritically as a rousing anthem for the hippie counterculture. Their "Woodstock" is a stomping hoedown. But Joni Mitchell's interpretation of the song on her album *Ladies of the Canyon* (also 1970), where she accompanies herself on electric piano, is completely different. With its slow, jazz-inflected pacing, her "Woodstock" is a moody and at times heartbreakingly melancholy art song. It shows the heady visions of the sixties counterculture already receding and evaporating.

In the sleeve notes and other published sources, the verses of "Woodstock" are run together with few or no stanza breaks. Hence the song's wonderfully economical structure is insufficiently appreciated. My tentative transcription follows the sleeve in omitting punctuation but restores the ballad form by dividing lines where rhymes occur. "Woodstock" is organized in nesting triads: its nine stanzas fall into three parts, each climaxing in a one-stanza refrain. In Mitchell's recording, the three refrains are signaled by the entrance of background scat singers—her own voice overdubbed. At the end, this eerie chorus contributes two off-rhymed lines that I insert in italics.

Mitchell the poet and artist has cast herself in the lyric as a wanderer on the road to Woodstock, beckoning as a promised land for those fleeing an oppressive society. She meets another traveler, whose story takes up the rest of part one (1–12). Hence "Woodstock" opens with precisely the same donnée as does Shelley's "Ozymandias" ("I met a traveller from an antique land / Who said . . ."). Responding with her own story, Mitchell's persona repeats her companion's hymnlike summation ("We are stardust / We are golden") to indicate her understanding and acceptance of its message (13–24). Now comrades, they arrive at Woodstock and merge with a community of astounding size. From that assembly rises a mystical dream of peace on earth and of mankind's reconnection to nature (25–38).

The song's treatment by a male supergroup automatically altered it. The four musicians, bellying up front and center, are buddies—the merry, nomadic "rock 'n' roll band" whom the lyric's young man yearns to join (6). But Mitchell's radical gender drama is missing. Presented in her voice, the lyric's protagonist is Everywoman. The wayfarers' chance encounter on the road to Woodstock is thus a reunion of Adam and Eve searching for Eden—the "garden" of the song's master metaphor (12). They long to recover their innocence, to restart human history. The song's utopian political project contains a call for reform of sexual relations. Following Walt Whitman or Jack Kerouac, the modern woman writer takes to the road, as cloistered Emily Dickinson could never do. She and her casual companion are peers on life's journey. Free love—"hooking up" in sixties slang—exalts spontaneity over the coercion of contract.

The rambler is "a child of God," like Jesus' disciples on the road to Emmaus, because he desires salvation—but not through organized religion (1). He has shed his old identity and abandoned family, friends, property, and career. Like her, he is a refugee. Indifferent to his social status, she honors him in the moment. And she asks no favors or deference as a woman. Her question—"where are you going"—implies, Where is this generation headed (3)? Is it progressing, or drifting? Does it aim to achieve, or merely to experience? And if the latter, how can raw sensation be bequeathed to posterity without the framing of intellect or art?

He's on his way to "Yasgur's farm"—the festival site on six hundred acres of rolling pastureland in upstate New York, a working dairy farm owned by the paternal Max Yasgur (5). It is nowhere near the real Woodstock, an art colony town seventy miles away. Most of those who flocked to the three-day Woodstock festival were the white, middle-class children of an affluent, industrialized nation cut off from its agrarian roots. In Mitchell's song, their goal, "Yasgur's farm," becomes a hippie reworking of Yahweh's garden. The young man planning "to camp out on the land" to free his soul is a survivalist searching for primal nature (7–8). Michael Wadleigh's epic documentary film *Woodstock* (1970) records the violent gale and torrents of rain on the second day that turned the field into a morass. The "rock 'n' roll band" coveted by the traveler is ultimately the festival audience itself, united in music—an adoptive family of brothers and sisters who were rocked by lightning and who rolled in the mud.

"We are stardust / We are golden": the refrain is a humanistic profession of faith in possibility (9–10). Mankind was created not by a stern overlord but by sacred nature itself. It's as if the earth were pollinated by meteor showers. To be golden means to be blessed by luck: divinity is within. "We've got to get ourselves / Back to the garden": Woodstock pilgrims need no Good Shepherd or mediating priesthood (11–12). When perception is adjusted, the earth is paradise now. The woman wanderer is touched by the stranger's sense of mission: "Then can I walk beside you" (13)? Woman as equal partner rejects the burden of suspicion and guilt for man's Fall. She too is a truth seeker: she has "come here to lose the smog"—the smoke that gets in our eyes from romantic love and from the cult of competition and celebrity in our polluted metropolises (14). She feels egotistic preoccupations lifting as she becomes "a cog / In something turning"—the great wheel of karma or of astrological cycle (15–16). (Woodstock was initially called an "Aquarian Exposition" to mark the dawning of the harmonious Age of Aquarius.)

The impulse for migration to Woodstock could be "just the time of year," when summer juices surge and vacationers flock to mountains or sea (17). But if it's "the time of man" (a gender-neutral term), Woodstock's mass movement is an epochal transformation (18). The lyric's apocalyptic theme can be understood as a healing amelioration of the modernist pessimism of Yeats's "The Second Coming"—a poem that Mitchell would daringly rewrite for a 1991 album. Yeats's sinister beast slouching toward Bethlehem has become a generation embarked on a spiritual quest.

"I don't know who I am": the road to Woodstock leads to self-knowledge or self-deception (19). As a name, "Woodstock" is fortuitously organic, with associations of forest and stalk or lineage: streaming toward their open-air sanctuary, the pilgrims are nature's stock, fleeing a synthetic culture of plastics and pesticides. (In her raffish hit song "Big Yellow Taxi," Mitchell says, "They paved paradise / And put up a parking lot / . . . Hey farmer farmer / Put away that DDT now.") The festival-goers believe, rightly or wrongly, that music is prophetic truth. "Life is for learning," for expansion of consciousness rather than accumulation of wealth or power, "the devil's bargain" (compare Wordsworth's "sordid boon"; 20, 36). The returning refrain hammers the point home: we own everything in nature's garden but are blinded by ambition and greed.

The lyric seems to take breath when the pair, with near ecstasy, realize their journey has been shared by so many others: "By the time we got to Woodstock / We were half a million strong" (25–26). The first "we" is two; the second, by heady alchemy, has become a vast multitude. It's as if Adam and Eve are seeing the future—the birth of Woodstock nation, forged of Romantic ideals of reverence for nature and the brotherhood of man. As the two melt into the half million, there is an exhilarating sense of personal grievances and traumas set aside for a common cause. The crowd is "strong" in its coalescence, however momentary. "Everywhere there was song / And celebration": duty and the work ethic yield to the pleasure principle, as music breaks down barriers and inhibitions (27–28). The group triumphs, for good or ill.

The artist's "I" reemerges from the surging "we" of the Woodstock moment: "I dreamed I saw the bombers / Riding shotgun in the sky / And they were turning into butterflies / Above our nation" (29–32). Is this a shamanistic or psychedelic hallucination? Or is it a magic metamorphosis produced by the roaring engine of rock, with its droning amps and bone-shuddering vibration, eddying up from the earth? The bombers are the war machine then deployed in Vietnam. During her childhood, Joni Mitchell's father was a flight lieutenant in the Royal Canadian Air Force. Thus "Woodstock" aligns the modern military with mythic father figures and sky gods, as in William Blake's engraving *The Ancient of Days,* where Yahweh, crouched in a dark cloud, launches spears of sunlight from his rigidly out-thrust down-stretched hand.

"Riding shotgun" means guarding a stagecoach in the Wild West. Why are the bombers on alert—to smite foreign enemies, or to monitor domestic subversives? Rebel children are the nation's new frontier. The bombers, Pharaoh's pursuing chariots, can destroy but not create; they helplessly follow social change from a distance. Their alteration to butterflies "above our nation" suggests an erasure of borders, restoring the continental expanse of pre-Columbian North America. It's as if mistrust and aggression could be wished away and nationalistic rivalries purged around the world. The impossibility of this lovely dream does not negate its value. Perhaps the armored warplanes are chrysalises hatching evolved new men, the pilots floating down on parachutes to join the festival of peace. But we cannot live as flitting butterflies. Civilization requires internal and external protections and is far more complex and productive than the sixties credo of Flower Power ever comprehended.

In spatial design, "Woodstock" tracks along the wanderers' narrow path, then suddenly expands horizontally at its destination, where the half million have gathered. Buoyed by "song," the lyric now swells vertically to the sky, where it bewitches and exorcizes its harassers. Finally, it sweeps backward in time to take in geology: we are "million-year-old carbon" (34). Our Darwinian origins are a primeval swamp of lizards and plants, crushed to a fertile matrix. We are kin to rocks and minerals, the lowest of the low in Judeo-Christianity's great chain of being. What injects life into the song's stardust and carbon is not the Lord's breath but music. By affirming our shared genetic past, furthermore, Mitchell's metaphor conflates the races: we are carbon copies of one another. If at the cellular level we're all carbon black, then racial differences are trivial and superficial. And carbon under pressure transmutes to the visionary clarity of diamond.

The grandeur of Mitchell's lyric, with its vast expanse of space and time, is somewhat obscured in its carefree performance by Crosby, Stills, Nash and Young, who are true believers in the revolutionary promise of Woodstock nation. By literally re-creating the "song and celebration," their bouncy, infectious rock rendition permits no alternative view of the festival, even though by the time their record was released, the disastrous Altamont concert had already occurred, exposing the fragility of Woodstock's aspirations. (*Gimme Shelter,* the Maysles brothers' 1970 documentary on the all-day festival at Altamont Speedway near San Francisco, captures the discord and violence leading to a murder in front of the stage.) CSN&Y's evangelical version of "Woodstock" was meant to convert its listeners to pacifism and solidarity. But six months after release of their single, the group had bitterly broken up. They themselves couldn't hold it together. And Mitchell's love affairs with two band members (Crosby and Nash) also ended.

In the hesitations and ravaged vibrato of her recording of "Woodstock," Joni Mitchell confides her doubts about her own splendid vision. Partly because she did not perform at Woodstock, her version has more distance and detachment. Her delivery makes lavish use of dynamics, so that we feel affirmation, then a fading of confidence and will. This "Woodstock" is a harrowing lament for hopes dashed and energies tragically wasted. It's an elegy for an entire generation, flamingly altruistic yet hedonistic and self-absorbed, bold yet naive, abundantly gifted yet plagued by self-destruction. These contradictions were on massive display at Woodstock, where the music was pitifully dependent on capitalist technology and where the noble experiment in pure democracy was sometimes indistinguishable from squalid regression to the primal horde.

An extended coda begins, as if the song doesn't want to end. The lyrics dissolve into pure music—Woodstock's essence. The coda, with its broken syllables, is a crooning lullaby that turns into a warning wail. Mitchell is skeptical about groups; she longs to join but sees the traps. When her voice falls away, her reverberating piano goes on by stops and starts. The entire power of "Woodstock" is that what is imagined in it was *not* achieved. Woodstock the festival has become a haunting memory. Mitchell's final notes hang, quaver, and fade. Cold reality triumphs over art's beautiful dreams.

FINAL CUT: THE SELECTION

PROCESS FOR *BREAK, BLOW, BURN*

Break, Blow, Burn, my collection of close readings of forty-three poems, took five years to write. The first year was devoted to a search for material in public and academic libraries as well as bookstores. I was looking for poems in English from the last four centuries that I could wholeheartedly recommend to general readers, especially those who may not have read a poem since college. For decades, poetry has been a losing proposition for major trade publishers. I was convinced that there was still a potentially large audience for poetry who had drifted away for unclear reasons. That such an audience does in fact exist seemed proved by the success of *Break, Blow, Burn,* which may be the only book of poetry criticism that has ever reached the national bestseller list in the United States.

On my two book tours (for the Pantheon hardback in 2005 and the Vintage paperback in 2006), I was constantly asked by readers or interviewers why this or that famous poet was not included in *Break, Blow, Burn,* which begins with Shakespeare and ends with Joni Mitchell. At the prospectus stage of the project, I had assumed that most of the principal modern and contemporary poets would be well represented. But once launched on the task of gathering possible entries, I was shocked and disappointed by what I found. Poem after poem, when approached from the perspective of the general audience rather than that of academic criticism, shrank into inconsequence or pretension. Or poets whom I fondly remembered from my college and graduate school studies turned out to have produced impressive bodies of serious work but no single poem that could stand up as an artifact to the classic poems elsewhere in the book. The ultimate standard that I applied in my selection process was based on William Butler Yeats's "The Second Coming," a masterpiece of sinewy modern English.

Ezra Pound, because of his generous mentoring of and vast influence on other poets (such as T. S. Eliot and William Carlos Williams), should have been automatically included in *Break, Blow, Burn*. But to my dismay, I could not find a single usable Pound poem—just a monotonous series of showy, pointless, arcane allusions to prior literature. The equally influential W. H. Auden was high on my original list. But after reviewing Auden's collected poetry, I was stunned to discover how few of his poems can stand on their own in today's media-saturated cultural climate. Auden's most anthologized poem, "Musée des Beaux Arts," inspired by a Breughel painting, felt dated in its portentous mannerisms. A homoerotic love poem by Auden that I had always planned to include begins, "Lay your sleeping head, my love, / Human on my faithless arm." But when I returned to it, I found the poem perilously top-heavy with that single fine sentence. Everything afterward dissolves into vague blather. It was perhaps the most painful example that I encountered of great openings not being sustained.

Surely the lucid and vivacious Marianne Moore, so hugely popular in her day, would have produced many poems to appeal to the general reader. However, while I was charmed by Moore's ingenious variety of formats, I became uncomfortable and impatient with her reflex jokiness, which began to seem like an avoidance of emotion. Nothing went very deep. Because I was so eager to get a good sports poem into *Break, Blow, Burn* (I never found one), I had high hopes for Moore's beloved odes to baseball. Alas, compared to today's high-impact, around-the-clock sports talk on radio and TV, Moore's baseball lingo came across as fussy and corny.

Elizabeth Bishop presented an opposite problem. Bishop is truly a poet's poet, a refined craftsman whose discreet, shapely poems carry a potent emotional charge beneath their transparent surface. I had expected a wealth of Bishop poems to choose from. With my eye on the general reader, I was keenly anticipating a cascade of sensuous tropical imagery drawn from Bishop's life in Brazil. But when I returned to her collected poems, the observed details to my surprise seemed oppressively clouded with sentimental self-projection. For example, I found Bishop's much-anthologized poem "The Fish" nearly unbearable due to her obtrusively simmering self-pity. (Wounded animal poems, typifying the anthropomorphic fallacy, have become an exasperating cliché over the past sixty years.) Even splendid, monumental Brazil evidently couldn't break into Bishop's weary bubble, which traveled with her wherever she went. It may be time to jettison depressiveness as a fashionable badge of creativity.

Charles Bukowski was another poet slated from the start to be prominently featured in *Break, Blow, Burn*. (Indeed, he proved to be the writer I was most asked about on my book tours.) I had planned to make the dissolute Bukowski a crown jewel, demonstrating the scornful rejection by my rowdy, raucous 1960s generation of the genteel proprieties of 1950s literary criticism, still faithfully practiced by the erudite but terminally prim Helen Vendler. I was looking for a funny, squalid street or barroom poem, preferably with boorish knockdown brawling and half-clad shady ladies. But as with Elizabeth Bishop, I could not find a single poem to endorse in good faith for the general reader. And Bukowski was staggeringly prolific: I ransacked shelf upon shelf of his work. But he obviously had little interest in disciplining or consolidating his garrulous, meandering poems. Frustrated, I fantasized about scissoring out juicy excerpts and taping together my own ideal Platonic form of a Bukowski poem. The missing Bukowski may be the surly Banquo's ghost of *Break, Blow, Burn*.

Feminist poetry proved a dispiriting dead end. Grimly ideological and message-driven, it preaches to the choir and has little crossover relevance for a general audience. Adrienne Rich's "Diving into the Wreck," a big anthology favorite, is symptomatic of the intractable artistic problem. A tremendously promising master metaphor—Rich uses deep-sea diving to dramatize modern women's confrontation with a declining patriarchal civilization—collapses into monotonous sermonizing and embarrassing bathos. The poem's clumsiness and redundancy are excruciating (risible "flippers," for example, loom large). I was more optimistic about finding a good feminist poem by Marge Piercy, who treats her woman-centric themes with spunky humor. Piercy's work is full of smart perceptions and sparkling turns of phrase, but her poems too often seem like casual venting—notes or first drafts rather than considered artifacts. I finally chose for *Break, Blow, Burn* two forceful, lively poems by Wanda Coleman and Rochelle Kraut that are not explicitly feminist but that express a mature and complex perspective on women's lives.

I had glowing memories of dozens of poets whom I had avidly read (or seen read in person) after my introduction to contemporary poetry in college in the mid-1960s: Denise Levertov, Randall Jarrell, Muriel Rukeyser, Robert Duncan, John Berryman, W. D. Snodgrass, Robert Creeley, John Ashbery, and Galway Kinnell, among many others. But when I returned to their work to find material for *Break, Blow, Burn,* I was mortified by my inability to identify a single important short poem to set before the general reader. Live readings seem to have beguiled and distracted too many writers from the more rigorous demands of the printed page—the medium that lasts and that speaks to posterity. All of the above poets deserve our great respect for their talent, skill, versatility, and commitment, but I would question how long their reputations will last in the absence of strong freestanding poems. Beyond that, I was puzzled and repelled by the stratospheric elevation in the critical canon given to John Ashbery in recent decades. "Self-Portrait in a Convex Mirror" (1974), Ashbery's most famous poem, is a florid exercise in strained significance that could and should have been compressed and radically reduced by two-thirds. Can there be any wonder that poetry has lost the cultural status it once enjoyed in the United States when an ingrown, overwrought, and pseudo-philosophical style such as Ashbery's is so universally praised and promoted?

Given my distaste for Ashbery's affectations, it would come as no surprise how much I detest the precious grandiloquence of marquee poets like Jorie Graham, who mirrors back to elite academics their own pedantic preoccupations and inflated sense of self. That Graham, with her fey locutions and tedious self-interrogations, is considered a "difficult" or intellectual poet is simply preposterous. Anointing by the Ivy League, of course, may be the kiss of death: Nobel Prize winner Seamus Heaney, another academic star, enjoys an exaggerated reputation for energetically well-crafted but middling poems that strike me as second- or third-hand Yeats. As for the so-called language poets, with their postmodernist game-playing, they are co-conspirators in the murder and marginalization of poetry in the United States.

For the contemporary poems in *Break, Blow, Burn,* my decisions were based solely on the quality of the poem and never on the fame of the poet. As I stumbled on a promising poem in my search, I photocopied it for later consideration. Once the finalists were assembled, I pored over them again and again to see if they could hold up to sequential rereading. Did a poem retain its freshness and surprise? Some of my finds were soon dropped when I noted how a powerful opening was not sustained by the rest of the text. It was highly distressing to see what might have been a remarkable poem self-destruct or wither away, as if the poet failed to keep pressure on his or her own imagination—or perhaps to hold the poem back long enough to let it develop and ripen on its own.

An example of this latter problem is William Stafford's "The Color That Really Is." The poem begins stunningly: "The color that really is comes over a desert / after the sun goes down: blue, lavender, / purple. . . . What if you saw all this in the day?" Stafford sees the rays of the sun as swords that "slice—life, death, disguise—through space!" These amazing, even shamanistic perceptions about existence are followed by an arresting second stanza sketching a stark scene of chilling specificity: the poet glimpses a woman's "terrible face" under the light of a casino table in Reno. That ravaged face reveals "what a desert was / if you lived there the way it is." The juxtaposition of sublime, visionary images with a gritty slice-of-life portrait is brilliant and daring. But then Stafford attaches a jarring finale—a stanza awkwardly inserting himself in a posture of mawkish piety: "Since then I pause every day to bow my head." What a waste!

Again and again, there were poems that had provocative or inspired first lines but that then fell flat, as if the poet were baffled about how to proceed. For example, Bill Knott's "More Best Jokes of the Delphic Oracle" (wonderfully sly title) begins, "I vow to live always at trash point." What satiric pleasures that bold line promises, but the poem never delivers. Sometimes an ambitious poem would find its natural architecture but then neglect smaller details of workmanship or tone. An example is Bob Kaufman's "To My Son Parker, Asleep in the Next Room." An African-American Beat poet, Kaufman, like his colleague Allen Ginsberg, was directly influenced by Walt Whitman. This memorable poem is an epic chant that surveys human history from "shaggy Neanderthals" marking "ochre walls in ice-formed caves" to artists and priests in far-flung cultures from Egypt and Assyria to China, Melanesia, and Peru. The rhythms are forceful and insistent and the images compellingly visual or visceral. The poem ends in an exalted if uneven coda celebrating freedom.

After working with Kaufman's poem, however, I became disillusioned by its needlessly simplistic politics: India is "holy," while Greece is "bloody"—as if India's soil has not been equally drenched in blood. And there are rote hits at "degenerate Rome" and "slave Europe." These angry value judgments, exalting all non-Caucasians over Europeans, have become so hackneyed through political correctness since the 1960s that they undermine the poem, whose ultimate theme is human aspiration and artistic achievement. The poet would have served his poem better with a more expansive, forgiving, and authentically Whitmanian vision. As is, it is too close to a rant. Kaufman's sadly self-limiting poem demonstrates how progressive American poetry began to isolate itself from general society in the last half of the twentieth century. When poets defensively cluster in a ghetto of homogeneous opinion, they lose contact with their larger audience. Great poetry never requires a political litmus test.

A poem that emerged from a quite different social milieu is Morris Bishop's "The Witch of East Seventy-Second Street," which was published in *The New Yorker* in 1953. Though my primary critical sympathy remains with the rude, rebellious Beat style, I find Bishop's poem far more effective than Kaufman's in reaching its artistic goal:

"I will put upon you the Telephone Curse," said the witch.
"The telephone will call when you are standing on a chair with a
    Chinese vase in either hand,
And when you answer, you will hear only the derisive popping of
    corks."

But I was armed so strong in honesty
Her threats passed by me like the idle wind.

"And I will put upon you the Curse of Dropping," said the witch.
"The dropping of tiny tacks, the dropping of food gobbets,
The escape of wet dishes from the eager-grasping hand,
The dropping of spectacles, stitches, final consonants, the
      abdomen."
I sneered, jeered, fleered; I flouted, scouted; I
      pooh-pooh-poohed.

"I will put upon you the Curse of Forgetting!" screamed the
      witch.
"Names, numbers, faces, old songs, old joy,
Words that once were magic, love, upward ways, the way home."
"No doubt the forgotten is well forgotten," said I.

"And I will put upon you the Curse of Remembering," bubbled
      the witch.
Terror struck my eyes, knees, heart;
And I took her charred contract
And signed in triplicate.

Catering with its chic uptown address, well-appointed decor, and so-
phisticated whimsy to the affluent readers of the glossy *New Yorker,*
"The Witch of East Seventy-Second Street" nevertheless manages to
tap archetypal imagery for eerily unsettling effect. Poet and witch
have an odd intimacy: she breaks into his ordered routine like an am-
bassador from elemental nature. Is she a malign proxy for mother or
wife, as in fairy tales? She speaks in ominous parallelism, like the
witches of *Macbeth*—four curses in four stanzas, culminating in the
parodic "triplicate" business contract, "charred" by hellfire and
signed by the defeated poet.

    As with Jaques's melancholy speech about the seven ages of man in
Shakespeare's *As You Like It,* human life is mapped as a series of

losses, with the elderly regressing to an infantile state. The witch's "Curse of Dropping" attacks the body (fingers and hands stiffen; the belly sags), while her "Curse of Forgetting" attacks the mind (memory lapses, especially costly to poets with their bardic mission). Everything valuable in life—emotion as well as sensation—seems to recede. But the worst is the "Curse of Remembering," which overwhelms the mind with regrets. Remembering is too crushing a burden. Better to remain in the fenced preserve of quaint connoisseurship (the Chinese vases), into which modern technology can barely penetrate (the sputtering telephone). The poem presents the poet as isolated, refined, and removed from collective joys (the "popping of corks" at unattended parties), but open to attack from mythic forces. It's as if, with their active imagination, poets are the point in modern civilization, where the archaic can invade and retake spiritual territory.

Bishop's poem, for all its virtues, finally seemed too arch or pat for *Break, Blow, Burn*. A poem that came very close to inclusion, however, was Gary Snyder's "Strategic Air Command." (I decided to use Snyder's "Old Pond" instead.)

The hiss and flashing lights of a jet
Pass near Jupiter in Virgo.
He asks, how many satellites in the sky?
Does anyone know where they all are?
What are they doing, who watches them?

Frost settles on the sleeping bags.
The last embers of fire,
One more cup of tea,
At the edge of a high lake rimmed with snow.

These cliffs and the stars
Belong to the same universe.
This little air in between
Belongs to the twentieth century and its wars.

VIII, 82, Koip Peak, Sierra Nevada

Snyder's opposition of serene nature to ethically distorted society is classically High Romantic. The two men camping out in the Sierra Nevada mountains hear the "hiss" of a military jet, the serpent in the garden as well as an avatar of impersonal industrial mechanization. The jet's passage near the planet Jupiter in the constellation and astrological sign of Virgo suggests that male authority figures (as in William Blake) have become cruel or sterile. God's periodic encounter with a virgin (as in Yeats) can lead to a destructive new birth. The rogue satellites are the all-seeing eyes of government surveillance, agents of a global system of mutual hostility and fear.

The visitors seek a spartan simplicity. They have stripped down to essentials in order to purify themselves, like tea-drinking Buddhist monks at the "high lake rimmed with snow." The fading fire (as in Shakespeare's Sonnet 73) represents an elemental reality, like the frost settling on the sleeping bags, prefiguring the beds of the dead. The men's humble comforts, with their tactile immediacy, contrast with the jet's dehumanized perfection and arrogance. Earth, air, water, and fire: these endure, while political events flare up and disappear, like the jet. The poet contemplates the largeness of the universe, compared to the narrow band of the earth's atmosphere, where the jet, representing the war-torn twentieth century, cruises. Skeptical questions could certainly be asked: would Snyder return society to the preliterate nomadic era, when humans lived desperately hand to mouth and were helplessly vulnerable to accident and disease? But that does not invalidate his protest. The poem is prophetic: machines, dazzling artifices of the mind, may gradually be robbing humanity of free will, but nature is ultimately unreachable, unperturbed by human folly. Wars, like the jet's "flashing lights," are mere dying sparks in nature's harmony.

Because Allen Ginsberg had made such a huge impact on me in college, I confidently expected him to play a prominent role in *Break, Blow, Burn*. But *Howl*, my favorite Ginsberg poem, proved thornily difficult to excerpt: the notorious opening section (starting "I saw the best minds of my generation destroyed by madness, starving hysterical naked") seemed too strident and unsupported on its own. Ginsberg's oft-anthologized "A Supermarket in California" was a possibility, but

I found its prosy humor a bit too blatant. There was an obscure early Ginsberg poem, however, that obsessed me—"The Blue Angel." But its traditional format (six four-line stanzas) is so unrepresentative of Ginsberg's work as a whole that I felt it would mislead a general audience. Furthermore, because the theme is Marlene Dietrich, it might seem as if I had chosen the poem merely because it's about a movie star—a charge that might well have been true! (My first book, *Sexual Personae,* argued that cinema, prefigured in Plato, is the master principle of Western culture.)

The title refers to Dietrich's breakthrough 1930 film, *The Blue Angel*, where she plays a cabaret femme fatale. The poem begins: "Marlene Dietrich is singing a lament / for mechanical love." Ginsberg portrays Dietrich as "a life-sized toy, / the doll of eternity." She is a streamlined objet d'art: her hair is "shaped like an abstract hat / made out of white steel." But her face is ghoulishly "whitewashed and / immobile like a robot," with a "little white key" protruding from the temple. Her eyes, with their "dull blue pupils," are "blank / like a statue's in a museum."

Ginsberg's poem works on multiple levels—cultural, biological, and psychological. First of all, the Dietrich doll, like a surreal construction by Salvador Dalí (who did mock-ups of Mae West and Shirley Temple), represents the artificial projections of Hollywood, the studio-created stars whose machine-made images infatuated audiences around the globe. White-blonde Dietrich is a modernist abstraction, an *idea* of sex removed from the sensory. She is eternal because her celluloid image will never age.

More disturbingly, Ginsberg also portrays female sexuality as a brute, fascist imperative. That there is personal projection here seems proved first by a tagline identifying the poem as a dream that Ginsberg had in Paterson in 1950, and second by the despairing coda, introduced by a hasty dash: "—you'd think I would have thought a plan / to end the inner grind, / but not till I have found a man / to occupy my mind." A startlingly frank gay revelation for that repressed period. But after so vividly hallucinatory a poem, what strangely bland language. Here Ginsberg plainly suggests that his homosexuality was a route of escape from the drearily grinding occupation of his mental space by demanding, domineering women—above all his mother, whose mental breakdown and institutionalization he would memorialize in *Kaddish*. Walt Whitman's longings for a male comrade were couched in far more effusive and tender language. But in Ginsberg's poem, all of the drama and glamour belong to a pitiless female automaton.

Related questions: is Dietrich, with her "lament / for mechanical love," a personification of random, anonymous gay sex, with which Ginsberg was perhaps feeling fatigued or disillusioned? As a gay male icon at the time, was Dietrich a symbol of gay men's own enforced, artificial construction of self? Is Ginsberg implying that gay male love is a flight from real women—a jailbreak toward male identity and freedom? Woman's image here is godlike yet cold and terrifying (like Yeats's desert beast with its "blank and pitiless" gaze in "The Second Coming"). Dietrich sings, but she does not speak. Was poetry Ginsberg's way of reclaiming and liberating language?

Gay men's cultish attachment to movie stars in the closeted era before the 1969 Stonewall rebellion, which sparked the gay liberation movement, is also registered in a sprightly little untitled poem by Frank O'Hara that begins, "Lana Turner has collapsed!" O'Hara, who always wrote quickly, tossed it off on the Staten Island ferry on his way to a 1962 reading where he scandalized Robert Lowell by impudently reciting it. I was very tempted to use this increasingly popular poem in *Break, Blow, Burn* but decided instead to treat another O'Hara poem, "A Mexican Guitar," which has never to my knowledge received critical comment or even been publicly noticed.

At the time O'Hara wrote his Lana Turner poem, most intellectuals accepted European cinema as an art form but still dismissed Hollywood glamour movies as trash or kitsch. The "Method," ultra-serious and socially leftist, was the prestige style in acting. But splashy Hollywood movies, with their ferocious or suffering divas (Bette Davis, Judy Garland) and their frivolity and excess (Busby Berkeley, Carmen Miranda), were defiantly central to gay male "camp." Andy Warhol's hyper-colored silk screens of Elizabeth Taylor and Marilyn Monroe cheekily turned movie stars into Byzantine icons.

Angst-ridden, suicide-studded confessional poetry was then at its height. Lana Turner, fresh from a series of lurid scandals, was a symbol of glitzy tabloid celebrity and not remotely an appropriate subject for a poem. "Lana Turner Collapses on Movie Set" was an actual headline, a version of which O'Hara evidently spotted on a New York newsstand. The poet describes the weird muddle of rain, snow, and city traffic through which he hurries, distracted. The headline, with its boldface visual clarity and exclamatory, telegraphic diction, breaks on him like an electrifying epiphany. The grey mediocrity of everyday life seems transformed, and the slippery ambiguities of language and definition in which a poet dwells are temporarily transcended. Lana Turner's soap opera traumas are like a ritual martyrdom, a sacrament avidly witnessed by her millions of fans. O'Hara's last line: "oh Lana Turner we love you get up." Who is "we"? Presumably gay men, who found themselves sympathetically bonding as fans with a vast audience of mainstream movie-lovers who normally ostracized them.

Lynn Emanuel's poem "Frying Trout While Drunk" is far more sober. Instead of the kinetic urban landscape of O'Hara's fancy-free sophisticates (the Lana Turner poem refers to "lots of parties" where the poet "acted perfectly disgraceful"), we are now in a crimped realm of psychological entrapment and wounded memory.

> Mother is drinking to forget a man
> Who could fill the woods with invitations:
> Come with me he whispered and she went
> In his Nash Rambler, its dash
> Where her knees turned green
> In the radium dials of the '50s.
> When I drink it is always 1953,
> Bacon wilting in the pan on Cook Street
> And mother, wrist deep in red water,
> Laying a trail from the sink
> To a glass of gin and back.
> She is a beautiful, unlucky woman
> In love with a man of lechery so solid
> You could build a table on it
> And when you did the blues would come to visit.

I remember all of us awkwardly at dinner,
The dark slung across the porch,
And then mother's dress falling to the floor,
Buttons ticking like seeds spit on a plate.
When I drink I am too much like her—
The knife in one hand and in the other
The trout with a belly white as my wrist.
I have loved you all my life
She told him and it was true
In the same way that all her life
She drank, dedicated to the act itself,
She stood at this stove
And with the care of the very drunk
Handed him the plate.

As autobiography, if it is that, Emanuel's poem seems influenced by Robert Lowell's seminal *Life Studies* (1959). (I used a Lowell poem from that book, "Man and Wife," instead of this one.) Admirably condensed and finely written, "Frying Trout" distills an entire life of helpless observation and pained reflection. Food, drink, and sex are literally and symbolically intertwined. Everyday routine and rituals, such as cooking, are punctuated by erratic and impulsive breaches of convention. The daughter both admires and pities her mother and tries to understand her weaknesses and compromises, which she fears she has inherited via the time-dissolving act of drinking. The mother is betrayed and humiliated by her own desires and foolish trust. She accepts exploitation and betrayal as the price of sexual pleasure, a mime of love.

Emanuel's intense imagery, skillfully underplayed, is tremendously evocative. The knife and white-bellied trout suggest sex but also a masochistic vulnerability. Exquisitely caught details abound in quick scenarios: the mother's knees turning green in the car's radio light; bloody water trailing to a gin glass; buttons of a fallen dress "ticking like seeds spit on a plate." Flesh is fruit here, carelessly devoured. This poem patiently, methodically offers its story without sentimentality or melodrama. There is no flinching from harsh facts and yet no gratuitous self-dramatization either. Emanuel's technique is quiet, steady, and scrupulously exact. "Frying Trout While Drunk" is a tour de force of courageous truth-telling.

Two poems about women rockers nearly made the final cut. In "Marianne Faithfull's Cigarette," Gerry Gomez Pearlberg describes a scene of charged suspension and voyeurism. Spare and ritualistically structured, this poem has a cool Baudelairean perversity. Marianne Faithfull, "bored," is chain-smoking while a crew of daft academics is "talking, talking, talking." The poet is transfixed by the singer's discarded cigarette, branded with its "ring of lipstick." There is an idolatrous fetishism in her desire for the butt, but she asks someone else to fetch it. Abashed, she herself will not cross the aesthetic distance to the enthroned star, whose insouciance is wonderfully caught.

The poem becomes the words that the poet could not speak in the star's presence. I love the gap between the academics' inflated discourse and the squalid litter of Faithfull's red-smeared cigarettes— a tainted beauty that the fascinated poet tries to capture. However, I did not include Pearlberg's poem, which so perfectly captures my own cultic attitude toward stars (such as Elizabeth Taylor, Catherine Deneuve, or Daniela Mercury), because I was uncertain about its interest to a general audience. Furthermore, I had qualms about the finale: "Watching her light up was like seeing the Messiah. / Or Buddha's burning moment under leaves of cool desire." This is way too much. Faithfull's oblique, imperious divinity is already well caught by the poem. We don't need the Messiah and Buddha, with their centuries of accumulated associations, to come crashing in like colossi. All the poem needs at the end is a haiku effect, words floating off like smoke.

Alice Fulton's "You Can't Rhumboogie in a Ball and Chain" is a tribute to Janis Joplin. ("Ball 'n' Chain," a blues song by Big Mama Thornton, was Joplin's hallmark.) The first two stanzas are a knock-out:

You called the blues' loose black belly lover
and in Port Arthur they called you pig-face.

The way you chugged booze straight, without a glass,
your brass-assed language, slingbacks with jeweled heel,
proclaimed you no kin to their muzzled blood.
No chiclet-toothed Baptist boyfriend for you.

Strung-out, street hustling showed men wouldn't buy you.
Once you clung to the legs of a lover,
let him drag you till your knees turned to blood,
mouth hardened to a thin scar on your face,
cracked under songs, screams, never left to heal.
Little Girl Blue, soul pressed against the glass.

The heavy sprung rhythms and eye-popping imagery, rattling the reader with hard consonants and alliteration, are reminiscent of the poet-priest Gerard Manley Hopkins, whose ecstatic techniques are deployed here for far earthier and more carnal purposes. Even Fulton's rugged slang scintillates. Through a series of sleazy snapshots, Joplin's pain and defiance and her bold explorations of the netherworld are rivetingly captured.

If it had continued at this sensational level, "You Can't Rhumboogie" would, in my view, have become a contemporary classic. But over the next four stanzas, the sense of urgent compression is lost. We get tantalizing glimpses of seedy diners, "nameless motels," and bad memories of senior proms, but the bruising shocks of the wonderful opening stanzas are repeated and done to death. "Blood" pops up in every stanza; there are simply too many traumas and tortures for the beleaguered reader to process. Instead of sympathizing with Joplin, we feel resentfully penned in a gore-spattered emergency room. While the powerful rhythms and images did all the work at the start, there's now a turn toward editorializing and psychoanalysis ("self-hatred laced your blood").

The final stanza is clever but makes too radical a shift in tone:

Like clerks we face your image in the glass,
suggest lovers, as accessories, heels.
"It's your shade, this blood dress," we say. "It's you."

Well, we've sure left Texas. That's Sylvia Plath coming through the door—a far more middle-class and coyly ironic voice. Fulton has unfortunately abandoned the proletarian percussiveness of her opening, which explodes with the vernacular.

David Young's "Occupational Hazards" still enchants and intrigues me. It draws its inspiration from riddles, fairy tales, children's songs, and emblematic chapbooks with roots in medieval allegory:

> *Butcher*
> If I want to go to pieces
> I can do that. When I try
> to pull myself together
> I get sausage.

> *Bakers*
> Can't be choosers. Rising
> from a white bed, from dreams
> of kings, bright cities, buttocks,
> to see the moon by daylight.

> *Tailor*
> It's not the way the needle
> drags the poor thread around.
> It's sewing the monster together,
> my misshapen son.

> *Gravediggers*
> To be the baker's dark opposite,
> to dig the anti-cake, to stow
> the sinking loaves in the unoven—
> then to be dancing on the job!

> *Woodcutter*
> Deep in my hands
> as far as I can go

> the fallen trees
> keep ringing.

The poet's pure pleasure in improvisational, associative play with language is registered in the mercurial puns and quirky metaphors. Young's catalog of occupations echoes the children's limerick "Rub-a-dub-dub, three men in a tub" ("The butcher, the baker, the candle-stick-maker"). However, each vocation here—butcher, baker, tailor, gravedigger, woodcutter—can be read as an analogue to the practice of poetry.

The butcher going to pieces is the poet exploring his or her emotional extremes, out of which may come "sausage," the inner life ground up, processed, and strung together in linked stanzas. Such a life requires intestinal fortitude. Rising long before dawn, bakers (normally beggars) "can't be choosers"; like writers wrestling with their material, they are under compulsion to knead their sticky, shapeless dough. With a strangely active dream life, the bakers see metaphorically: "buttocks" and "moon" prefigure the raw white loaf (compare the slang term "buns" for buttocks; flashing one's buttocks is "mooning"). Poets, the "kings" of their own "bright cities," have a tactile intimacy with language, while their sources of inspiration range from the coarsely material to the celestial.

A tailor at work resembles the poet cutting, trimming, and stitching his verse. The needle is the sudden penetration of insight, while the flexible thread, assuring continuity and shape, is dragged in the rear as a secondary process. The result is "my misshapen son": art-making by men is an appropriation of female fertility. The end product, like Frankenstein's "monster" with his stitched-up face, may seem ugly or distorted (in an avant-garde era). But the artwork is the artist's true posterity, a child of the intellect rather than the body—a distinction made by Plato.

Young wittily says that the merry gravedigger ("the baker's dark opposite") must "dig the anti-cake" and "stow the sinking loaves in the unoven"—as if the bakery has gone through Alice's looking-glass and turned into a graveyard. Cake and corpses: this morbid mingling of sweets and rot is a brilliant conflation of motifs from *Hamlet*, with its jovial gravedigger and its satirical imagery of the murdered king's body served up as "funeral baked meats" at a too-hasty wedding banquet, where the main dish is the queen (*Hamlet* 1.2.180). Meditating on elemental realities, the poet faces death and turns it into artistic sustenance and pleasure ("dancing on the job"). Finally, the woodcutter is the poet who ruthlessly topples his lofty forebears to clear mental space for himself. But their words still ring in his mind. They have seeped into his bones, to the deepest layers of his psyche. Poetry, a form of making, is a mission he cannot escape. The battered hands of the craftsman dictate to the soul.

I often regretted not including David Young's marvelous poem in *Break, Blow, Burn*. But in perfect truth, I wondered if I could do it justice. It was weighed against May Swenson's "At East River," which has a similar listlike format and childlike sense of wonder. I ultimately went with Swenson because of her poem's intriguing parallelism with Wordsworth's panoramic sonnet about a modern metropolis tranquilly embraced by nature, "Composed Upon Westminster Bridge," which appears earlier in my book.

A. R. Ammons' "Mechanism" upset me severely and still does. This poem should have been the dramatic climax of *Break, Blow, Burn*. In fact, it should have been one of the greatest poems of the twentieth century. Its vision of complex systems operating simultaneously in human beings and animal nature is at the very highest level of artistic inspiration. But in execution, the poem is a shambles, with weak transitions and phrasings that veer from the derivative to the pedantic. "Mechanism" is my primary exhibit for the isolation and self-destruction of American poetry over the past forty years:

Honor a going thing, goldfinch, corporation, tree,
     morality: any working order,
   animate or inanimate: it

has managed directed balance,
     the incoming and outgoing energies are working right,
   some energy left to the mechanism,

some ash, enough energy held
        to maintain the order in repair,
    assure further consumption of entropy,

expending energy to strengthen order:
        honor the persisting reactor,
    the container of change, the moderator: the yellow

bird flashes black wing-bars
        in the new-leaving wild cherry bushes by the bay,
    startles the hawk with beauty,

flitting to a branch where
        flash vanishes into stillness,
    hawk addled by the sudden loss of sight:

honor the chemistries, platelets, hemoglobin kinetics,
        the light-sensitive iris, the enzymic intricacies
    of control,

the gastric transformations, seed
        dissolved to acrid liquors, synthesized into
    chirp, vitreous humor, knowledge,

blood compulsion, instinct: honor the
        unique genes,
    molecules that reproduce themselves, divide into

sets, the nucleic grain transmitted
        in slow change through ages of rising and falling form,
    some cells set aside for the special work, mind

or perception rising into orders of courtship,
        territorial rights, mind rising
    from the physical chemistries

to guarantee that genes will be exchanged, male
    and female met, the satisfactions cloaking a deeper
racial satisfaction:

heat kept by a feathered skin:
    the living alembic, body heat maintained (bunsen
burner under the flask)

so the chemistries can proceed, reaction rates
    interdependent, self-adjusting, with optimum
efficiency—the vessel firm, the flame

staying: isolated, contained reactions! the precise and
    necessary worked out of random, reproducible,
the handiwork redeemed from chance, while the

goldfinch, unconscious of the billion operations
    that stay its form, flashes, chirping (not a
great songster) in the bay cherry bushes wild of leaf.

The pretty goldfinch flitting in and out of the poem symbolizes nature unconscious of itself. Flashing through the cherry bushes in the last line, it carries a valedictory blessing like the ones in Wordsworth's "Tintern Abbey" and Wallace Stevens' early poem "Sunday Morning" (which ends with flocks of birds sinking "on extended wings").

But it is the doggedly philosophical late Stevens, notably in "The Auroras of Autumn" and "An Ordinary Evening in New Haven," who is exercising a baleful and crippling influence here on Ammons, as on so many other American poets of his generation, including John Ashbery. (Two examples of luminous early Stevens appear in *Break, Blow, Burn.*) Over time, Stevens's language tragically failed him. He ended his career with a laborious, plodding, skeletal style, employed in self-questioning poems of numbing length. Gorgeous images or lines still abound, but pompous, big-think gestures have become a crutch.

The obtrusive "ideas" in late Stevens have naturally provided grist for the ever-churning academic mill. But poetry is not philosophy. Philosophic discourse has its own noble medium as prose argumentation or dramatic dialogue. Poetry should not require academic translators to mediate between the poet and his or her audience. Poetry is a sensory mode where ideas are or should be fully embodied in emotion or in imagery grounded in the material world. Late Stevens suffers from spiritual anorexia; he shows the modernist sensibility stretched to the breaking point. Late Stevens is not a fruitful model for the future of poetry.

In Ammons' "Mechanism," Whitman's influence can be felt in the cosmic perspective and catalog of organic phenomena. But there isn't nearly enough specificity here. Whitman was able to invoke nature's largest, most turbulent forces along with the tiniest details of straw, seeds, or sea spray. Ammons was on the verge of a major conceptual breakthrough in his willingness to consider the intricacies of human organizations, corporations, and management as expressions of the nature-inspired drive toward order. Whitman's melting, all-embracing Romantic love is no longer enough for a modern high-tech world. Connecting sexual "courtship" to state-guaranteed "territorial rights," Ammons is using an anthropological lens to focus on the ancient birth of civilization itself in law and contract. And by conflating history, science, economy, and art, he would end the war between the artist and commercial society that began with the Industrial Revolution and that has resulted in the artist's pitiful marginalization in an era dominated by mass media.

"Mechanism" approaches a view of consciousness itself as a product of evolutionary biology. The minute chemistry of enzymes and platelets is made almost psychedelically visible. The poem makes us ponder huge questions: are we merely flitting goldfinches in nature's master plan? Is free will an illusion? Is art too a product of natural design? But the poem is fatally weakened by its abstruse diction, bombastic syntax, and factitious format. Why did Ammons choose these untidy staggered triads? They seem forced and arbitrary, out of sync with his own music. While David Young's cryptic "Occupational Hazards" uses a concrete, vigorous, living English that connects us to the sixteenth century, "Mechanism" relies on a clotted, undigested academese that strains at profundity.

And the poem is too long. Shakespeare's sonnets, bridging his piercing emotional experiences with his wary social observations, demonstrate the beauty and power of high condensation. In his great sonnet "Leda and the Swan," Yeats showed how a vast historical perspective could illuminate shattering contemporary events. Perhaps "Mechanism" should have been a sonnet, a worthy heir to Shakespeare and Yeats. But the poem shows the increasing distance of the poet from general society, which Ammons is analyzing but is no longer addressing in its own language. It prefigures what would happen to American poetry over the following decades, as the most ambitious poets became stranded in their own coteries and cultivated a self-blinding disdain for the surrounding culture.

PAUL BLACKBURN (1926–71)
Born in St. Albans, Vermont. Mother abandoned family after winning
Yale Younger Poets series in 1929. Her son was raised by grandparents
and educated at New York University and the University of Wisconsin.
Mentored by Ezra Pound. Published translations of troubadour poetry.
Taught in Provence, then moved to Spain and began translating Spanish
poetry. Afterward based in New York and allied with Black Mountain
and Beat poets. Founded poetry reading programs, such as the Poetry
Project at St. Mark's Church.

WILLIAM BLAKE (1757–1827)
Son of a London hosier. Was home-schooled and apprenticed to an en-
graver. Studied briefly at Royal Academy. Suffered extreme poverty dur-
ing a career as an engraver and illustrator. Had visions as a child; began
writing poetry at age twelve. Incised his illuminated poems on copper
plates and painted the prints with watercolor. Politically radical, he
was neglected during his lifetime. Among his major works: *Songs of
Innocence; Songs of Experience; The Marriage of Heaven and Hell*
(1789–94).

WANDA COLEMAN (1946–)
Born in Watts, Los Angeles. Showed early talent as a violinist and pi-
anist. Worked as a secretary, editor, journalist, and TV scriptwriter;
won Emmy for *Days of Our Lives*. Has published a novel and numer-
ous volumes of poems and stories, including *Mercurochrome* (2001)
and *Ostinato Vamps* (2003). Renowned for her live readings (available
via commercial recordings). Literary influences: Nathanael West, Ann

Petry, Charles Bukowski. Other influences: American popular music (blues, jazz, country and western) and Mexican language and culture.

SAMUEL TAYLOR COLERIDGE (1772–1834)

Son of a Devonshire clergyman. At Cambridge with Robert Southey, planned never-realized utopian commune, Pantisocracy, in Pennsylvania. Verses published in newspapers (1793–95). Met Wordsworth in 1795. They cowrote the revolutionary *Lyrical Ballads* (1798). Coleridge's "mystery" poems, "Kubla Khan" and "Christabel," written in 1797 but held back until 1816. *Biographia Literaria* (1817) contains Coleridge's literary criticism and theory of art as beauty and pleasure. Analyzed politics and endorsed German philosophy. Plagued throughout life by depression and opium addiction.

EMILY DICKINSON (1830–86)

Born in Amherst, Massachusetts. Daughter of a lawyer in a prominent, prosperous family. Locally well educated in humanities and science. Became a recluse but was an active letter-writer. A few of her poems, altered by editors, were published anonymously during her lifetime. Over 1,000 poems found in a locked box after her death. Her first three posthumous collections (1890–96) were hugely successful. But accurate transcriptions of the poems were not available until Thomas H. Johnson's three-volume edition was published in 1955.

JOHN DONNE (1572–1631)

Son of a London ironmonger. Raised Roman Catholic and educated at Oxford and Cambridge. Traveled abroad on naval expeditions. Wrote provocative love poetry, then religious poetry. Secretary to Sir Thomas Egerton, lord keeper of the great seal, who was enraged by Donne's secret marriage to his wife's niece. Impoverished for the next decade. Took holy orders in the Church of England in 1615 and became chaplain to James I. In 1621, appointed dean of St. Paul's Cathedral, where he won fame for his sermons and is entombed.

GEORGE HERBERT (1593–1633)

Born at Montgomery Castle, Wales. Son of Sir Richard Herbert and brother of Lord Herbert of Cherbury. Donne was his mother's friend. Public orator at Cambridge and a representative to Parliament. In 1630, took holy orders in the Church of England and became a country parson at Bemerton, near Salisbury. Wrote but did not publish 160 religious poems, collected as *The Temple*. When dying from tuberculosis at age forty, he sent the manuscript to a friend, who published it after Herbert's death to huge acclaim.

LANGSTON HUGHES (1902–67)

Born in Joplin, Missouri. Raised in Kansas by grandmother with Abolitionist family past. Graduated from Lincoln University. Worked as a cook, busboy, and seaman. Early poetry in *Crisis* (NAACP magazine). First book, *The Weary Blues* (1926). A leader of the Harlem Renaissance. His *Mulatto* (1935) was the first Broadway play by an African-American. Promoted use of black vernacular in literature. In the 1950s, suffered U.S. government investigation for his leftism and his visit to Russia in the 1930s.

ROCHELLE KRAUT (1952–)

Born in a Displaced Persons camp in West Germany; raised in Chicago. Majored in medieval art and architecture at University of Illinois, Chicago. Active with *Milk Quarterly* poets and Paul Sills's Body Politic Theater. Moved to New York in 1973; joined Poet's Theater and the Poetry Project at St. Mark's Church. Published two books of poetry and wrote and performed in many avant-garde plays. Co-published *Frontward Books* with Bob Rosenthal (husband). Literary influences: haiku, Catullus, Ted Berrigan, and James Schuyler.

ROBERT LOWELL (1917–77)

Born in Boston into old, distinguished New England family. Transferred from Harvard to Kenyon College and then attended Louisiana State University, where he studied with the New Critics, including Cleanth Brooks. Converted from Episcopalianism to Roman Catholicism in 1940. Jailed as a conscientious objector during World War II. Early poetry was formal. The more colloquial *Life Studies* (1959) revolutionized American poetry and became the canonical book of the "confessional" school. Repeatedly hospitalized for manic depression. Active in protests against the Vietnam War.

ANDREW MARVELL (1621–78)
Born near Hull, Yorkshire. Son of a clergyman. Educated at Cambridge. Spent four years in Europe, mastered many languages. As a tutor at Nun Appleton House, wrote "The Garden" and other poems celebrating country life. Was John Milton's assistant in the Latin Secretaryship to Cromwell's Council of State; later helped free Milton from prison. M.P. for Hull (1659–78). After the Restoration, became a political satirist. Most of his poetry was unpublished before a post-humous 1681 collection.

JONI MITCHELL (1943–)
Born in Fort Macleod, Alberta, and raised in Saskatchewan. Mother a schoolteacher; father a grocery manager and former military officer. Childhood illnesses, including polio. Showed early talent for painting. Attended Alberta College of Art. Became folk singer in college; moved to Toronto and United States to perform. Her original songs were widely covered before first album released (1968). Leading figure in Los Angeles music scene. Turned toward jazz/rock fusion in 1970s. Has had immense influence on women singer-songwriters.

FRANK O'HARA (1926–66)
Born in Baltimore; grew up near Boston. Studied piano at New England Conservatory. Two years in Navy during World War II. Entered Harvard; switched major to literature. Became an editor of *Art News* and a curator at the Museum of Modern Art. Belonged to the New York School of poets who allied with Abstract Expressionist and Action painters in 1950s. *Art Chronicles* (1975) contains his art criticism. Killed at age forty by a dune buggy on Fire Island.

SYLVIA PLATH (1932–63)
Born in Boston. Daughter of a German immigrant professor and a highschool teacher. First poems published before she entered Smith College. Nervous breakdowns began in college. In England on a Fulbright scholarship in 1955, she met poet Ted Hughes and married him. Attended Robert Lowell's workshop in Boston in 1959; deeply influenced by *Life Studies*. First book, *The Colossus* (1960). *Ariel* (1965), a literary sensation, collected poems written before her suicide at age thirty in London. Her novel, *The Bell Jar* (1963), first published under a pseudonym, was autobiographical.

RALPH POMEROY (1926–99)

Born in Evanston, Illinois, and raised in nearby Winnetka. Attended School of the Art Institute of Chicago and University of Illinois. At eighteen, published poem in *Poetry* magazine. Pursued painting in Paris in late 1940s. Was an editor, art critic, curator, and exhibiting artist in New York City. Active in San Francisco poetry scene of late 1950s. Taught in the United States and abroad. Published essays, monographs, catalogs, and three collections of poetry, plus an illustrated book of poems with Andy Warhol.

THEODORE ROETHKE (1908–63)

Born in Saginaw, Michigan. Immigrant German father and uncle owned commercial floral greenhouse, where he played as a child. Educated at University of Michigan. Repeatedly hospitalized for manic depression and given shock treatments. Influenced by Blake, Wordsworth, Emerson, Whitman, and Yeats. First book, *Open House* (1941), was well received. *Words for the Wind* (1958) is a classic collection of his poems. Taught at various colleges but mainly the University of Washington, where he mentored many young poets.

NORMAN H. RUSSELL (1921–)

Born in Big Stone Gap, Virginia; raised in western Pennsylvania. Ancestry Scotch, English, and Cherokee. Attended Slippery Rock State Teachers College and University of Minnesota (Ph.D. in botany). Four years (two in India) in Army Air Force in World War II. Taught biology and poetry at various colleges and universities; extensive publications in science as well as poetry. Retired from University of Central Oklahoma. Literary influences: Carl Sandburg, e. e. cummings, John Dos Passos. Central theme of his poetry: mankind's relationship to the environment.

WILLIAM SHAKESPEARE (1564–1616)

Born at Stratford-upon-Avon and educated at free grammar school. By the early 1590s, was working as an actor and playwright in London. Cofounded Globe Theatre in 1599. Wrote thirty-seven known plays. His first published poems, *Venus and Adonis* (1593) and *The Rape of Lucrece* (1594), had controversial erotic themes. An edition of 154 of his sonnets (which had circulated in manuscript) was published in

1609. The first collection of his plays appeared seven years after his death.

PERCY BYSSHE SHELLEY (1792–1822)

Born in Sussex to a prominent, affluent family. Expelled from Oxford after publishing a pamphlet titled *The Necessity of Atheism*. Endorsed free love. Scandalously abandoned first wife (who committed suicide) for Mary Godwin, daughter of a socialist and feminist. Summered with Byron in 1816 in Switzerland, where Mary wrote *Frankenstein*. After moving to Italy in 1818, Shelley wrote such poems as "Ode to the West Wind" and *Prometheus Unbound*. He drowned at age thirty while sailing off Viareggio.

GARY SNYDER (1930–)

Born in San Francisco; raised in Pacific Northwest. Published first poems at Reed College, where he majored in literature and anthropology; senior thesis on North American Indian myth. Worked as logger and forest ranger. Moved to San Francisco in 1952; studied East Asian languages at Berkeley and befriended Beat poets. A model for hero of Jack Kerouac's *The Dharma Bums*. Studied Zen Buddhism in Kyoto (1956–68). First book: *Riprap* (1959). Sees poets as shamanistic truth-tellers. Exponent of environmentalism; critic of Western militarism and materialism.

WALLACE STEVENS (1879–1955)

Born in Reading, Pennsylvania. Attended Harvard and tried journalism in New York City. Father discouraged his desire for a literary career. Stevens took a law degree and accepted a quiet, lucrative, lifetime job with a Hartford insurance company. First poems published by *Poetry* magazine in 1914. First book, *Harmonium* (1923), showed the influence of French Symbolism and the visual arts. Later work became more philosophical. Hailed as a major writer when his *Collected Poems* was published (1954).

MAY SWENSON (1913–89)

Born in Logan, Utah. Parents were Swedish immigrants and Mormons. Father taught engineering. She published poems in literary magazine at Utah State University. Moved to New York City in 1936; worked as stenographer and editor. First book, *Another Animal* (1954), was well received. Influenced by Emily Dickinson, e. e. cummings, and Marianne Moore. Known for her wordplay, painterly descriptions of nature, and visual experiments and "iconographs" (shaped poems). Taught writing and also published drama, children's literature, and translations from the Swedish.

JEAN TOOMER (1894–1967)

Born in Washington, D.C. Son of a Georgia farmer. Restlessly attended universities in Wisconsin and New York. Published poems and prose in literary magazines and frequented avant-garde circles in New York City. In 1921, taught in Sparta, Georgia, to explore his Southern roots. From that experience came *Cane* (1923), a multigenre work about the black experience that helped trigger the Harlem Renaissance. Later studied George Gurdjieff's spiritual philosophy, made a pilgrimage to India, and joined Quaker meetings in Pennsylvania.

CHUCK WACHTEL (1950–)

Born in Brooklyn. Graduated from City College of New York. Traveled in Europe; in Mallorca, encountered the work of Catalan modernist poet J. V. Foix, whose titles can be longer than his texts. Other literary influences: Charles Reznikoff; Muriel Rukeyser; Hubert Selby, Jr.; Grace Paley. Published five volumes of poems and short prose, a collection of stories, and two novels, *The Gates* and *Joe the Engineer*. Teaches in the Graduate Creative Writing Program at New York University.

WALT WHITMAN (1819–92)

Born on Long Island, New York, to a family with seventeenth-century roots in America. Son of a carpenter and a beloved mother of Quaker ancestry. Little formal education. Was a printer's apprentice, then a teacher, journalist, and editor. Influenced by Emerson, notably about America's cultural independence from Europe. First edition of *Leaves of Grass* (1855) was self-published; there were six more expanded editions. The sexual explicitness of Whitman's poetry made him notorious. He worked as a volunteer in hospitals during the Civil War.

WILLIAM CARLOS WILLIAMS (1883–1963)

Born in Rutherford, New Jersey, to an English father and Puerto Rican mother. Began writing poetry in high school. Attended medical school in Philadelphia, where he met Ezra Pound, later his literary adviser. Was a family doctor in Rutherford for forty years. A founding member of Imagism. Also wrote fiction, drama, essays. Opposed the elitism and dominance of T. S. Eliot. Became a mentor to the Beat poets. His five-volume epic, *Paterson* (1946–58), reinterpreted American history.

WILLIAM WORDSWORTH (1770–1850)
Born in Cumberland, in the Lake District of northern England, which fostered his love of nature. Son of an attorney. His mother died when he was eight, a traumatic loss. Educated at Cambridge. Radicalized by visits to Europe after the French Revolution but became disillusioned and increasingly conservative. Met Coleridge in 1795. They cowrote *Lyrical Ballads* (1798), a landmark of Romanticism. Sought to reclaim the speech of the "common man." Appointed poet laureate in 1843. Autobiographical poem, *The Prelude*, published posthumously.

WILLIAM BUTLER YEATS (1865–1939)
Born in Dublin. Son and brother of painters. Studied at the Metropolitan School of Art in Dublin. Edited William Blake's poems (three volumes, 1893). Major figure in the Celtic Revival; cofounded the Irish Literary Society and Irish National Theatre, for which he wrote plays. Early poetry was in Pre-Raphaelite style. Studied occultism and believed wife was a medium. Fierce nationalist during period of political violence. Senator of Irish Free State (1922–28). Won Nobel Prize for literature in 1923.

These publications by Camille Paglia address issues discussed in the introduction.

Sexual Personae: Art and Decadence from Nefertiti to Emily Dickinson (Yale University Press, 1990; Vintage Books, 1991). Ch. 1: Nature and art. Chs. 2–4: Beauty and form. Chs. 5–7: the Renaissance. Chs. 8–14: High Romanticism. Chs. 15–24: Late Romanticism.

Sex, Art, and American Culture: Essays (Vintage Books, 1992).

"Junk Bonds and Corporate Raiders: Academe in the Hour of the Wolf," from *Arion* (Spring 1991). Critique of poststructuralism and proposals for educational reform.

"*Sexual Personae:* The Cancelled Preface." A theory of literary criticism.

"East and West: An Experiment in Multiculturalism." A humanities course co-created with Lily Yeh at the University of the Arts.

"Milton Kessler: A Memoir," from *Sulfur* (Spring 1991). On the poet/professor who introduced Paglia to contemporary poetry.

Vamps & Tramps: New Essays (Vintage Books, 1994).

"The Nursery School Campus: The Corrupting of the Humanities in the U.S.," from *Times Literary Supplement* (May 22, 1992).

"Love Poetry," from *The Princeton Encyclopedia of Poetry and Poetics,* ed. Alex Preminger and T. V. F. Bogan, 3rd ed. (1993).

"No Law in the Arena: A Pagan Theory of Sexuality." A dissident feminist view of controversial social issues, including pornography, prostitution, rape, sexual harassment, and homosexuality.

The Birds (British Film Institute, Film Classics Series, 1998). A scene-by-scene close reading of Alfred Hitchcock's 1963 film.

"Sex," in *The Spenser Encyclopedia,* ed. A.C. Hamilton et al. (University of Toronto Press, 1990). On erotic language and symbolism in Edmund Spenser's *The Faerie Queene.*

"The Mighty River of Classics: Tradition and Reform in Modern Education," *Arion* (Fall 2001). A lecture given in 2001 at Santa Clara University.

"Dispatches from the New Frontier: Writing for the Internet," in *Communication and Cyberspace: Social Interaction in an Electronic Environment,* ed. Lance Strate, Ron L. Jacobson, and Stephanie B. Gibson (Hampton Press, 2002). On Paglia's methodology as a columnist for Salon.com from its debut issue (1995–2001).

"The North American Intellectual Tradition," *Media Ecology Association Journal* (June 2002). The Second Annual Marshall McLuhan Lecture given in 2000 at Fordham University.

"Cults and Cosmic Consciousness: Religious Vision in the American 1960s," *Arion* (Winter 2003). Expanded version of a lecture given in 2002 at Yale University.

"The Magic of Images: Word and Picture in a Media Age," *Arion* (Winter 2004). Expanded version of a lecture given in 2002 at York University, Toronto.

ACKNOWLEDGMENTS

Thanks above all are owed to my family, Alison Maddex and Lucien Harry Maddex. I am very grateful to my editor, LuAnn Walther, for her stalwart support and expert advice throughout this long project. John Siciliano and Chuck Antony provided invaluable editorial assistance. Kent Christensen and John DeWitt generously reviewed and corrected the manuscript. While writing this book, I benefited from conversations about art, literature, education, and media with the following people, in alphabetical order: Katharine Barrett, Glenn Belverio, Tina Bennett, Robert Caserio, Herbert Golder, Kristoffer Jacobson, Ann Jamison, Mitchell Kunkes, Lenora Paglia, Lance Strate, and Helen Vermeychuk.

Quotations from Shakespeare's plays are from *The Complete Signet Classic Shakespeare* (1972), ed. Sylvan Barnet. Spelling and punctuation in poems by Donne, Marvell, and Blake have sometimes been slightly modernized.

SEXUAL PERSONAE
Art and Decadence from Nefertiti to Emily Dickinson

Is Emily Dickinson "the female Sade"? Is Donatello's David a bit of pedophile pornography? What is the secret kinship between Byron and Elvis Presley, between the Medusa and Madonna? How do liberals and feminists—as well as conservatives—fatally misread human nature? This audacious and omnivorously learned work of guerilla scholarship offers nothing less than a unified-field theory of Western culture, high and low, since the Egyptians invented beauty—making a persuasive case for all art as a pagan battleground between male and female, form and chaos, civilization and daemonic nature. *"Sexual Personae* [is] an enormous sensation of a book, in all the better senses of 'sensation.' There is no book comparable in scope, stance, design or insight"(Harold Bloom).

Women's Studies/Art Criticism/978-0-679-73579-3

VAMPS AND TRAMPS
New Essays

With her brilliant bestsellers *Sexual Personae* and
Sex, Art, and American Culture, Camille Paglia be-
came America's first internationally recognized pub-
lic thinker since the 1960s. Her best work combines
Olympian learning with dazzling rhetoric and a com-
mon sense that's as invigorating as a double espresso.
In this unfettered new book of essays, never before
published in book form, Paglia brings her visceral in-
telligence to bear on subjects that range from Bill and
Hillary Clinton to Madonna, from *Frankenstein* to
the novels of D. H. Lawrence, and from feminist icon
Catharine MacKinnon to First Amendment flasher
Howard Stern. *Vamps and Tramps: New Essays* gives
us Paglia as a bold transgressor of intellectual bound-
aries, conflating biology, homoeroticism, and culture
into "A Pagan Theory of Sexuality." There's Paglia
the omnivorous commentator, whose curiosity en-
compasses Germaine Greer and Princess Di. And not
least of all, we see the prankish provocateuse who
trades outrageous true confessions from the gender
front with Lauren Hutton and dishes all of down-
town with drag queen Glennda Orgasm.

Essays/Popular Culture/978-0-679-75120-5

VINTAGE BOOKS
Available at your local bookstore, or visit
www.randomhouse.com